Queering Drag

Queering Drag

REDEFINING THE DISCOURSE OF
GENDER-BENDING

MEREDITH HELLER

INDIANA UNIVERSITY PRESS

This book is a publication of

Indiana University Press
Office of Scholarly Publishing
Herman B Wells Library 350
1320 East 10th Street
Bloomington, Indiana 47405 USA

iupress.indiana.edu

© 2020 by Meredith Heller
All rights reserved

No part of this book may be reproduced or utilized in any form or by any means, electronic or mechanical, including photocopying and recording, or by any information storage and retrieval system, without permission in writing from the publisher. The paper used in this publication meets the minimum requirements of the American National Standard for Information Sciences—Permanence of Paper for Printed Library Materials, ANSI Z39.48-1992.

Manufactured in the United States of America

Cataloging information is available from the Library of Congress.

ISBN 978-0-253-04565-2 (hardback)
ISBN 978-0-253-04566-9 (paperback)
ISBN 978-0-253-04567-6 (ebook)

1 2 3 4 5 24 23 22 21 20

CONTENTS

Acknowledgments   vii

Preface   xi

1 What's in a Name?
   Redefining the Discourse of Gender-Bending   1

2 "Masculine Women, Feminine Men":
   Variety and Vaudevillian Male Impersonators   40

3 Mythical, "Sexless" Characters:
   Identity Borders in El Teatro Campesino   77

4 The "First Punch" at Stonewall:
   Counteridentification Butch Acts   115

5 Bent Means "Not Quite Straight":
   Kinging as Disidentification   152

   Conclusion:
   Bending Rhetoric   193

Bibliography   203

Index   217

ACKNOWLEDGMENTS

I WOULD BE honored to acknowledge the contributions of the following people, groups, and institutions to the process of constructing this book:

My most respected and trusted mentors: Laury Oaks and Paul Jagodzinski.

My best friends and most trusted collaborators: Rose Elfman and Ryan Bowles Eagle.

My interlocutors: Richelle South; Andrew Henkes; The Beauty Kings; the performers, audience participants, and organizers of Bent and the Drag King Contest; and the individuals who accompanied me to drag shows.

My colleagues: Julie Moreau, Nishant Upadhyay, core and affiliated Women's and Gender Studies faculty and staff at Northern Arizona University, and Sanjam Ahluwalia, who has been extremely supportive of this project.

My community: the much loved and missed Maxine Heller, Cynthia Heller, Matt Rudig and Sitka Rudig, Megan Coe, Lisa Cohen, Christy Simonian Bean, Kane Anderson, Dave Eagle, Julio Pérez Centeno, Steve Attewell, the Eagle family, the Bowles family, and the Fields family.

My dissertation committee at the University of California, Santa Barbara (UCSB): Christina McMahon, Leila Rupp, and

Suk-Young Kim; many thanks also to my Feminist Studies graduate advisors, Leila Rupp and Phoebe Rupp.

The reviewers of this manuscript, who offered kind critiques and insightful suggestions while also raising up a junior colleague. And the supportive staff, editors, and board members of Indiana University Press.

The students in my graduate course on the politics of gender-bending, whose conversations about queer worldmaking helped me work through several theoretical positions; the many students who watched drag videos in my classes and debated their queer aspects and genderfucking potential; the brilliant and eager undergraduate students I have worked with who continually remind me of the value and importance of my job.

Many archival resources: the Queer Music Heritage Archives, developed and curated by JD Doyle; the California Ethnic and Multicultural Archives, specifically the El Teatro Campesino collections; and the UCSB Library, especially the staff and services that facilitated loans of microfilmed historical newspapers. The Harry Ransom Center at the University of Texas at Austin, the Music Division of the New York Public Library Digital Collections, the open-content program through the J. Paul Getty Museum and the Getty Research Institute (the Getty), and Vanessa Adams all generously allowed the use of images.

The College of Social and Behavioral Sciences at Northern Arizona University, which supported the final stage of this project with a book-finishing grant. At the dissertation-completion level, this project was financially supported by UCSB through a summer research travel grant, a Graduate Opportunities Fellowship, a Doctoral Scholars Fellowship, and a Dean's Advancement Fellowship. I also wish to acknowledge the graduate teaching assistantships I received from the departments of Theater and Black Studies and the graduate teaching assistantships and postgraduation adjunct teaching work I received from the Department of Feminist Studies. I especially thank Eileen Boris and Ingrid Banks for giving me some of these critical work opportunities.

The UAW Local 2865—the union that organizes TAs, readers, and tutors across the UC system—which helped me thrive in a safe and equitable work environment.

A portion of chapter 3 appeared as "Gender-Bending in El Teatro Campesino (1968–1980): A *Mestiza* Epistemology of Performance," in *Gender and History* 24, no. 3 (2012): 766–781 (John Wiley and Sons). A portion of chapter 5 appeared as "Female-Femmeing: A Gender-*Bent* Performance Practice," in *QED: A Journal of GLBTQ Worldmaking* 2, no. 3 (2015): 1–23 (© 2015 Michigan State University). Ideas related to this project and its future directions appeared briefly in "Is She He? Drag Discourses and Drag Logic in Online Media Reports of Gender Variance," in *Feminist Media Studies* 16, no. 3 (2016): 445–459 (Taylor and Francis). I presented portions of this research at the following conferences and institutions: the Association for Theatre in Higher Education, the American Society for Theatre Research, the Popular Culture/American Culture Association, the National Women's Studies Association, and UCSB.

I completed this project on a nontenure faculty track, mostly teaching a 4/4 course load while completing significant service and other research. Thus this project was made possible by stealing from my leisure time, carving around grading sessions and committee work, and waking ever earlier to write. Without disregarding my own tenacity and sacrifice, I must also point out that I completed this project because I had unearned resources and advantages such as food and housing security, affordable health care, labor protection, institutional access, freedom from state violence, and networks of people who could gift me their uncompensated intellectual labor. Those in contingent faculty positions with less access to these critical resources because of racist, sexist, heterosexist, cis-sexist, and ableist barriers might not be able to complete such a project, despite tenacity and sacrifice. The work we do to explore cultural structures and social relations and then create community knowledges is crucial. My hero Audre Lorde says that without community, there can be no liberation. Our own community must become a coalitional pathway that lifts everyone up to intellectual liberation.

Finally, I thank George Heller for valuing the education and intellectual achievement of young people.

PREFACE

I WAS INVITED to speak on the NPR-hosted Southern California Public Radio show *AirTalk* for a segment called "Is Drag Degrading to Women?" Mary Cheney had posed this question on Facebook after watching a commercial for *RuPaul's Drag Race*. Cheney wondered if drag might parallel blackface minstrelsy in dehumanizing and degrading the subject performed. Cheney's post was polarizing. One side—comprising journalists, performers, academics, and RuPaul herself—argued that drag queening did not degrade women because, as a form of queer identification, celebration, and pride, it was specifically about tearing down gender walls.[1] The other side took a more ambivalent position: drag could perhaps degrade women if that were the intention of or effect from a misogynistic performer, or even a performer who was not fully vigilant about noting and combating sexism.[2] In this view, drag queens must have consciously antisexist intentions and use careful performance methods to ensure that this important queer community ritual does not become a sexist spectacle.[3]

I assume I was asked to participate in the segment because of my faculty position in women's and gender studies. My co–guest commentator was professional drag queen Miz Cracker (now even more famous for being the fourth runner-up on season ten of *Drag Race*). I suppose it would have been ideal for us to argue opposing sides, but it turned out we largely agreed. Rather than offering up a definitive "yes, sexist" or "no, never," Miz Cracker and I talked about the scope of theatrical gender-bending practices that do not (in fact, currently cannot) fit into the popular image of drag cultivated on *Drag Race*:

Drag performance is not just a simple version of drag queening as a man performing as a woman or drag kinging as a woman performing as a man. Drag means bending identities like gender, sex, sexual orientation, queering those relationships and those identities.... Some drag queens perform with full beards; we don't see that on *RuPaul's Drag Race*. We don't see any drag kings on *RuPaul's Drag Race*, we see very few trans individuals performing drag on *RuPaul's Drag Race*. So the type of drag that Mary Cheney was talking about, which is what she sees on *RuPaul's Drag Race*, might be degrading to women ... but it's certainly not the breadth and scope of the type of drag that is performed.[4]

So, is drag degrading to women? It really depends on what we mean when we say "drag." Chandra Mohanty reminds us of the "urgent need to examine the *political* implications of *analytic* strategies and principles."[5] So this book illuminates the scope of drag practice, questions the popular discourse on drag, and then offers up new ways of thinking about, talking about, and spreading these practices.

NOTES

1. For examples of this position, see Scudera's "Dear Mary Cheney" and Tracer's "RuPaul's Perfect Response." Walker, who did not weigh in on this particular debate, refers to drag queening as "perhaps the quintessential performance of [queer] visibility" because queens are popularly contextualized as displaying their gay sexual orientation via acts of gender-bending (*Looking Like What You Are*, 7).

2. For example, see Miz Cracker's excellent *Slate* article "Drag Isn't Like Blackface."

3. I draw here on hooks's distinction between a publicly enacted ritual and an entertaining but vapid spectacle (*Black Looks*, 150).

4. Heller, interview on "Drag Queen Asks: Is Drag Degrading to Women?" February 18, 2015.

5. Mohanty, "Under Western Eyes," 336.

Queering Drag

ONE

What's in a Name?

Redefining the Discourse of Gender-Bending

THEATRICAL GENDER-BENDING, ALSO referred to in this book as *drag*, is a genre of performance that most people in the contemporary West have been—at least tangentially—exposed to.¹ Perhaps, like Mary Cheney, they know the drag queen contest show *RuPaul's Drag Race*. Maybe some know the political drag queen troupe the Sisters of Perpetual Indulgence or the popular (now defunct) San Francisco–based drag queen club *Finocchio's*. But even people unaware of these iconic examples may know of comedienne Dame Edna, Divine's appearance in *Hairspray*, John Travolta's appearance in the remake of *Hairspray*, Gwyneth Paltrow's role in *Shakespeare in Love*, the historical fact that Shakespeare's plays were traditionally cast with men, the documentary *Paris Is Burning*, Tyler Perry's *Madea* films, or Lady Gaga's Joe Calderone persona. In plays, club performances, and pride parades as well as on TV, film, and social media, gender-bending—as both a stage performance and a conceptual discourse about gender flexibility—is part of mainstream consciousness.

This book explores a swath of theatrical gender-bending practiced in the past 150 years of US history: male impersonation, "sexless" mythical characters, queer butch acts, and contemporary drag kinging. Obviously, this list does not constitute the whole of the genre. But even within the delimited time and geography of my study, the full range of gender-bending is much more extensive than what I cover. And yet, despite the vastness of this practice, popular public knowledge about drag is narrow and premised on (and, I argue, bounded and limited by) a myopic vision of the genre. To be blunt, *drag* is often assumed to mean "performing as a drag queen." And *drag*

Fig. 1.1. Season six finalists of *RuPaul's Drag Race*. Left to right: Adore Delano, Bianca Del Rio, and Courtney Act.

queening is predominantly characterized as an over-the-top, glamorous doing of hyperfemininity by a man who will eventually reveal his underlying "boy body."[2] Indeed, this type of queening is the primary form of drag on *RuPaul's Drag Race*. Many types of drag do not make it to *RuPaul's Drag Race* but are nevertheless lovingly and skillfully practiced in small theater forums or queer spaces. For many—including non-gender-conforming, trans, and otherwise queer people—drag not only enhances their lives but also reduces and combats their vulnerability to external violence or early death. In fact, many theatrical drag practices in Western entertainment history do not resemble drag queening in the slightest. However, the drag that makes it to *RuPaul's Drag Race* does hold a hegemonic, if not singular, position in the cultural imagination: our popular discourse on gender-bending is always filtered primarily through the ideological representation Laurence Senelick dubs "the adult male decked out in seductive feminine frippery."[3] Ask people around you what drag is and very likely you will get a description that would make it onto *RuPaul's Drag Race* (see fig. 1.1).

This book grapples with a critical disconnect between what Diana Taylor characterizes as the archive and the repertoire.[4] There is a vast drag repertoire, some of which can be learned about experientially by attending live performances. But the archiving of performance is significant in the "production and transmission of knowledge," especially for practices that are no longer occurring (have no current repertoire).⁵ So how drag is textually classified, linguistically named, and rhetorically used is as important as the act itself. I argue that current popular knowledge about drag is circumscribed, specifically because of an archival limitation I term *drag discourse*. I use *discourse* to reference textual and oral language practices that name, classify, explain, and analyze ideological or physical phenomena. Although discourse may encompass nonlinguistic or experiential modes of transmission, the term primarily encapsulates how language is used to form and exchange thoughts about phenomena. Drag discourse refers to both the process of translating drag performance into oral and written language and also the use of ideas linked to this language for creating and spreading knowledge about the genre.

There are drag performances that elude language and known methods of classification, and, for some, the potential of drag resides in this illegibility. Gender-bending encompasses a generative and rich potential in that it can build community, create safer spaces, and, over time, lead to more possibilities for queer lives. But the most popular, common, and established knowledges about drag have been shaped not by what occurs in the repertoire but by what has been formally and informally archived. To facilitate the spread of a personal experience at a drag show beyond the "bracketed" geographic location of the repertoire, people translate it into standard "linguistic or literary codes."⁶ This book illuminates the many ways that drag performers construct, reproduce, bend, and challenge identity. It also acknowledges how these practices have been discursively mapped into archival collections, written histories, scholarship, and news stories. It is not my position that people who produce drag archives cannot see the nuances of drag or are unwilling to acknowledge its complexities. Rather, I argue that we simply do not have a sufficient discourse on this practice yet, and thus we lack vital rhetorical tools to name such nuance and analyze such complexity.

Let me lay out exactly what the discourse on drag is and why it constrains our ability to capture complex knowledges. In *The Drag Queen Anthology*, Steven P. Schacht and Lisa Underwood define *drag queens* as "individuals who publicly perform being women in front of an audience that knows they are 'men' regardless of how compellingly female—'real'—they might appear otherwise."⁷ Here, a drag queen is defined as a drag queen because she looks "compellingly female" onstage *and also* because she is really a man offstage. In other words, drag queening is a theatrical presentation of a gendered persona that is not real but rather a parody of reality (the resulting logic is that, in reality, men are not actually feminine). Thus, drag queening is discursively materialized not by reference to the part of the stage presentation that bends or queers identity but rather by direct reference to the performer's assumed stable cisgender identity in contrast to the gender seen onstage.[8] Although Schacht and Underwood's anthology illustrates a range of drag practices, this definition appears in the introduction and is framed as a legitimate, general, or, at least, objective description.

I do not fault Schacht and Underwood for offering this definition, because it is a very standard way of describing drag. Almost identical definitions can be found in textual descriptions of drag kinging, cross casting, and male and female impersonation. Though common, such definitions are premised on questionable cultural assumptions about the body, including what I find most problematic: the notion that performing bodies are "really" either male or female—or at least can be assumed so. This definition is also problematically tethered to the idea that gendered aesthetics are actively done, but assigned gender—in this book, what I refer to as *sex*—is ontological and static and thus what you really are. Gender is a cultural construction that is both performed and performative, and theatrical gender-bending can certainly demonstrate this. But other identities, in this case the body's sex classification as either male or female, are also a form of cultural gendering, albeit a medically accomplished one.[9] I discuss Western methods of articulating and maintaining the binary sexed (male or female) body shortly. For now, it suffices to say that many modes of identification and taxonomy—gender, race, ability—have been culturally developed and applied to the unique body.

Many scholars emphasize the great potential of theatrical gender-bending to reveal how identities are not biological mandates but rather cultural ideologies that we do—and thus can undo or do differently.[10] Yet, the tools we use to name and define this potential directly reference the assumed biological mandate of sex and its normally or naturally connected cisgender attribution. This is a completely uncomfortable discursive position, and I am not the only one who feels this way. Schacht and Underwood reveal their own awareness of the problem and perhaps discomfort with it when they bracket the words "men" and "real" with quotation marks. Other scholars hedge as well: J. Halberstam defines a *drag king* as "female" but qualifies it with "(usually)."[11] Esther Newton does not qualify her essentialist engagement with sex but does bracket her reference to the "reality" or "essence" of maleness with quotation marks.[12] Here, progressive scholars are attempting to define *gender-bending* as "an act that bends or breaks identity categories." And yet, their linguistic method of doing so proves my point: no matter how uncomfortable they might be with assuming what performers "really" are, they nevertheless employ this concept in their definitions—and employ it via the construct of biological sex. As Leila J. Rupp and Verta Taylor put it, "Although we argue that drag queens and drag performances break down the boundaries between woman and man, gay and straight, we continue to use these categories, however flawed they might be, to identify people. In part, the language gives us no choice."[13]

Drag discourse has the power to affect the people doing the act, watching the act, and learning about the act remotely. In their study of the drag queens at the 801 Cabaret, Rupp and Taylor lay out the possibility that certain cultural entertainment like drag "expands and problematizes identity" in a way that "promotes resistance to domination."[14] A drag act that reimagines identity can be, as Cathy J. Cohen articulates, a "defiant behavior, and [also an act of] political resistance."[15] Lauren Berlant and Michael Warner use the term *queer worldmaking* to describe the formation of a space that allows for the centralization and celebration of nonnormative bodies and practices.[16] Drag actions that participate in queer worldmaking contribute to the framing of nonconformity as something legitimate within a specific space, but they can also spread this ideology beyond the geographic "bracket" of that microsphere.[17] For those deemed queer, the spread of a physical or ideological queer world allows more room in which to live tolerable or joyous existences, practice "self-fashioning," and avoid the dangers of a phobic majoritarian world.[18] This is no trivial thing for trans or gender-nonconforming people, especially those who are not White, as their exceedingly high death rates from murder and suicide would suggest. Queer worldmaking is not a project that all drag acts consciously take up. But as José Esteban Muñoz notes, performance can certainly accomplish such goals; specifically, "minoritarian performance" such as drag already "labors to make worlds—worlds of transformative politics and possibilities."[19] Theatrical gender-bending has the potential to be a source of individual or group strength for deeply marginalized people as well a source of large-scale political resistance and cultural change. The discursive component of drag is so important because it factors into drag's capacity to enact these spaces and changes on a macrolevel. And this potential is stagnated by our current methods of translating drag into a spreadable taxonomy.

Current drag discourse frames the taxonomy of what is—and, by extension, what is not—gender-bending. Taxonomies are tricky things: they are organized around cultural biases but also frame biases as objective and essential truths. In line with Michel Foucault's argument about sexual classification in *The History of Sexuality*, I see how organizing and labeling queer practices, even within an expanded taxonomy, is binding to them.[20] But while I do not wish to limit queer performance, I also do not want to continue using the terms presently available to describe and explore drag. Therefore, I am cautiously dedicated to expansively reworking the discursive parameters of drag and thus the shape of our drag taxonomy. The fact is that drag is already deeply embedded in the Western imagination and lexicon. Judith Butler discusses the potential of "resignification" projects, or the expansion of terms by adding meanings that do not necessarily "retain and reiterate the abjected history of the term" and might even "perform a reversal of effects."[21] Butler's example is "queer."[22] Historically used to identify the strange or out of sync, in the twentieth century it was engaged to brand and punish people whose sexual practices did not conform to compulsory heterosexuality. Yet, *queer* is now often self-deployed to celebrate one's gender or sexuality as existing apart from the hegemony but within a shared counteridentification. And at my university, students can minor in queer studies if they desire to explore how institutionally stratified norms displace people. In all these iterations, "queer" retains its core shape: it names what does not align with hegemonic structures and expectations. But other time- and place-specific meanings chained to this term—a slur, a negative attribute, a word that groups many people under one umbrella, a field of inquiry—have shifted. We need not abandon *queer* because of its very real problematic connotations. Instead, we should see our discourses as malleable modes of communication that can be reordered and infused with new content.

So, the first major project of this book is to scrutinize drag discourse and explore how it has been used to classify, archive, explain, and analyze gender-bending. In this regard, my project primarily focuses on how drag is translated from that primary moment of transmission at the actual show. Some of the coolest gender-bending acts I have seen spoke to me in ways that words alone could never do justice. Nevertheless, these acts are translated into words when archived or described in news stories, anthologies, histories, and scholarly monographs like this one. In each chapter of this book, I compare the words and ideas most often used to characterize gender-bending to actual gender-bending acts. What becomes painfully apparent are the gaps between the complexities and the nuances of these practices and the reductive discourse used to archive them. This is not to say that drag language forecloses us from articulating drag's potential. Just the opposite: as I demonstrate in the next chapter, the way we characterize historical male impersonation, for example, has led to inflated conclusions about its queer cultural impact. What I argue is that the existing drag language is limited, so an act that fits well within its definitional parameters could ultimately reify the status quo while an act that might not even appear to be drag could be pushing boundaries in significant ways. The taxonomy formed by drag discourse matters not only because of its inclusionary and exclusionary power but also, critically, because of how it is an analytic. That is to say, we use it to help us logically conclude whether acts are truly defiant, resistant, or build toward a queerer world.

The second major project of this book is an offshoot of the first: I develop new definitional guidelines for naming an act as gender-bending (or having a gender-bending process). This is a reformulation of drag taxonomy, to be sure, but one that undoes some harmful reductions and exclusions. (For instance, the reformulation is grounded in what occurs onstage; moreover, it acknowledges the cultural construction and import of identities without foregrounding any one identity as the primary reality or truth.) Here it is: if a performer displays identities, bodies, or actions that are out of sync with hegemonic cultural formations of the normal, natural, or ideal, then the act is bent. Likewise, if a performer deploys identities, bodies, or actions that confront or actively break down hegemonic cultural formations of the normal, natural, or ideal, then it is bent. This expansive definition forms a rather broad taxonomy that might include a large number of theatrical practices that are not traditionally understood to be drag. In fact, my purpose is to do just that: to expand the taxonomy in ways that dilute the singularity of certain hegemonic identifications (sex and gender) contextualizing bentness. Consequently, our understanding of drag will no longer rely on what may be interpreted or presumptively read about the performer's body vis-à-vis their act; instead, it will derive from what the performer intends to communicate with their body onstage and how the performer methodologically goes about doing it. From this discursive location, we can then begin to communicate more deeply about what such acts might truly be accomplishing.

DRAG DISCOURSE

The drag examples I explore in this book might be known tangentially by some but are not extensively documented in popular or scholarly texts. In this regard, I hope to grow the scope of what is known about drag, in general, and especially about these practices that have been marginalized in other accounts of drag. But my project is not to craft a holistic picture of gender-bending (this book would have to be ten times thicker).[23] Relatedly,

I acknowledge that theatrical performance can transmit meaning experientially and also replicate said meaning through a continued repertoire. What I am primarily interested in here is comparing a range of meaningful drag practices to the discursive process of naming said practices as drag (or not) and then forming a classification system that carries specific knowledge to mass publics. So, let me now speak about the power of discourse and, specifically, what Taylor describes as the "dominance of language and writing."[24]

A common neoliberal axiom states that "sticks and stones may break my bones, but words will never hurt me." Butler argues the opposite: certain speech acts lead to very real emotional, psychological, and physical injury (i.e., hate speech can trigger violence).[25] In the vein of feminist materialism, Butler extends this to argue that *discourse*—which she defines as "speech acts linked to significant legal or social consequences"—actually "materializes" all that is knowable.[26] So the primary way we recognize our bodies as having meaning is through language-based discourse, which also forms the basis of the knowledge that allows us to be "recognizable" to others.[27] New materialist theorists articulate how the body is also a key agent in this process. Donna Haraway's theory of situated knowledges explicitly characterizes the body as an "actor and agent" rather than "a blank page of social inscriptions," and Karen Barad notes a key relationship between "the body's materiality—for example, its anatomy and physiology—and other material forces [that] actively matter to the processes of materialization."[28] But in both materialist and new materialist theories of the body, discursive practices, specifically language and writing, are key to individuals' ability to interpret themselves and their actions within the culture.

In mass publics not composed of feminist theorists, though, discourse is generally framed more basically as a type of language that helps individuals move through space, understand other individuals, accomplish daily tasks, and avoid (or enact) frictions or dangers. For example, the phrase *women's restroom* supplies necessary basic information about the function of a space and who can use it. But few words are simple one-to-one representational signs;[29] rather, most terms or speech acts are "sign-chains" in that they are only fully knowable and actionable if one already has complex cultural fluency.[30] Take again that straightforward phrase *women's restroom*. Such a term presumes we all share a common understanding of who a woman is, how to identify a woman, and what the appropriate reaction is to an individual in a women's restroom who is identified as not a woman. The fact that this language is omnipresent in and around public space also presumes agreement with or at least acknowledgment of the (culturally constructed) notion that there is a fundamental, binary sex difference and that men and women cannot mix in these spaces because of their heterosexual attractions (I guess). Thus, even simple descriptive terms such as *women's restroom* are chained to and part of a larger discourse about gender, bodies, sexuality, and difference.

In a parallel vein, the definition for gender-bending seems to supply straightforward explanatory information about who is doing the act and why it is a unique theatrical practice. But these unchallenged words are sign-chains: they trade in complex meanings about what such an act is in relation to social norms and therefore what the actor is accomplishing in cultural time and space. And if one desires to argue that drag is a progressive deconstruction of identity (as many scholars do), one must draw on a particular body of words that are tightly chained to particular cultural discourses about gender, bodies, sexuality, and difference. Editors and contributors of *The Drag King Anthology*, Eve Shapiro writing about the drag king troupe the Disposable Boy Toys, and Rupp and Taylor in *Drag Queens at the 801 Cabaret* express displeasure with the limited tools available to describe drag.[31] It is no coincidence that all three of these projects centralize acts that do not fit well into traditional gender-bending definitions, and thus their analyses are not being fully served by the discourses chained to drag language. But most works on gender-bending, and specifically the most popular and canonical studies, categorically employ standard drag words, terms, and phrasings. I have already discussed Schacht and Underwood's definition of drag queens. Similarly, Newton's 1972 *Mother Camp*, one of the first and best-known drag ethnographies, sums up the process of drag queening: "The oppositional play is between 'appearance,' which is female, and 'reality,' or 'essence,' which is male."[32] In *Female Masculinity*, Halberstam defines a drag king as "a female (usually) who dresses up in a recognizably male costume and performs theatrically in that costume."[33] As previously mentioned, the parentheses and quotation marks signal authors' awareness of and perhaps discomfort with the limitations of these definitional terms. Yet, language issues are not addressed beyond these punctuation markers, and no other way of describing drag is offered.

Newton, Halberstam, and Schacht and Underwood are what I consider canonical sources because of how often and prominently they are referenced in drag scholarship. However, these linguistic patterns are employed in other (and newer) scholarship as well. In a 2004 essay on Canadian drag clubs, Fiona Moore explains that drag, "in its simplest form," is "men dressing in female clothing for the purposes of performance."[34] In the 2010 *Sex, Drag, and Male Roles*, Stephen Bottoms references co-contributor Diane Torr's definition of contemporary drag kinging as an extension of the "tradition of female-to-male theatrical cross-dressing"; he also offers as his own definition, "The performance of male characters by female-bodied performers."[35] In a 2012 article for *Signs*, Katie R. Horowitz reproduces standard drag language by writing that "generally speaking queens are biological males who perform as women and kings are biological females who perform as men."[36] Horowitz also qualifies this definition: "(although even this comparison is questionable at best, given the increasingly vocal and critical presence of genderqueer and transgender drag performers at various stages of transition)."[37] This notation acknowledges the diversity of people who do drag but become totally invisible when standard drag language is employed to describe the genre. But like Halberstam, Newton, and Schacht and Underwood, Horowitz still uses these words even while articulating their critical limitations. All such texts fail to produce any other language that might better denote the scope of either practices or performers.

To be clear, I am not disparaging these scholars or their work. Just the opposite: I have referenced these texts specifically to demonstrate how even detailed characterizations of drag by progressive and aware scholars materialize through a reductive drag discourse. Drag scholars use language they are wary of because we lack other ways to approach written or oral characterization of these practices. But this book advances the argument that any critical, sustained, and expansive engagement with gender-bending must be accomplished by a more inclusive and less essentialist discourse. Our words must be able to fully characterize the scope of the genre, fully acknowledge diverse forms of bending, and fully articulate why certain acts do not challenge the status quo and others spread queerness. The development of and consistent engagement with a different type of drag discourse will be a process, to be sure, but it is a crucial one if we desire to spread more comprehensive knowledge about drag and also if we do not wish to foreclose the spreadability of a queer practice.

METHODS AND APPROACH

My approach to this endeavor is to trace four types of US-based gender-bending practice: male impersonation in variety and vaudeville (1860–1920), sexless mythical characterizations by El Teatro Campesino's teatristas (1968–1980), butch expressions by queer Black nightclub performers (1910–1969), and contemporary drag kinging in California (2008–2012). I illuminate these practices via semiotic and textual analyses of archival materials such as candid, publicity, and performance photographs; newspaper reviews, advertising materials, and programs; sound and video recordings; internal unpublished documents; social media content; and interviews and other autobiographical materials. For my chapter on drag kinging, I also use ethnographic participant observation as well as interviews and conversations I conducted. Drawing on such an expanse of data is useful for articulating a complex picture of these acts. At the same time, it allows me to reflexively interrogate materials that have made it into the archives and how those curated sources are used in popular and scholarly work to form definitive accounts of drag. In coming to my own conclusions about the impact of each of these practices, I heavily factor in performers' expressed or demonstrated intents: why certain performers may not have wanted to (or could not) fully recast identity, may have wanted to create identity disobedience, or may have desired to present alternate identity pictures. Each chapter also attends to the performers' geographic and temporal locations. Furthermore, I ask what it means when drag is done as commercial entertainment, for general and like-minded or like-identity audiences, to advance political goals, or to build community space.

I chose these particular gender-bending examples because each practice I explore has already been linguistically coded or archived as done by women or as a women's practice. Therefore, my examples currently reside within a drag taxonomy defined in part by essentialized sex difference. While I acknowledge that sex difference has been and continues to be a powerful locating force, I do not claim that all individuals I study are ontologically female, only that they have either self-identified as such or been identified in these terms by those who wield the power of definition (archivists, reporters, scholars). But with that said, here is why I chose to investigate "women's drag practices": there is a staunch feminist position in theater scholarship that maintains, with an increasing volume of scholarly analysis on women's performance practices, a larger range of radical performance methods will be uncovered. Specifically, this position proposes that women's gender-bending work might be a subtler form of identity manipulation and thus more effective at queer worldmaking. In grounding my own investigation in these practices, I work within what is often presumed to be the most potentially progressive iteration of the genre. However, I demonstrate the limits of this position: even if these practices hold great potential for radically queering identity categories, our uncritical classification of them as women's practices roots our analysis to sex essentialism.

I argue that our discourse on drag has left us without sufficient rhetorical tools to parse the potentiality of when an act of bending ultimately reinforces cultural structures and when it leans toward radical breakage and change. No doubt there are experiential ways to find this out, but not everyone is able to attend drag shows. And when drag acts are recorded, the discourse used to describe them leads easily to interpretations of these acts as overwhelmingly culturally defiant. Gender-bending can be a simple or complicated act; it can involve layered forms of identity bending; and it can be done for commercial gain, self-expression, group solidarity, entertainment, self-fashioning, survival, or politics. Some bending is widely accepted because its queerness occurs only within particular nonthreatening spaces or contexts. Other bending is confrontational because of how its queerness makes people profoundly uncomfortable. I investigate the disconnect between these multivalent intents, methods, and impacts and the logic paths most often triggered by drag discourse. Specifically, I question how drag discourse ideologically positions sex as a form of embodied authenticity distinct from other forms of bendable, doable gender. And I contest the narrative that a bent or queer practice is always culturally confrontational or radical. To fully apprehend bent acts—and, importantly, to be able to holistically communicate about them on a macroscale—we must have a discourse that illustrates the multifarious bent capacities of gender-bending without automatically infusing radical progressiveness into such a description.

WHY DISCOURSE MATTERS TO GENDER

A foundational flaw in the definition of *drag* is in its characterization of the act as—at its core—a binary sex-gender division for which gender flexibility is knowable only in opposition to the performer's stable sex designation. This is not just a drag discourse problem; these assumptions appear in much of contemporary Western discourse. In this section, I explicate more fully the relationship between participatory discourse and gender materialization and detail the cultural habit of removing sex from this equation. Let me start with a famous performance example. The play begins when a police officer verbally hails a pedestrian walking along the street. When the officer yells "Hey, you there!" the pedestrian stops and then turns to acknowledge the officer.[38] Curtain. Short as it is, Louis Althusser's "little theoretical theatre" encapsulates a key materialist theory about identity production and maintenance. Physical bodies are unique and have biological differences and natural capacities; Althusser allows that a "concrete individual," which I take to mean the corporeal capacity of the functioning body, exists before the culturally defined "concrete subject."[39] But our capacity for understanding and thus making meaning out of bodily functions and capacities is interpellated through differentiation (you/me), location (citizenship), ideological acknowledgment (I am "you"), and participatory response (I stop, I turn).

Butler uses a similar framework to explore why some individuals feel their gender is an expression of a fixed, precultural inner core—or, to put it more bluntly, why we think gender is who we are rather than what we do.[40] For Butler, this perception comes from "the stylized repetition of acts," or the muscle memory formed by habitual participation in preestablished cultural identities and their meanings.[41] Butler analogizes this to a play for which the script has been written, the lines memorized, and the scenes rehearsed; the night-after-night performance "actualize[s] and reproduce[s] reality once again."[42] Such a vision of gender production has been critiqued for its implication that humans are passive subjects in this process. Not so. Humans understand and communicate about their bodies (i.e., are the actors in the play), but they do so via the ideological and cultural discourses available to them (i.e., the playscript).[43]

We know, then, that gender is what we do (though there is still debate about why we do it). However, I am also concerned with how Western culture elevates "sex," the medical classification of bodies as either male or female, to a position above and apart from gender. Kate Bornstein argues that sex is simply one more form of cultural gendering, but it is considered a measure of the precultural self because of its grounding in biology and science.[44] Although this might be common knowledge to my reader, it bears repeating that, while bodies are material and such corporeality contains objective knowledges, binary sex difference is a translation of bodily specificity into a cultural belief system. Indeed, *intersex* is the term used to name bodies that have what medical professionals label indeterminate or "non-dimorphic" sexual development, or a mixture of "male" and "female" chromosomes, hormones, gonads, and genitals. Intersex bodies that cannot be so easily grouped into medically defined male or female sex categories are common—Katrina Karkazis estimates perhaps 1 in 1,000.[45] Because the medical realities of intersex bodies do not align with the cultural "truth" of binary sex difference, the existence and prevalence of intersex people is often concealed from public knowledge and many intersex individuals are surgically or hormonally altered to fit into one category. In an attempt to linguistically characterize the medical assignment of sex as a form of body gendering, Bornstein suggests we reterm sex as *biological gender.*⁴⁶ In spite of Bornstein's excellent proposition—offered over two decades ago—as well as the current trend of using the term *assigned sex* to highlight this process, binary sex difference retains its prime position in the cultural imagination as an objective truth; binary sex is easily and often evoked as a baseline for the reality of the self as well as a launching point for discussions about other gender doings.

Sex is not just a means of understanding and organizing the body; it is a key tool for understanding and organizing the body's performance of gender. Let me illustrate this "sex logic" with a story. There is an eighteenth-century oil painting by Nicolas de Largillière that depicts a child and a dog in a forest (see fig. 1.2). The child wears a voluminous pink cape fastened with a bejeweled brooch, a golden tunic, and laced, open-toed sandals. A halo of fluffy white-blonde curls encircles the child's head. Sitting with legs crossed and toes pointed, this pink-lipped, flushed-cheek child wraps both arms lovingly around the dog. I first saw this painting, *Portrait of a Boy in Fancy Dress*, at the J. Paul Getty Museum. As I examined it, a father and his young child stopped to look, too. A lively discussion erupted between them. The child proposed that the figure's named identity in the title of the painting was conflicting with the figure's gender aesthetic of pink clothing, apparent makeup, long eyelashes, and gentle embrace of the dog. The father explained that the figure's outwardly feminine gender signifiers did not negate the figure's named identity, clearly stated by the title, because there was another way to understand such an aesthetic. The exchange sounded like this: The child, "But how can he be a boy?" The father, "He's a fancy boy." They moved on.

This vignette illustrates, first, the common belief that people can "do gender" in various ways.⁴⁷ Although there are culturally appropriate and inappropriate ways to do gender, gender is not invariably presumed to be a totally rigid and immovable quality. Second, it illustrates the common belief that sex is a totally rigid and immovable quality and thus a secure launching point for discussions about doing gender. The father never wavered in his belief that the subject was male—the sex identification of "boy" could not be undone by any "fancy" (meaning feminine) gender presentation. But the boy's gender presentation could be and was evaluated in relation to his sex designation (he was fancy, for a boy). Discussions about how certain forms of gender become marked as appropriate or inappropriate via their relationship to certain sex designations are important.⁴⁸ But discussions that unequivocally position sex as a stable means of explaining how gender is being done leave no room for also questioning the role or capacity of sex itself. In other words, sex becomes the baseline bearer of a body's truth.

Fig. 1.2. *Portrait of a Boy in Fancy Dress* by Nicolas de Largillière. *Courtesy of the Getty's open-content program.*

The production and accomplishment of gender are both quotidian and fantastic. Gender can affirm or alter people's locations within society, define relationships, build personal perspectives, and even change culture. Gender is in the things we take on (roles such as jobs or hobbies) as well as in how we are read by others (attributions such as body language or pronouns).[49] Candace West and Don H. Zimmerman frame gender as a critical communication and conveyance tool: part of key interactional endeavors among humans.[50] And Marlon M. Bailey illustrates various doings of gender within ballroom spaces that lead to self-fashioning and joyful play that enhances queer life. Outside these ball spaces, gender performance is also a crucial method for nonconforming queer folk to blend in and survive.[51] But, I argue that such varied articulations of gender are still necessarily predicated on the unshakable cultural dogma that sex is not the same as gender and also that sex is a valid anchor for naming and evaluating such gendered capacities.

Please note that while the father and child at the Getty put considerable effort into identifying the boy's sex so as to better characterize his gender, no such effort was made for the dog. Judith Lorber argues that humans and nonhuman animals share some physical and biological traits but our attribution of gendered meaning to these traits is a distinctly human mode of organization.[52] In basic terms, locating the dog's sex would not allow for richer insights into whether and how it was presenting itself rightly or wrongly. In a related vein, factors such as age, historical and geographic location, socioeconomic and class status, and race/ethnicity would have explained a great deal more about the child's presentation than his sex identity could. And yet, none of these qualities were primarily drawn on to make conclusions about him. Instead, the figure's sex was engaged as the first and seemingly most useful gateway for the ensuing gender evaluation.

I will add one more layer before getting to the bending of gender. As exemplified with the fancy boy, assigned sex is frequently elevated above gender when gauging how and why people do gender the way they do. On the flip side, gender interests are sometimes also engaged to ascertain a person's "true" sex if it is not already clear. This is illustrated in Anne Fausto-Sterling's account of the sexing of intersex person Levi Suydam. The year was 1843, the place was Salisbury, Connecticut, and Suydam had cast the winning vote for the Whigs. A public melee ensued about whether Suydam was qualified to vote because, in 1843 Connecticut, a minimum (although not sole) voting qualification was maleness. After two medical exams revealed that Suydam had both a penis and a vaginal opening, Suydam's sex was ultimately classified due to "feminine propensities, such as fondness for gay colors, for pieces of calico, comparing and placing them together, and an aversion to bodily labor."[53] Predilections and interests chained to time- and place-specific gender beliefs were used to gauge Suydam's "true" sexed self when it was in question. Similar logic models are deployed in contemporary accounts of trans individuals seeking medical or legal services. Dean Spade discusses how people are forced or coerced into producing narratives of always having known they were a woman or a man because of early attractions to gendered toys, clothes, spaces, and (hetero)sexual partners.[54] In both cases, binary gender stereotypes can be occasionally used as part of an ontological revelation of "true" (even if not assigned) sex.

Ideally, any discussion about the bending of gender would be foundationally built on how a body's bent expression calls specific gender meanings into question. In this ideological frame, "bending gender" actually bends the parameters of gender taxonomies rather than simply allowing a subject to traverse them. For instance, if Suydam liked both colorful fabric and doing manual labor, this might illustrate how one body could indeed participate in opposing gender activities. Suydam's act of "bending gender" would contest the nature of the gender categories themselves as well as question how one's category alignment (or misalignment) could ever possibly define one's "true" sexed self. But actually, this is not how the bending of gender has been ideologically or discursively formulated. Instead, bending actions have been defined as those that accomplish opposite gender scripts from the ones attached to an individual's sex assignment. For example, one might say that Suydam was "bending gender" because Suydam was a man who liked feminine things. Or that Suydam was "bending gender" because Suydam appeared masculine but was really a woman. These language patterns do illustrate how interests and appearances are culturally gendered and also how bodies may do various forms of gender as they please. But this language does not call into question the assumption that certain interests or appearances are good measures of gender affiliation; nor does it destabilize the position of sex as the primary organizing factor. Instead, interests and appearances remain either masculine or feminine, and we know Suydam is bending only if we know Suydam is "really" a woman or man.

As both a formal stage practice and an action done in everyday life, "bending gender" is a method of physically stretching, changing, denying, reinventing, or otherwise manipulating cultural gender mores. The body is critical in setting and maintaining "what is real" about gender.[55] Words do not make our bodies, but words do help us work through ideas, express complex thoughts, and archive those ideas and thoughts in written canons of knowledge. The issue is broader than what Suydam did or what gender benders do; it also includes how those doings are interpreted and then institutionalized by the doctors and judges and scholars who have power over them. As Barad puts it: "Discourse is not what is said; it is that which constrains and enables what can be said."[56]

In that case, does a discursive method exist for acknowledging the cultural import of sex and the role it plays in the gendering process while also denying sex "ontological status apart from the various acts which constitute its reality"?[57] If so, it is not employed to the extent it should be. Scholars have raised this question in regard to trans and intersex studies that evoke maleness or femaleness as a foundation for gender analysis. David Valentine asserts that many otherwise progressive theorists cannot conceive of ways to critique identity formation apart from contrasting it to an ontological baseline "about bodies and practices, about the relationship between signifier and signified."[58] Raine Dozier is critical of studies that build identity critiques by characterizing "sex as the 'master status' or 'coat rack' on which gender is socially constructed."[59] Karkazis argues that when one type of identity is situated as more authentic or stable than others (in her work, this is sex), it becomes the basis for continued institutional stratification.[60] Even the most well-intended scholarly text aimed at revealing the falseness of identity essentialism can have the unintended consequence of reifying identity essentialism if, as an analytic tool, it discursively frames the body as ontologically sexed.

At this point, the whole business is beyond any basic materialist "we are all constructed" or essentialist "culture is formed through biological truths" argument. Theorizing the human as "either pure cause or pure effect" leaves little room for the messy and complex realities of life or the intersectional relationship between culture, embodiment, and experience.[61] Gender, race, and sexual orientation are social constructions because they are products of cultural imagination and historical experience. Nevertheless, these designations—and the material consequences of their intersections—matter a great deal. Sex likewise matters a great deal in the doing and understanding of quotidian gender performance. In conjunction with these realities, though, it is important to unpack how and why we have developed identity legibility through various forms of discourse, including unrelenting reference to binary sex classification. To be frank, I find it unethical to universally locate the bodies and identities of drag performers within discursive paradigms that frame them as "really men" or "really women." I ask that we deploy a drag discourse that focuses on what performers do rather than who they are, thus crediting them with the impacts of their carefully constructed and deployed bending. This book demonstrates how to do so.

BUILDING THE CANON

The conventional definition of theatrical gender-bending is braced by two assumptions that function as central pillars. The first is that what is seen onstage is fictive play, which may influence or reflect but does not wholly comprise everyday reality. This is actually an assumed attribute of all cordoned theater spaces and practices. Audiences attending a play are generally aware that the kitchen they see onstage is not actually a working kitchen in a real house but rather a representation of a kitchen. Likewise, if audiences witness a murder onstage, they do not generally believe the victim is actually dead and the murderer a killer. The cultivated general understanding that theatrical performance is a meaningful yet symbolic representation for the primary purpose of message transmission is commonly called "willing suspension of disbelief."[62] Audiences are invited to temporarily ignore their logic and suspend their perception of reality for the sake of experiencing the entertainment, narrative, and emotional impact of theater.

But the second assumption makes gender-bending unique among theater practices. Drag relies on the notion that what appears onstage is not only not real but actually in direct contrast to the performer's reality. Audiences at a drag queen show are assumed to carry the "explicit recognition that the individual publicly performing femininity and *being a woman* is also simultaneously acknowledged to be a man and *not a woman*."[63] Audiences who watch an actor perform a detective character might assume the actor is not really a detective. However, they can accept and enjoy this representation whether or not they know the actor's true self includes being a detective. In this context, audiences do not need to know anything about the reality of the actor in order for the actor's acting skill and presentation to be a success. This is not so for drag. Audiences' comprehension and enjoyment of gender-bending largely depends on their recognition of it as such, which, Pamela Robertson argues, "depends upon our shared recognition that the person behind the mask is really another gender."[64] Thus, drag queening is defined as a fictive representation of gender (first pillar) that directly contrasts with the everyday sex and gender of the performer (second pillar). These two pillars do not apply to all forms of gender-bending, but they are deeply embedded in our drag discourse. And it is my position that they were formed and solidified by the way gender-bending was (and continues to be) historicized. The characterization of drag in history has profoundly shaped both public and canonical scholarly knowledge about this practice. So, as befitting my theater degrees,

I now dive deep into theater history to illustrate why the two-pillar model became both foundational and framed as born of necessity.

I learned theater's origin story (i.e., the story adopted by the West) as a high school freshman, and I encountered it again in the first chapters of all the theater textbooks I read in college. Here it is: in ancient Greece, around 534 BCE, a man named Thespis stepped away from his dithyrambic storytelling chorus and used his individual voice and body to represent one of the story's characters. After this revelation—that individual people could play the individual people in the stories—actors began performing as specific characters. More stories were written with lines for individual characters/actors, and popular play competitions developed around these scripts. Greek playwrights Aeschylus, Sophocles, and Euripides wrote plays about gods, villagers, heroes, villains, and, yes, even women. Greek woman characters were integral to many play narratives, but actual Greek women were not legally or socially allowed to perform in (maybe not even attend) public plays. Thus, this origin story for theater is the origin story for theatrical gender-bending. In this account, gender-bending is not born of a desire to bend identity or create a disjointed effect; rather, it emerges because Greek actors had to perform every character in a given script and only men could be actors. Oscar Brockett and Franklin J. Hildy's *History of the Theatre* succinctly states, "All actors were men, all actors wore masks, all actors played more than one role."[65] *The Longman Anthology of Drama and Theater* explains that actors "customarily played more than one role in a play (including those of women)."[66] The perfunctory tone of these entries reflects the first pillar: all performances are fictive representations anyway, and the show must go on. Because Greek theater has a primary position in the Western theater canon, premises and assumptions tied to this practice have transferred to gender-bending performance in general.

This gender-bending historicization also appears in feminist theater history critiques. For example, Sue-Ellen Case argues that Greek plays and acting methods have little relevance to women because men wrote and performed woman characters via stereotypical tropes, language, gesture, and dress.[67] These shallow character qualities and expressions were the methodology Greek actors used to mark themselves as fundamentally different from their woman characters (second pillar). Such performative gestures made it explicit to audiences that the production was honoring cultural prohibitions against women participating in plays. They also distanced the actor from any implication that his bending actions represented his desire to bend gender roles or elevate women's identities and lived experiences (as noncitizens, women occupied lesser social positions). Case proposes that Greek gender-bending had nothing to do with actual women or altering women's cultural positions but was, in fact, a method of reinforcing stratified institutional sexism.[68]

The historicization of gender-bending as a device built to support rather than deviate from established gender mores appears in other prominent theater accounts. For example, one narrative starts with early Japanese Kabuki (ca. 1600–1629 CE), wherein all actors were women and thus performed all roles. After 1629 CE, the Tokugawa shogunate established Kabuki as a men's performance practice, and the woman roles were acted first by adolescent male wakashu and later by adult male onnagata. Similarly, China's Beijing Opera employed male dan performers to enact stylized woman types. This practice was established during the Qing dynasty (ca. 1636–1912) because, during that time, women did not participate in the performance genre.[69] Another example is from Elizabethan England: women were prohibited from acting in public theaters, so William Shakespeare's heroines were performed by adult or adolescent men. These historical narratives come from diverse times and locations, but their significance to gender-bending is that they frame the practice as a "purely functional" means of working around and actually maintaining cultural gender beliefs and regulations.[70] This book focuses on gender-bending acts in the past 150 years of US history, thus does not explore performances that were cultivated or deployed under these historical prohibitions against men or women being onstage. Nevertheless, the overarching drag framework I work with and against was strongly established by these archival examples.

This is a good point to draw some important distinctions among forms of gender-bending before looping back to its historicization. There is a difference between theatrically staged gender-bending and quotidian forms of gender that are performative in nature, and which people perform daily. Gender performance is part of what we do to communicate, navigate space, validate selfhood, and represent who we are to others. Bailey also articulates how poor, queer people of Color who are part of the Detroit ballroom scene use gender performance to present themselves as heterosexual and cisgender in public space, thus avoiding homophobic and transphobic violence.[71] Spade likewise outlines how trans individuals perform gender-conforming narratives to access medical and surgical services.[72] However, in this book, I do not refer to everyday gender doings (gender performance) as theatrical performance or theatrical acts of "gender-bending." Newton argues that expressing a queer identity in public is "utterly serious, always 'for real,' completely different in feeling and tone from the fabulous and bittersweet excesses of the camp drag queen."[73] Likewise, Butler notes a distinction between how a gender-bending stage performer "can compel pleasure and applause" and how a trans or gender-nonconforming person "on the seat next to us on the bus can compel fear, rage, even violence."[74] There is a difference in context and consequence between everyday identity performance and identity performances enacted within the cordoned space of the theater with its corollary willing suspension of disbelief.

In this book, I use *theatrical* to refer to conscious doings that occur in delineated public performance arenas, such as theaters and stages, and have the intent of communicating a message to an aware audience. In my conclusion, I complicate the assumed safety and delimitations of this formal theater space as well as extend theatrical analysis into more broadly conceived performance arenas. But in this book my focus is on gender-bending practiced in known theatrical spaces because of the two central pillars: (1) theatrical performance does not constitute reality and thus is able to be consumed by audiences within willing suspension of disbelief; (2) theatrical gender-bending constitutes an opposition to the performer's lived reality. It is extremely interesting how key lines of reality and permissibility become occluded (though not absent) when located in a space reserved for fantasy and telling stories about the fantastical. Such spaces are often assumed to be free from "punitive and regulatory social conventions" like gender norms.[75] They are not.

Referring to a person's quotidian performance or expression of queer gender as a "gender-bending performance" overlays qualities of the theater onto it.[76] I am specifically troubled by the attendant implications that these personal identity expressions are not "real" or that there is a different "reality" under the "act." With that said, I also acknowledge the connection between gender-bending theater practices and the lives of the performers. For example, the experiences, identities, and politics of many gender or sexually queer drag performers inform their stage work.[77] Bailey argues that the theatrical space of the ballroom allows for gender self-determination: a form of identity labor that does not just inform ballroom stage practices but also expands the gender possibilities of ballroom members.[78] Shapiro argues that the drag king collective Disposable Boy Toys was an "identity incubator": individuals used the context of drag performance to experiment, which led not only to a more expansive personal understanding of identity but also to personal identity shifts.[79] There is certainly overlap among what performers bring to the stage, what occurs in the theatrical space, and what performers and audience members take and use in their daily lives.

In addition to the key distinction between lived gender performance and theatrical gender-bending, there are important contextual differences among clearly defined stage practices. The historical cross casting I have referenced in this section is not the same as the individualistic gender-bending acts I examine in the rest of the book. However, few works mark much of a difference. Gender-bending that results from a scripted plot twist or from a playwright's or director's vision or public gender prohibition is called cross casting: this is when an actor, clearly identified as a man or woman, is placed into a scripted role that is not the same as his or her personal sex identity. Sometimes this bending is simply a convention of the scripted narrative. For example, in Shakespeare's *Twelfth Night*, a woman character, Viola, poses as a young man to gain entrance into men's spaces. In this regard, the woman character is the one "bending gender" and, although the woman playing Viola must bend as well, the actor is one step removed from the bending implications of the action.

More often, though, theatrical cross casting is connected to public gender prohibitions or an articulated vision of the director or playwright. As previously mentioned, plays produced during England's Elizabethan era (such as *Twelfth Night*) were publicly performed by men. Thus, the part of Viola (who poses as a young man) was cross-cast with a man actor. Because of the mandate for willing suspension of disbelief, audiences accepted that Viola was meant to be a woman character even though they could clearly see that a man was playing the part. This particular casting impetus is much less prevalent in contemporary settings but still present in certain work—for example, that of the Takarazuka Revue, an all-woman acting troupe based in Japan and known for elaborate musical productions. Jennifer Robertson argues that part of the popularity of the revue is that women audiences can fantasize about men characters without the implication that they are engaging in inappropriate (heterosexual) feelings.[80] In other contemporary theater contexts, cross casting is a decision made by the director or playwright to advance the message of the production. For instance, in a contemporary production of *Twelfth Night*, a director might decide to cast a man as Viola to create a jarring visual contrast between the actor's body and the limited and stifling gender roles that compel Viola to pose as a man.

Theatrical cross casting can surely bend boundaries of identity and thus is important in the theatrical gender-bending canon. But when cross casting is the result of a plot twist, public gender prohibition, or production decision, it is not directly connected to the vision or desires of the actual performer. In fact, cross-cast actors are explicitly removed from the impetus (and thus the full implication) of their own bending actions. In contrast, I define gender-bending acts as theatrical representations that necessarily hinge on the actor's vision and desire as well as technique and skill. Such acts are generally autonomous creations not beholden to formal external scripts, not part of a larger plot narrative, and not carried out at the behest of a higher power such as a director or playwright. A gender-bending act is centralized around the performance of identity incongruity, although it might be secondarily focused on portraying a particular character. This more individualized and less scripted context enables the gender-bending actor to build and exercise their vision for a successful act. I examine gender-bending acts in this book because, first, acts yield a range of expansive and diverse stage products, generally more so than when the bending is guided by a director, script, or public gender prohibition. Second, it is easier to trace the impacts of the performance back to the intentions of the performer and the methods they use to carry it out.

There are certainly commonalities among bending practices, but in marking their differences, I emphasize the nontransferable aspects of cross casting that are nevertheless centralized in the definition of gender-bending. Cross casting was historically the most socially justified and supported type of bending practice: we have rich details about Greek, Chinese, Japanese, and British cross casting because they were popular, state-sanctioned practices that produced a protected archive of playscripts, performance reviews, and social or legal edicts. Gender-bending acts are not often part of a larger formalized script, so they have left less of a paper trail. And while cross-casted performances often obtained notoriety by being produced at large public theater houses and play festivals, it is not outlandish to conjecture that gender-bending acts were also being produced but in less reputable or more private spaces. The historical visibility of cross casting is not proof that this is how the genre originated nor can it be used to argue for primacy in organizing gender-bending discourse.

For example, a supposedly universal feature of gender-bending is that the audience knows crucial information about the performer's offstage self (second pillar). This would make sense if all gender-bending were like historical cross casting, where the audience's awareness of the actor's offstage identity was tied to its awareness that the performer and performance were complying with gender regulations. To be fair, this particular feature is part of some other forms of gender-bending as well. In certain drag acts, awareness of the actor's offstage self is accomplished through a "reveal": an action deployed onstage to dissolve the performance image. Drag actors do reveals by showing sex characteristics such as breasts or gender attributes such as short hair. Reveals share actors' offstage sex and gender, but they also highlight the actor's performance skills. This latter quality is related to "disguise and reveal" folktales and children's stories, in which characters, such as Aladdin, Cinderella, Jasmine, Mulan, or Ariel, disguise themselves as a noble or a commoner or a soldier or a human.[81] When the character finally reveals their true self to be a commoner or a noble or a woman or a fish, chaos ensues but is quickly followed by a "happily ever after" ending. Tracing the stage reveal from this lineage, Moe Meyer argues that reveals are ultimately vehicles for showcasing the "hero's" skill and cleverness.[82] So a theatrical reveal is really intended to highlight the skilled construction of the character and therefore the performance talent of the enactor.

Reveals are important pieces of methodological evidence that illustrate the intentions and goals of a gender-bending process I term *identification*. But a standard reveal—or any disclosure of a sexed or gendered offstage self—is not intrinsic to all gender-bending practices. As this book explores, gender-bending encompasses several other processes that I term *revisionary identification, counteridentification,* and *disidentification*; in these, a standard reveal is much less useful and could even obscure the import of race, community, socioeconomic status, and sexuality in the act or for the actor. Troublingly, however, drag conventions like the reveal are bandied about as universal methods for explicating efficacy, or measuring the accomplishments of a drag performance. This is illustrated in Meyer's account of a postoperative woman (assigned male at birth) performing a Barbara Eden / *I Dream of Jeannie* act at a drag show. According to Meyer, the audience went wild over the campy feminine illusion, but, when the performer executed a full strip, the audience was stunned into silence. Meyer attributes the audience's intense response to the popular notion of what gender-bending, particularly drag queening, is. The performer's feminine presentation led audiences to assume the performer was "really" a man (second pillar). Audiences were thus poised to witness the reveal of a "boy body" and then congratulate the performer on her excellent skills of fictive gender production (first pillar). When they saw body parts associated with women, the audience no longer apprehended the presented femininity as a fictive and fundamentally different identity and thus judged the act not to be gender-bending at all.

This audience's response illustrates my key concern with the gender-bending archive: it elevates a set of knowledges that, in turn, have serious implications on drag reception in general. The *I Dream of Jeannie* performer presented femininity queerly, as an act of high camp. The femininity presented was also bent from the performer's lived reality, as she is neither Barbara Eden nor a genie. So, it *was* drag in fundamentally bent and queer ways, despite its lack of a simple and crisp division between onstage gender and lived sex. Instead of loving the act for its skillful and entertaining execution or its campy queerness, however, the audience stopped enjoying their experience as soon as they classified it as not drag. According to Meyer, the director came out shortly after the *I Dream of Jeannie* number to announce: "Don't get yourself too worked up over her. It's all man-made."[83] In other words, the director urged the audience to consider this as a gender-bending act because the performed femininity was opposed to the male identity the performer had been assigned at birth. Linguistically reframing the act to conform to a traditional definition of gender-bending made the audience more able to accept it. Discourse does indeed play a big role in framing both drag knowledge and how drag is received. More than any other partial perspective acquired through experience or participation, the discourse formed and cemented via the canon of historicized gender-bending guides the analysis of its potential.

CANON IN ANALYTIC PRACTICE

The dominant historicization of gender-bending has limited our capacity to analyze its cultural impact; my primary concern, therefore, is to establish a sex-gender discourse that defines drag in ways that illustrate such effects. To elucidate my position, I draw on two different but equally canonical scholarly studies. In her analysis of Caryl Churchill's play *Cloud 9*, Elin Diamond asserts that the scripted cross casting of Victorian housewife Betty with a man actor estranges audiences from what they are used to seeing as normal cisgender behavior. The actor's body serves as a *gestus* (a readable feeling or attitude): when audiences see how alien and awkward Victorian femininity is on the actor's form, they apprehend how it is universally constraining. This staged bending transmits an impactful cultural message without direct words or phrases. As the performance visually marks how gender is often undesirably imposed onto certain sexed bodies, the audience can palpably feel its wrongness.[84] The second piece is Jill Dolan's mid-1980s discussion about drag queen shows, which employs a similar framework but takes an opposite position. Dolan argues that audiences always remain hyperaware that the individual doing femininity is a man and that femininity is not natural or normal for this body to do. But rather than claiming that this awareness leads audiences to develop a sympathetic ethos, Dolan argues that the actor's body under the feminine drag is a constant signifier of men's socially superior gender position. While drag queening may illuminate the constructed nature of feminine gender, Dolan concludes, drag audiences will not associate this with the plight of women forced into certain gender roles. Rather, both performer and audience simply take a mocking pleasure in the artifice of a man choosing to do things that only women have to do.[85]

No doubt Diamond's and Dolan's arguments resonate with many and inflame a few, but my intent is not to debate their conclusions per se. Rather, I have two other reasons for highlighting these particular texts. The first is to show how both pieces assume there is a universal and known definition for gender-bending and also that gender-bending can have important cultural impacts. In fact, both arguments start with the baseline position that men performing as women could theoretically break the stable relationship between gender and sex in audience members' minds. Second, both texts make important and complex conclusions about gender-bending's effect by uncritically referencing the privilege and stability they attribute to male sex designation. In both studies, performers are assumed to be forever and always men under their gender acts. This ideological positioning of the performer's body is the only way the authors articulate the act's impact: the immovable fact that the actors are men is the foremost catalyst that either deconstructs cisgender identity relationships or reinforces them. Thus, while these texts debate the actors' expressions of stage gender, neither author queries whether her assumption about the actors' cisgender designation is even correct. And even if this assumption were true, neither study questions whether this one particular identity, uninflected by other factors such as race, sexuality, and socioeconomic status, is the key to illuminating the acts' effects.

These texts are certainly not outliers: almost all scholarship on gender-bending presumes performers are either male or female (men or women) and then uses this nonintersectional iteration of identity to characterize the efficacy (or lack thereof) of the gender bend. An exception is Butler's work, likely because of her training in phenomenology and materialism. In *Gender Trouble*, Butler scrutinizes her own beloved simile of "gender performativity as theater production" by querying whether theatrical or public performances can actually illuminate quotidian gender performativity. Her brief mentions of public cross-dressing, butch/femme role play, and drag queening led some scholars to frame drag as a highly effective means of deconstructing essentialist identity structures.[86] Perturbed with this turn of events, Butler clarifies in *Bodies That Matter* that drag queening might be a form of gender performance, but, rather than permanently troubling identity scripts, most bending—both quotidian and staged—reifies ideological formations of sex, race, and heterosexuality.[87] Butler argues that drag specifically does not dismantle identities as much as it creates a dangerous ideological separation between what is considered performance/performable (gender) and what is considered real. Drag can certainly disrupt gender, sexuality, and even racial ideologies temporarily, but if it evokes the "real" in relation to these practices, drag ultimately becomes a "vehicle for a reconsolidation of hegemonic norms."[88]

Butler's primary focus is on discourse, which leaves little room for addressing what meaning might have experientially traveled between audience and performer. Instead, she highlights the meaning that travels through archival materials (literature and film), popular speech acts (utterance, discussion, announcement), and scholarly accounts (criticism of drag representations). Like Taylor, Butler acknowledges the power of the archive in shaping and facilitating the spreadable influence of a particular message. Without discounting the significance of what can be communicated in the absence of textual or oral mediation, it is often only the archive, the speech acts, and the scholarly accounts that are accessible to mass publics. For instance, despite participating in cross-casted plays and attending drag shows, I acquired the majority of my own knowledge about gender-bending from scholarly and ethnographic books and articles and curated images and videos in print and digital archives. In exploring drag beyond its immediate repertoire, then, Butler creates a path to trace how certain drag narratives are shaped through privileged discursive practices that then become the gold standard for explication and analysis.

My final task in this section is to illustrate a particular subset of scholarly drag analysis that employs sex-gender discourse not only to illustrate efficacy but also to fundamentally define radical practice. As mentioned earlier, the more progressive track in gender-bending theater studies focuses on women performers and women's practices. Actually, there is already a rich but occluded history of women doing theatrical gender-bending. I noted how the earliest form of Kabuki was enacted by women troupes and also how women play both otokoyaku (men) and musumeyaku (women) parts in contemporary Takarazuka. Relatedly, young British women played "principal boys" in nineteenth-century burlesque and Christmas pantomime shows (this is where the tradition of casting Peter Pan with a woman comes from). When famous Western actors such as Sarah Bernhardt and Charlotte Cushman wanted to demonstrate their talent, they took on "trouser roles" such as Hamlet. Some of the highest wage earners in US variety and vaudeville shows were male impersonators. And while I have only discussed the dramatic cross casting of Betty in *Cloud 9*, a woman actor always plays Betty's young Victorian son Edward.

Women's gender-bending is often framed in the literature as more effective at creating lasting macrocultural gender shifts specifically because the performances are visually subtle and therefore less immediately alienating. This assertion is based on Western androcentrism, or the notion that men's standards of dress, presentation, and behavior are an invisible ideal. Thus, men who present in feminine-coded ways are immediately noted for their gender deviation, while women presenting in masculine-coded ways are marked as non–gender compliant much less quickly, if at all.[89] Let me give an example of this. A friend and I wore bright vintage dresses and heavy makeup to one of the Drag King Contest shows I document in chapter 5. Most of those around us were in dark jeans, suspenders, black boots, and jackets, along with the occasional hard part haircut, long sideburns, or thin goatee. Looking at each other in dismay, my friend exclaimed: "Nobody else is dressed up!" Halberstam comments on the contemporary Western habit of noting femininity as something visibly done (as evidenced by the compliments my friend and I received) while presuming masculinity—especially the White cismasculine looks I describe here—as something that "just is."[90] In reality, the majority of the audience was dressed up and engaging in gender play just like us but with stylized or stereotypical versions of White masculinity rather than high-camp femininity. It was pretty embarrassing that I, a drag scholar, did not immediately note how the people around us were "bending gender." But here I prove the argument of women's drag scholarship. A woman's drag masculinity might be taken, at first glance, as androcentrism rather than drag. But when audiences do finally come to realize what they have been watching is a form of drag, they also realize that they have been integrating and accepting such a bend into their worldviews all along.

To illustrate this form of analysis, I return to Diamond's *Cloud 9* study. In addition to examining the gestus produced when Betty is cast with a man, Diamond also explores the casting of young Edward with an adult woman actor. Diamond argues that there is not so much of a visual contrast between

Edward's young masculinity and the woman actor's body because, in the audience's contemporary world, White Western women and young men often wear similar outfits or have similar physiques and hairstyles. Diamond asserts that Edward's embodied representation has a prosaic rather than upsetting gestus, and herein lies its potential: a cross-cast Betty estranges gender from sex to demonstrate an important aspect of its oppressiveness, while a cross-cast Edward demonstrates how cultural divisions between men and women can be overlooked and thus must not be that important. Both Betty and Edward represent forms of gender-bending, but Edward's impact on the audience is framed as more effective in large-scale gender dismantling.

Because Diamond is investigating scripted cross casting, it makes sense that she assumes the actors are "really" men or women (the script calls for that) and also that the impact of the bending is connected to the divergence between the actors' identity and the scripted performance of gender. But as I have mentioned, scholarly modes of analyzing cross casting are not universally translatable to all other forms of gender-bending. Models that foreground the fixity of offstage sex to reveal the impact of the gender performance should be employed only if and when this relationship is explicitly highlighted in the script, by the director, or by the performer. And while work on women's practices confronts the gender-bending canon in important ways, there is still a problem if it presumes certain performers are women and then frames such an identity as an inevitable catalyst for radical efficacy. The task of the feminist drag scholar is, first, to go back to that part about if and when; that is, to explore why certain drag performers foreground particular information in their acts and how such information supports their overall goals. In redefining drag discourse, we shift away from analytic models that force us to identify a performer according to standardized and assumed bodily categories and focus instead on exploring how performers build meaning around their own bodies.

REDEFINING DRAG DISCOURSE

Once, at an academic conference, I was asked to explain the main difference between drag queens and the performers I study. I got nervous and said that drag queens were generally male-identified or men who performed exaggerated or queer femininities, while the drag kings and male impersonators I study are usually female-identified or women. In other words, I defined my own project with the reductive discourse that my project fundamentally argues against. I did so because those words were connected to popular information about cultural categorical differences and so they quickly and comprehensibly separated the practices. This discursive shortcut momentarily served me, but it did not explain the mosaic of drag I study, acknowledge all performers who do these acts, or give credit to their intents and methods. The shortcut did do something useful, though: it led me to think about the actual main difference between drag queening and the acts in this book. If we remove sex from its position of definitional primacy (i.e., drag queens are men and I study women's practices), is there a significant difference between these practices? Certainly, they look different and different people do them, but almost all gender-bending varies according to the presentation and performer. And not all gender-bending acts done by people who share an offstage sex identity are significantly related. The drag queening that Mary Cheney saw on *RuPaul's Drag Race* differs greatly from that described in *Drag Queens at the 801 Cabaret*. Both are stage presentations of femininity done by people who primarily identify as men, but, beyond that, these acts are not aligned in politics, location, socioeconomic status, intersectional engagement, or even a vision of femininity. It makes little sense to give sex the final say when intent, methodology, and impact are much more meaningful data points. So, we need a way to more clearly emphasize which drag differences and drag similarities really do matter.

I have already argued the stakes of this project: to prevent drag discourse from foreclosing the spreadability of queer acts and also prevent our rhetoric from attributing worldmaking capacity to acts that bend but ultimately are a "reconsolidation of hegemonic norms."[91] There is one more important stake: existing drag discourse invalidates many of the people who do drag. In my embarrassing conference conversation, I was also asked if trans, nonbinary, or gender-variant people could participate in drag. The asker, I think, knew that these people do drag; the question seemed less about the actual performers than with my discourse that made no space for them. My study is fundamentally focused on exploring the potential capacity of bent stage practices to build a queerer world. And yet, the prevailing discourse does not provide linguistic tools to acknowledge the queerness of the performers who work to accomplish these feats. Disregarding or occluding the queerness of drag performers simply because they do not fit with the cisgender identity arrangements in drag discourse is the very definition of an injurious rhetorical act.

Queer theory is, at its core, the study of how power flows through such identification practices. A queer critical engagement necessarily examines who has authority to name, how naming defines self and practice, and how those meanings are used to constrain and stratify. Analytic queer lenses such as

Lisa Duggan's "homonormativity" reveal how some people in the contemporary LGBT community—for example, those who are wealthy and White and have domestic priorities such as getting married and having children—are not estranged from or oppressed by hegemonic sexuality frameworks.[92] Conversely, other individuals who do not identify as LGBT—for example, poor, Black single mothers on welfare assistance—are gravely stigmatized for their sexual practices and lifestyles. Cathy J. Cohen concludes that contemporary iterations of queerness are often just a "single-oppression framework" of gay versus straight that fails to account for multifarious and intersectional forms of sexual marginalization and privilege.[93] This is why Muñoz frames queerness as something that must remain "not quite here."[94] Bodies, practices, or objects may eventually be normalized, but queerness itself delineates a state of abjection defined in relation to norms, even if those norms shift.

Following Cohen's lead, this book marks a division between the current popular use of "queer"—specifically as an umbrella for Western-centric minoritarian LGBT identities—and the concept of radical queerness, which nods to Muñoz's "not quite here" periphery and also does not "focus on integration into dominant structures but instead seeks to transform the basic fabric and hierarchies that allow systems of oppression to persist and operate efficiently."[95] As Cohen's description of radical queerness reflects, "queer" serves as both an adjective for various marginalizations and a verb for actions that break down and fundamentally alter marginalizing structures. In this latter sense, then, "queer" identifies actions that have the explicit intention of spoiling or ruining cultural norms and, in doing so, setting the stage for a "forward-dawning futurity."[96] To engage Audre Lorde's famous "the master's tools will never dismantle the master's house" metaphor, queer actions illuminate the structure of the house—showing how some people are located in the master bedroom and others in the basement—and then provides tools to burn the house down in preparation for a new space.[97]

In the spirit of radical queerness, I propose a redefinition for drag that fundamentally alters the drag taxonomy. My purpose is to develop a discourse around drag that does not unintentionally limit or alter its complex and pointed meanings. Such a tool is critically necessary, even though redefinitions work from within the house and taxonomies have serious limitations and power imbalances.[98] The first step in this process is a step away from an unquestioned reliance on sex difference. This does not mean ignoring the cultural role of sex, its significance in gendering the body, or the reality that sex identity continues to be an organizing factor in some gender-bending. But sex and its relationship to other forms of gender can no longer be the sole anchor for drag discourse. Instead, I choose to identify gender-bending in any theatrical act that portrays a queer version of identity or portrays identity relationships queerly. Thus, gender-bending includes any staged performance that has the intention and takes the steps to cultivate a queer gestus. This includes all acts that centrally portray identities, bodies, or actions as out of sync with the cultural framework of normal, natural, or ideal. This also includes all acts that centrally deploy identities, bodies, or actions to confront or actively break down notions of what is normal, natural, or ideal. In both contexts, the bentness of the act rests on the performer's clear presentation of readable identity disjointedness: the performer must communicate how the presented identity does not align with hegemonic scripts of identity congruence.

This forms a broad taxonomy encompassing many theatrical acts that are not currently considered gender-bending. But a crucial strength of this framework is that while it creates a multifarious data set, it simultaneously defines gender-bending very narrowly, via performers' own expressed intentions and methods. The performer conceives of the bending, does the bending, and is responsible for cultivating awareness of said bending in audiences. The audience is not in charge of classifying the act or using their knowledge or presumptions of sex identity to fit the act to the taxonomy. A performer might create an act that contrasts lived cismasculinity to feminine presentation, but, in that case, the performer is responsible for showing the audience this contrast in whatever way he finds most effective or compelling. If instead the performer desires to communicate the fallacy of connecting certain body parts to certain identities, then the performer must explicitly do that. It can all be drag. But, ultimately, it is the performer who must define and express the act as drag, and then audiences must take this definition at face value.

I intend for this book to honor many types of gender-bending, including acts that do not accomplish macrolevel identity resistance or revision. In fact, my next chapter outlines a form of gender-bending that was deployed mainly as a hegemonic, commercial form of entertainment. Make no mistake: these acts are drag because they present a (temporarily) queer iteration of identity. But they have also been theorized as queer worldmaking based on their display of a disjunction between sex and gender. In positioning my central analytic focus on the performers' intents and methods rather than rote sex-gender discrepancy, I can better articulate why these bent acts actually reconsolidated gender norms. Relatedly, I can then explicate why some other bent acts are able to elude or discourage simplistic identity classifications. It is this latter kind of accomplishment that Berlant and Warner conceptualize as a queer worldmaking process.[99] I argue that a key aspect of queer worldmaking is its spreadability, or its ability to change other public and private spaces and impact a range of people and systems of thought. If this is drag's radical potential, we must have a discourse that allows us to explain why some drag acts accomplish it and others do not.

THE NEXT CHAPTERS

The next chapters illuminate four types of US-based gender-bending, which I refer to as male impersonation, sexless mythical characters, queer butchness, and contemporary drag kinging. These practices are grouped according to shared performance intents and methods, for which I use the terms *identification / cross identification, revisionary identification, counteridentification,* and *disidentification*. The classification and analysis of drag practice within its respective process is my path toward analysis: such a frame allows me to assess how each act of bending was produced to reify, bend, alter, or disavow identity formations, including but not limited to sex and gender. Chapter 2 is about the most successful male impersonators in US variety and vaudeville (ca. 1860–1920). Annie Hindle's and Vesta Tilley's drag practices have been theorized as queer worldmaking in that they created space for women to pursue nonheterosexual and noncisgender interests, self-presentations, and romances. Drawing on publicity photographs, newspaper articles and advertisements, performance reviews, and magazine op-eds, I evaluate the intents and methods of top male impersonators, giving particular attention to how they utilized popular notions of race, gender, and socioeconomic status to build commercial products. The most successful impersonators employed the drag processes of identification and cross identification to highlight their status as normal women even when performing a male act. Thus, while their careers enabled them to have personal measures of flexibility, their acts transmitted identity transgression as momentary and unnatural. When these impersonators could no longer support their narrative of bent conformity, they lost that personal flexibility, too.

The next two chapters explore public or commercial gender-bending primarily intended to express racial or sexual solidarity, pride, community, and politics. Chapter 3 makes central the performance innovations of El Teatro Campesino's teatristas, the Chicana members of this theater troupe (ca. 1968–1980). Close analysis of a previously restricted archive of photographs, recorded interviews, and internal paperwork illuminates how and why teatristas crafted what I am calling sexless mythical characters such as *calaveras* (skeletons) and *diablos* (devils). Existing scholarship has characterized these performances as limited alternatives to the unequal gender representation and opportunities offered by the troupe repertoire. Drawing from Gloria Anzaldúa's theory of mestiza consciousness, I illustrate how sexless acts demonstrate a revisionary process that could remove teatristas from the constant obligations of embodying Chicana stereotypes without nullifying their racial-gendered identities or cultural-political connections. Chapter 4 also illuminates a gender-bending process that challenges and revises identity formation. From 1955 to 1969, Stormé DeLarverie was master of ceremonies for the Jewel Box Revue. Homosexual and Black audience members could easily locate DeLarverie's masculine stage aesthetic within the tradition of queer butchness popularized by Harlem Renaissance performers (1910–1930s). Drawing on performance and publicity images, news and magazine sources, Jewel Box Revue programming materials, and primary testimonials, I argue that DeLarverie's methods constitute counteridentification: a process that frames a drag aesthetic as a disclosure of queer minoritarian affiliation. Referencing DeLarverie's own statements and historical accounts of the Stonewall Rebellion, I speculate that DeLarverie's violent treatment by police officers demonstrates how DeLarverie's counteridentification drag was a conscious act of queer oppositional consciousness.

Finally, chapter 5 focuses on a variety of drag acts at drag king shows or queer drag spaces that feature drag kings (2008–2012). Combining ethnographic participant observation and interviews with evidence from digital video and social media archives, I argue that these practices exemplify a disidentification process in which queer stage pictures work to expand or dismantle majoritarian and minoritarian identity concepts such as, for example, that a person with breasts is a woman. Although the "anything goes" context of these spaces can embolden performers to create racist and sexist acts, disidentification drag is ultimately intended as a radically queer practice and carried out with the goal of queer worldmaking.

NOTES

1. Later in chapter 1, I mark the differences among gender-bending: individual theatrical acts, bending as a theatrical plot twist, scripted cross casting, and everyday gender performance. This study most often uses the term *drag* interchangeably with the first of these, individualized theatrical gender-bending acts.

2. "Boy body" is a frequently deployed phrase on *RuPaul's Drag Race*.

3. Senelick, *Changing Room*, 295.

4. This phrase forms the title of Taylor's book, *The Archive and the Repertoire*.

5. Taylor, *Archive and the Repertoire*, 23.

6. Ibid., 3–4, 25.

7. Schacht and Underwood, "Absolutely Flawless," 4.

8. Schilt and Westbrook define *cisgender individuals* as having "a match between the gender they were assigned at birth, their bodies, and their personal identity" ("Doing Gender, Doing Heteronormativity," 461). I use *cisgender* for an individual who was assigned either male or female at birth and is also comfortable being identified as a man or a woman, respectively, via various masculine or feminine ideologies. Following Enke's articulation of the term, I also use it to denote an individual's compliance with or privilege in hegemonic gender systems ("Education of Little Cis," 63–68).

9. Bornstein, *Gender Outlaw*, 30–31.

10. Most commonly cited is Butler's reference to drag queening in *Gender Trouble* (174), but other examples include Aston's "Male Impersonation in the Music Hall" and Torr and Bottoms's *Sex, Drag, and Male Roles*.

11. Halberstam, *Female Masculinity*, 232.

12. Newton, *Mother Camp*, 101.

13. Rupp and Taylor, *Drag Queens at the 801 Cabaret*, 5.

14. Ibid., 218.

15. Cohen, "Deviance as Resistance," 33.

16. Berlant and Warner, "Sex in Public," 558.

17. Taylor, *Archive and the Repertoire*, 4.

18. Bailey, *Butch Queens Up in Pumps*, 17–18.

19. Muñoz, *Disidentifications*, 195.

20. Foucault, *History of Sexuality*, 42. See also Code's concern that "classificatory systems sustain and reinforce social-political power structures" and "perpetuate hegemonic patterns of expertise and authority" ("Introduction," xvi).

21. Butler, *Bodies That Matter*, 223; *Excitable Speech*, 14.

22. Butler, *Bodies That Matter*, 226.

23. A few texts catalog a variety of historical and global gender-bending stage practices, such as Senelick's *Changing Room*.

24. Taylor, *Archive and the Repertoire*, 25.

25. Butler, *Excitable Speech*, 2.

26. Butler, *Bodies That Matter*, 239–240.

27. Butler, *Excitable Speech*, 5.

28. Haraway, "Situated Knowledges," 591–592; Barad, "Posthumanist Performativity," 809.

29. Webb, *Understanding Representation*, 2.

30. Butler, *Bodies That Matter*, 224.

31. Troka, LeBesco, and Noble, *Drag King Anthology*; Shapiro, "Drag Kinging and the Transformation of Gender Identities"; Rupp and Taylor, *Drag Queens at the 801 Cabaret*. See also Heller, "Gender-Bending in El Teatro Campesino (1968–1980)" and "Female-Femmeing."

32. Newton, *Mother Camp*, 101. Newton reproduces similar language in her 1996 critique of the exclusion of lesbians from the Cherry Grove homecoming drag queen competition ("Dick[less] Tracy and the Homecoming Queen," 169–171).

33. Halberstam, *Female Masculinity*, 232.

34. Moore, "One of the Gals," 103.

35. Torr and Bottoms, *Sex, Drag, and Male Roles*, 9.

36. Horowitz, "Trouble with 'Queerness,'" 306.

37. Ibid.

38. Althusser, *Lenin and Philosophy and Other Essays*, 174.

39. Ibid., 173.

40. Note that Bailey also uses this linguistic framework in his examination of "what members of the Ballroom community do as opposed to who they are" (*Butch Queens Up in Pumps*, 23).

41. Butler, "Performative Acts and Gender Constitution," 519.

42. Ibid., 526.

43. In fact, West and Zimmerman see great value in framing "gender as an accomplishment" because it shifts the analytic focus from "matters internal to the individual" to the overarching cultural contexts and "institutional arenas" that necessitate such doings ("Doing Gender," 126).

44. Bornstein, *Gender Outlaw*, 30.

45. Karkazis, *Fixing Sex*, 23. Karkazis uses her own rubric for defining intersex bodies and references Fausto-Sterling's work on newborns that undergo surgical treatment to estimate this particular number. An example of a well-known intersex person is world-class runner Caster Semenya, who was assigned female at birth, was raised as a woman, and identifies as a woman but who was discovered through mandatory sports gender testing to have hyperandrogenism and thus was barred from competing in some "women's" events.

46. Bornstein, *Gender Outlaw*, 30.

47. West and Zimmerman, "Doing Gender," 126.

48. For example, such conversations help illustrate how gender was used as a method of colonization and also how marginalized individuals use gender to strategically enact defiance or accomplish daily survival.

49. Bornstein, *Gender Outlaw*, 26–30, 45.

50. West and Zimmerman, "Doing Gender," 131.

51. Bailey, "Gender/Racial Realness," 369–374.

52. Lorber, *Paradoxes of Gender*, 15–16.

53. Quoted in Fausto-Sterling, "Five Sexes," 20.

54. Spade, "Resisting Medicine, Re/modeling Gender," 24.
55. Barad, "Posthumanist Performativity," 802.
56. Ibid., 818.
57. Butler, *Gender Trouble*, 173.
58. Valentine, "I Went to Bed with My Own Kind Once," 125.
59. Dozier, "Beards, Breasts, and Bodies," 298.
60. Karkazis, *Fixing Sex*, 10.
61. Barad, "Posthumanist Performativity," 812.
62. This term was first coined by Samuel Taylor Coleridge in *Biographia Literaria*, 365.
63. Schacht and Underwood, "Absolutely Flawless," 4.
64. Robertson, "What Makes the Feminist Camp?" 273.
65. Brockett and Hildy, *History of the Theatre*, 19.
66. Greenwald, Schultz, and Pomo, *Longman Anthology of Drama and Theater*, 62.
67. Case, "Classic Drag," 321–322.
68. Ibid., 327.
69. For more information on these practices, see Tian, "Male Dan"; Morinaga, "The Gender of Onnagata as the Imitating Imitated"; Robertson, *Takarazuka*.
70. Wandor, "Cross-Dressing, Sexual Representation," 170.
71. Bailey, "Gender/Racial Realness," 373–380.
72. Spade, "Resisting Medicine, Re/modeling Gender," 19–23.
73. Newton, "Dick(less) Tracy and the Homecoming Queen," 164.
74. Butler, "Performative Acts and Gender Constitution," 527.
75. Ibid.
76. For extended discussion on this point, see Heller, "Is She He?"
77. For example, see Shapiro, "Disposable Boy Toys," 28; see Horowitz, "Trouble with 'Queerness,'" 310–311, for a discussion of how some drag performances are considered "real" expressions of the performer's lived identity.
78. Bailey, *Butch Queens Up in Pumps*, 29–37.
79. Shapiro, "Disposable Boy Toys," 28.
80. Robertson, *Takarazuka*, 81–83.
81. Meyer, "Unveiling the Word," 70.
82. Ibid.
83. Ibid., 72.
84. Diamond, *Unmaking Mimesis*, 43–91.
85. Dolan, "Gender Impersonation Onstage," 5–11.
86. Butler, *Gender Trouble*, 174.
87. Butler, *Bodies That Matter*, 125.
88. Ibid.

89. Gender androcentrism is closely connected to heterosexist and racist standards. For example, the attribution of masculinity to a woman has been used to dehumanize or delegitimize women of Color, queer women, and disabled women.

90. Halberstam, *Female Masculinity*, 234. Halberstam's description of hegemonic standards of masculinity is based on White heterosexual identities.

91. Butler, *Bodies That Matter*, 125.

92. Duggan, "New Homonormativity," 179.

93. Cohen, "Punks, Bulldaggers, and Welfare Queens," 441.

94. Muñoz, *Cruising Utopia*, 1.

95. Cohen, "Punks, Bulldaggers, and Welfare Queens," 437.

96. Muñoz, *Cruising Utopia*, 1.

97. Lorde, *Sister Outsider*, 110–113.

98. Code argues that feminist taxonomy projects must work to avoid such issues by framing themselves as "working definitions" whose boundaries are "constantly being made and remade" ("Introduction," xvii).

99. Berlant and Warner, "Sex in Public," 558.

TWO

"Masculine Women, Feminine Men"
Variety and Vaudevillian Male Impersonators

ANNIE HINDLE STRIDES onto a platform in a bustling saloon, wearing a custom-tailored suit and with her short blond curls brushed severely to one side. She performs four song-and-dance numbers as a dandy or "swell" character: an upper-class man who drinks too much, goes out too much, and has an affinity for fashion and ladies. When parts of the songs pitch high, Hindle speaks the lines rather than raising her register or engages in "blue" (sexual or vulgar) asides. The *New York Clipper* declares that Hindle's "sex is so concealed that one is apt to imagine that it is a man who is singing."[1] Her audiences of working- and middle-class White men go wild for it. Hindle's popularity in the mid- to late nineteenth-century US entertainment genre of variety is due to her singing and acting talent, but, make no mistake, Hindle is no common "character delineator":[2] her popularity is based on the combination of her talent with a gender-bending process I call *cross identification*. Hindle's audiences love her because they see a realistic man onstage *and also* because they know this is a skillful illusion that evidences her theatrical prowess rather than her "real" sex identity.

A few decades later, Vesta Tilley makes her US debut at Tony Pastor's theater. Her song lyrics also depict a dandy. But she uses third-person pronouns that create distance between herself and the character, and she does not make blue asides when singing songs in her high soprano register. Her fashionable men's suits have been tailored just a bit at the waist and hips. A critic praises Tilley by declaring her "a delicate piece of Dresden china."[3] Tilley's popularity in turn-of-the-century US vaudeville is due to her singing and acting talent, but, make no mistake, Tilley is no variety-style male impersonator: her popularity is based on the combination of her talent with a gender-bending process I call *identification*. Tilley's audiences love her because of her "character studies" *and also* because the act never wholly conceals her purportedly natural predilection toward Victorian feminine respectability.[4]

This chapter considers the gender-bending work of successful variety and vaudevillian male impersonators. I am interested in detailing how the performers' expressed intentions and clear methods enabled them to shape particular audience responses, or at least influence popular narratives about themselves and their acts. While the term *male impersonation* could be applied to a range of gender-bending practices, it historically refers to a gender-bending act popularized in British and US stage entertainment during the nineteenth and twentieth centuries.[5] Variety and vaudeville comprised a range of entertainers and entertainments, from classically trained singers and dancers to curio animal and circus acts. Male impersonators were often talented singers and dancers, but no more so than many other variety and vaudeville performers. Thus, male impersonation was considered first and foremost a novelty act rather than a song or dance act. The novelty was that a middle-class White woman (occupying a racial-sexual position of social respectability) performed as a White man.[6] If we presume gender is always performative or done, then it is not hard to imagine a woman producing masculinity. However, if we follow the Victorian logic that gender is a fixed expression of an essentialist sex identity, then someone who can bend the capacity of their natural cisgender self is doing something special. Thus, the unique entertainment factor that male impersonators brought to their acts was contradiction: a woman who could sing and dance while simultaneously creating an illusory gendered character that fundamentally contrasted to her own gendered self.

In this chapter, I explore what audiences presumed or were told about male impersonators, how they came to this information, and how that knowledge allowed male impersonators to cultivate particular public sentiments. While British and US male impersonation has been discussed in other theater and cultural scholarship, it is rare for impersonators to be credited with building complex and nuanced acts in pursuit of a specific audience reaction. The active and self-selective decoder of the male impersonator's ambiguous and passive product is most often attributed to the audience's gaze. For example, Martha Vicinus says that male impersonation was "read in many different ways depending on the subjectivity of the viewer," and Aston claims that impersonators' gendered appearances "depend[ed] largely on their reception by the spectator."[7] If performers are credited with any agency, it is generally framed in terms of expanding middle-class White women's social spheres. But Aston and Vicinus agree that this effect depended "not so much on the intentions of the impersonator herself."[8] I argue the converse position; my analysis of impersonators' methodological processes develops a richer picture of both their individual intentions and their active cultivation of an impact on audiences.

Unlike some other acts I explore in this book, male impersonation was practiced largely before sound or video recording and photography capable of capturing live-action movement onstage. How, then, does one study the performance process of a performance with no contemporary repertoire and a limited archive? First, almost all successful entertainers posed for publicity photos as their most famous characters or showing off their most famous skills; these images were then used in commercial and advertising ventures, such as postcards, cartes de visite (portrait trading cards), and cabinet cards (larger size souvenir portrait cards), and were also printed in theater advertisements and annals of productions. Later, vaudevillian impersonators would take additional photographs as their "everyday" feminine selves for comparison. Evidence of performance processes can also be gleaned through content published in local and trade newspapers such as the *Clipper* and the *Sun*. Impersonators used these sources to advertise their upcoming engagements or special talents, and many papers also printed reviews and op-ed pieces about their shows. The most famous performers were mentioned in national gossip papers such as the *National Police Gazette*, and some savvy impersonators also contributed to their own news cycles by authoring poems and opinion pieces. Finally, vaudevillian performers gave personal interviews to papers and magazines about their private lives, opinions, and political leanings. While this archive cannot serve as a comprehensive outline of either male impersonators' stage acts or their private lives, it does offer a good amount of source material about their processes: exactly how and why impersonators became successful performers.

In using this archive to develop a nuanced picture of male impersonators' processes, I also necessarily engage with some popular narratives about male impersonators offered by historians, performance scholars, and theater practitioners. Male impersonation certainly does not play as prominent a role in gender-bending scholarship as, for instance, drag queening does. There are, however, more scholarly mentions of male impersonation than of any other act I explore in this book, and I argue that the boundaries and logic of drag discourse have led to some significant mischaracterizations about the impacts of these acts. This actually allows me a unique opportunity to examine the ways others have filtered these same archives through drag discourse and come to specific conclusions about this practice. Male impersonation generally makes an appearance in academic literature for two reasons. The first is to illuminate an occluded history of women's theatrical performances, and the second is to illustrate how these practices disrupted Victorian sexual or gender mores.[9] For instance, Lisa Duggan and Vicinus reference impersonators in studies about the history of same-sex desire, and Vicinus also suggests that male impersonation destabilized gender ideas.[10] Gillian Rodger asserts that "women in variety were not expected to adhere to middle-class ideals of the period."[11] It is true that some impersonators had public romantic relationships with women, were not legally sanctioned for dressing in men's clothing, and were not culturally stigmatized for having big public careers. So, the conclusion is often that male impersonation was a performance-based vehicle for cracking and expanding (or at least edging around) cultural gender and sexual limitations. But this conclusion overlooks a critical aspect of the act: male impersonators were successful only if their performances ultimately reconsolidated these norms. That is, these acts could be a "novelty" only if audiences believed Victorian mores were a justified standard for women, and especially for the women performers impersonating men.

I am not concerned here about *whether* male impersonation is a gender-bending practice; it clearly is, because the impersonators publicly identified as respectable White women and performed onstage as boozy playboys. Variety impersonators communicated this identity divergence to their audiences via a drag process I call *cross identification*. I derive cross identification from Muñoz's definition of identification, or the physical and ideological replication of hegemonic cultural norms.[12] Cross identification also delineates a culturally ideal form of embodiment and behavior. However, rather than directly exhibiting this social alignment, a cross-identification process evokes appropriate embodiment and behavior via their apparent absence. In drag terms, the more "manlike" an actor appears within the context of a male impersonation act, the more audiences will assume the man act is the skilled work of a nonman actor. Cross-identification drag is rooted in the logic and assumption that how the impersonator outwardly presents dichotomously opposes what the impersonator actually is. Variety impersonators accomplished cross identification by heavily advertising not only their drag specialty but also their offstage bodies and cultural positions, and then allowing audiences to leverage this knowledge while beholding an opposing representation.

Vaudevillian performers were similarly aligned with hegemonic standards of gender, sexuality, socioeconomic status, and race. However, a shift in mass popular perception about the relationship among gender, sex, and sexuality led to the cultivation of a more overt methodology I call *identification* drag. Vaudevillian impersonators encouraged audiences to think of them as skilled woman performers and also as innately feminine and (hetero)sexually respectable. Like their variety predecessors, vaudevillian performers actively cultivated public awareness about their offstage identities. However, in an era that often labeled "mannish" women sexual deviants, vaudevillian performers also designed stage personae that did not fully conceal their secondary sex characteristics or stereotypically feminine predilections. In this way, their stage masculinity never fully displaced the audience's ability to visually identify them both as female-bodied and as respectable ladies.

To be clear, I do not know if *only* people medically assigned female at birth performed as male impersonators, or if *all* male impersonators privately identified as female or women. However, the archives clearly indicate that the general public presumed male impersonators to be female-bodied and woman-identified people (in fact, this popular presumption led to Hindle's career demise when the public came to believe she was a man). The engagement of the "male impersonator" title functioned as a sexing cue to the mass public because it was known that only women performed this specialty. Furthermore, all male impersonators I have researched used women's pronouns in their advertising materials and were referred to in theater houses and news literature by women's titles and honorifics. In addition to documenting how impersonators gendered themselves, I also investigate how they cultivated an aura of gender-specific respectability, what Barbara Welter terms *true womanhood*.[13] Aston and Vicinus praise male impersonation for destabilizing or disrupting Victorian gender ideologies, but I make the opposite argument: male impersonation did not expand gender mores beyond the microspace of their own lives. In fact, impersonators' methodologies actually ensured that any personal outward masculine expression might benefit them but would not challenge quotidian gender and sex scripts at all.

Male impersonators also traded on their racial and socioeconomic positions to develop their aura of gender respectability. "Women performers" or "women's gender-bending practices" cannot be investigated without full attention to how gender operates in relation to race, sexuality, ability, location, and socioeconomic status. Yvonne Tasker and Diane Negra note that when a generic or universal female subject is referred to, such a subject is often "white and middle class by default."[14] In the case of male impersonation, that is absolutely true and absolutely relevant: male impersonators used tactics and traded on assumptions that were available to them specifically because they were White and middle class. So, this chapter draws on Kimberlé Crenshaw's model of intersectional analysis to explore how these performers' identities worked as a unit to locate them within a matrix of cultural, economic, and regulatory institutions, and also how such intersectionality led to their specific experiences and outcomes.[15]

In the following pages, I detail how an impersonator could lead audiences to see their bending as an act of cultural conformity. I also explore how drag discourse has cast these practices in the literature both as blank slates for audiences to layer private interests, tastes, and fantasies over and as important cultural transgressions. Audiences can actively decode performances in ways that do not align with the performer's preferred or intended message. But, in this book, I give primacy to the instigator of the message, especially as it is conveyed in a theater forum and with performance-based methodologies. Male impersonators gained and retained success only when they accomplished their communication agendas. Hindle was commercially successful because she clearly communicated her offstage gender respectability to her audiences by presenting herself as doggedly committed to crafting a male illusion. Tilley was commercially successful because of how she clearly communicated her affluent White heteronormativity to her audiences by letting it show through her male personae. The next sections catalog several ways male impersonators could build and deploy these successful identification or cross-identification gender-bending acts. And these intentions and methods primarily and necessarily shape my conclusions about the micro- and macroimpact of male impersonation.

VARIETY INTO VAUDEVILLE

The nineteenth century ushered in a wave of industry-related population increases in big cities like New York, Philadelphia, and Boston and port and river cities such as Milwaukee and Chicago.[16] This rise in urban population led to a rise in urban entertainment choices and opportunities. The respectable option for middle- and upper-class White amusement seekers was the theater: preferably scripted dramas and operas but also comedies and musicals. This was one of the more expensive entertainment choices, although a cheaper ticket would still pay for a standing spot as well as access to the "olio" acts performed on the stage apron during scenery changes.[17] Cheaper and more diverse entertainment options included minstrel shows, circuses, tableau shows, sports games, music concerts, and dime or curio museums. But for the working- or middle-class White man who liked a pint of beer and a cigar, concert saloons were the way to go. A concert saloon was a bar that offered regular entertainment nights such as sing-alongs accompanied by a professional musician or singer. As these nights became more popular, saloon managers began diversifying the events with dancers, comics, circus performers, impersonators, magicians, hat spinners, ventriloquists, knife throwers, and trained chimps. If several of these acts were strung together in a single night, it was a variety show. Rodger discusses how sweet and sentimental seriocomic songs were popular, but Peter Zellers characterizes variety shows as overarchingly "boisterous and unsophisticated; the comedy was low, robust, and often quite 'blue.'"[18] While some variety acts might have been sweet, the spaces of variety performance were branded in the press and by legislation such as the *Anti-Concert Saloon Bill* as hotbeds of "vices" such as drinking, smoking, fighting, scamming, thieving, and the selling and solicitation of sex.[19]

This atmosphere was less than appealing to middle-class White women performers who traded on having respectable reputations. Rodger says that, in the early days of concert saloons, women within these spaces were assumed to be prostitutes, lower-class sexualized workers called waiter girls, or family relations of the owner.[20] But concert saloons wanted to attract more women performers and would aggressively advertise for women piano players or "a good singing lady; must be attractive."[21] As this particular advertisement makes clear, women performers were not considered primarily sex workers but were treated nevertheless as sexual objects for the assumed heterosexual clientele. Many early concert saloons did not even have an elevated stage to physically separate women performers from the crowd, so "there was little to stop the men in the audience from molesting these women or treating them as prostitutes."[22] In spite of this, the amount of women venturing into variety performance contexts did grow for the very basic reason that the money, promotion, and stage time was better for women than in circus, olio, or ballet. For some performers, the solution was simple: as women's participation in variety grew, so too did a specific song-and-dance act that was, at first, called protean or character-change art, or character delineation. Later, it was almost universally referred to as male impersonation.

The concept of an adult woman performing a solo song-and-dance act as a man was a new one. Young women had been playing principal boys in Christmas pantomimes, and older women theater stars occasionally performed classic men's parts as "trousers roles." There is some mention in theater annals of man-woman sister acts as well as acts in which one woman wears partly men's garb and partly women's garb. However, these presentations appear to have been for the sake of singing a particular duet. And female impersonation (men presenting as caricatures of women), which had been quite popular in minstrelsy and circus genres, easily transitioned into variety hall forums. But there was no equivalent transition for women who had occasionally performed scripted men's roles or in men's clothing pieces. So Hindle, coming from different theatrical traditions in England, debuted something new in US entertainment when she advertised as "the original male impersonator."[23] Within three years of her debut, several women had shifted from ballet and seriocomic singing specialties to a near-identical male impersonation variety act. This was a White-centric practice. Unsurprisingly, the most popular commercial entertainment genres during the nineteenth century in the US were performed by and for White people or recent immigrants from Europe. And I have found no record of non-White male impersonators practicing as far back as the concert saloon era. In fact, we have few records of any variety-style theatrical practice by Black, Latinx, or Asian performers until high-profile news media began reporting on theater circuits such as the Chitlin' Circuit. Thus, it is safe to say that male impersonators paired gender ideologies with hegemonic racial standards when cultivating images of masculinity or sentiments of respectability.

The best variety male impersonators never expressed any quality onstage that audiences would consider feminine; nor did they wear costumes that showed off their legs, waists, or chests. This was very different from the costumes young women wore when performing as men in Christmas pantomimes or burlesques. Variety male impersonators wore straight or baggy suits and cut their hair short. A few uncorroborated mentions exist of Hindle encouraging the growth of facial hair by regularly shaving. A few references also point to Hindle and another famous variety impersonator, Ella Wesner, using lower singing voices and growing slightly stouter body figures.[24] Male impersonators would also spit, swear, smoke, and tell bawdy jokes. These behaviors were likely intended to appeal to the tastes of concert saloon patrons, but they also allowed male impersonators to frame themselves as "one of the guys" rather than as an object for the guys' sexual attentions. Impersonators often performed an upper-class man-about-town character called a fop, dandy, or swell. They also sometimes played laborers or soldiers, but the swell character was extremely popular with variety audiences, likely because of his high-class yet buffoonish status. Swell "character delineation"—the performance of a well-known caricature—was not the exclusive property of male impersonators; men performers such as Charles Vivian and Tony Pastor also frequently performed swells. In fact, male impersonators and men performers often swapped singing materials or copied each other's presentations.[25] But, whereas Vivian and Pastor were known for their skilled performances of specific caricatures of men, male impersonators were known for their skilled performances of maleness. The primary draw of male impersonation was not the singing, dancing, or funny character itself but the fact that a woman was pretending to be a man when accomplishing these things. And this particular novelty secured Hindle and Wesner bookings and rates rivaling or exceeding those of Vivian and Pastor.

The male impersonator's masculine persona seems to have offered its performers yet another benefit. Any unladylike performance material was all part of the illusion and thus not a reflection on the actor's real ladylike respectability. Nineteenth-century Victorian sentiments figured the ideal woman, what Welter terms the *true woman*, as genteel, sexually and religiously pure, and inclined toward the domestic.[26] A woman's respectability directly correlated with how well she embodied these attitudes and behaviors. Class and race prejudices precluded many women from these ideals regardless of their immaculate behaviors and presentations.[27] And not every middle-class White woman could achieve the true womanhood status either. Nevertheless, this idealized structure served as a primary measure for women's reputations. Male impersonators worked in disreputable spaces and performed vulgar and sexual acts, but the context of their performance novelty—high gender illusion—allowed them to separate the blueness of "men and manners of the day" from their personal reputations.[28] The efficacy of this is evident in *Clipper* and *Sun* reviews that praise impersonators for creating wonderful characters in spite of their own natural genteel selves. A variety impersonator's popularity and success, as well as her ability to maintain a standard of cultural respectability, were contingent on widespread public recognition that what she did onstage was the opposite of who she really was.

Around the 1880s, vaudeville began to overtake variety in mass popularity.[29] At first glance, the two entertainment genres appear similar in that they are fairly inexpensive and accessible urban entertainments comprising novelty and talent acts. But, whereas variety shows were an assemblage of separately booked independent performers and unrelated acts, vaudevillian performers frequently worked in troupes with a standard lineup and some acts that we interrelated. Not only was booking these troupes much easier than assembling a night's worth of acts in a piecemeal way, it also allowed entertainment hall managers to prescreen content and request changes in advance. Edwin Milton Royle describes a common vaudevillian edict: "You are hereby warned that your act must be free from all vulgarity and suggestiveness in words, action, and costume, while playing in any of Mr. ———'s houses, and all vulgar, double-meaning and profane words and songs must be cut out of your act before the first performance. [. . .] Such words as Liar, Son-of-a-Gun, Devil, Sucker, Damn and all other words unfit for the ears of ladies and children, also any reference to questionable streets, resorts, localities, and bar-rooms, are prohibited."[30] Such vetting offered a significant financial advantage: if a hall manager absolutely knew the whole show was absent of blue content, he could advertise it as "family friendly" and suitable for women and children, thus tripling its potential audience. The success of the family model was also fueled by popular sentiments about vaudeville in general. Royle reminisces: "Said a lady to me: 'They (the vaudeville theatres) are the only theatres in New York where I should feel absolutely safe in taking a young girl without making preliminary inquiries. Though they may offend the taste, they never offend one's sense of decency.'"[31] In short, vaudeville was considered the respectable version of variety-style entertainment.

Many established variety entertainers wanted to hitch themselves to vaudeville's rising star, but the genre's family-friendly reputation made this difficult for performers who specialized in blue material. In other words, male impersonators would have had to develop an act free of the spitting, swearing, and sexual jokes that brought them success in variety. To accomplish this transition, male impersonators had to alter their acts in another critical way as well, because the cultural context of respectability had also shifted due to the popularization of certain sexology theories. In the late nineteenth century, sexology emerged as a mode of scientifically theorizing and classifying people's nonhegemonic sexual or gender behaviors. Sexology's most popularly referenced conclusions are about people with same-sex desires, but the field also attempted to explain why some women were interested in men's clothing, jobs, or pastimes. Carroll Smith-Rosenberg documents how "women's rejection of traditional gender roles and their demands for social and economic equality" were suppressed by labeling these behaviors as masculine and connecting them to narratives about pathologically mannish women with same-sex desires.[32] And sexual and gender variation were not just labeled as an outward sign of a person's deviance; sexology actually defined them as indicative of a person's pathological identity.

Gender "inversion" was a theory popularized by sexologists such as Richard von Krafft-Ebing. This theory proposes that when women or men exhibited the gendered behavior and/or sexual desires of the so-called opposite sex, it is because of a congenital (or perhaps acquired) desire to become that other sex.[33] So, whereas an unfeminine woman had been considered disreputable before, a "masculine woman" at the end of the century was a figure with a diagnosable medical pathology, trapped in the wrong body and likely engaging in sexually deviant behavior.[34] Even a woman with racial and class privilege who expressed overt interest in men's things (politics, pants, paid labor) risked the stigma of gender pathology as well as the implication that she engaged in same-sex relationships. The novelty of variety male impersonation was that a woman *could* present herself like a man in all his stereotypical vulgarities and sexual tastes. But the vaudevillian male impersonator could not assume that simply advertising herself as a skilled performer would result in audiences cross-identifying her as a respectable woman rather than a mannish invert.

HINDLE'S VARIETY PROCESS

Variety impersonators received public praise and reward for their masculinity if and only if they successfully cultivated a strong cross-identification process. The most successful in this was Annie Hindle, who was billed (she likely billed herself) as "the original male impersonator, the model from which all others copy their feeble imitations."[35] While I know of no sound or image recording of any variety impersonator's stage performance, information about Hindle's characterization can be extrapolated from extant photographs and drawings. Because publicity images were intended to advertise the performer's talent, male impersonators often sat for them in costume and character. In one photo (see fig. 2.1), Hindle has her head positioned away from the camera and has focused her hooded eyes to the right of center. Her unsmiling and slightly pursed lips build tension along her jaw, and no other quality such as groomed eyebrows or long eyelashes feminizes her face. The *Sun* characterized Hindle's visage as "masculine in all its lines."[36] Hindle is, of course, dressed in a full men's suit and holds a bowler hat in hand, thereby leaving exposed her very short hair, combed severely to the side. The press

Fig. 2.1. Annie Hindle as "The Great Hindle." *Harry Ransom Center, University of Texas at Austin.*

lauded Hindle for keeping her natural hair "closely cropped" in a short men's style "which, on and off the stage, she parted on one side, brushing it away from the temples just like men do."[37] Prominent impersonator Ella Wesner followed Hindle's lead in terms of short hairstyle, while another, Alicia Jourdan, was at one point criticized in the press for "wearing her hair too long at the back of her head."[38] Hindle is also conveying characterization through body pose, as she sits backward on a chair and leans a crooked elbow against its carved wooden back. Newspapers reported that Hindle was of medium height and stature, but in this picture, she looks broad and tall.[39] Senelick explains that men performers frequently posed for publicity photographs sitting backward on chairs, and some male impersonators employed a similar "straddling pose in trousers" to evoke this familiar masculine presentation.[40] Articles that praised male impersonators referenced these meticulous details as evidence of their skill at the craft. Furthermore, male impersonators referenced these details—the permanent alteration of hair, the constant flawless presentation of masculinity—as evidence that they were dedicated women professionals.

Male impersonators in archival images might have been captured in their everyday street clothes or presentation. However, it is more likely that photos of impersonators in menswear depict a moment of their act or stage performance. This belief is partly based on how many photographs are labeled with both the performer's name and a particular song or character. Moreover, as advertising tools, images were a critical and primary way performers visually communicated their skill and novelty to an audience beyond the immediate theater. One of my favorite archival discoveries has been that some impersonators' publicity photographs keenly reflect the masculine stylings of either their relatives or well-known performance colleagues. In the case of Blanche Selwyn, she wears a huge handlebar mustache that looks awfully like J. H. Selwyn's.[41] Similarly, Hindle styled herself and her act in a way that mimetically reflected her variety star husband and manager, Charles Vivian. Hindle and Vivian were married two weeks after Hindle's arrival in the United States, and I have found no information about how Hindle physically presented after her US arrival but prior to her marriage. However, Rodger notes that during their marriage, "Hindle and Vivian performed practically identical acts," used a similar persona and song repertoire, and also physically styled themselves similarly.[42] I cannot say whether Hindle copied Vivian's look, Vivian copied Hindle's, or both were styling themselves in a popular masculine way. My point is that even if Hindle looked and acted masculine in her daily life, her styling and body language in photographs was performance based in that it was curated to transmit a readable masculine impression akin to Vivian's.

Apart from the context of publicity images, there is evidence that, if a male impersonator could frame her masculine aesthetic and behavior as part of her occupation, she could extend it beyond the immediate vicinity of the stage. Both Hindle and Wesner were known for wearing men's clothing in their everyday lives (often characterized in press coverage as stage costumes). In addition, the *National Police Gazette* printed a story about Hindle getting into a brawl with a man in a public house, and the *Sun* claims she was accidently addressed as "sir" from time to time.[43] These same papers also declare that the mark of a talented impersonator is that she can "easily walk Broadway in male attire without her sex being suspected."[44] I have found no publication that clearly identifies male impersonators as women performers *and also* negatively casts their offstage masculinity as a sign of their personal disreputability.[45] Instead, offstage masculinity is often framed as a continual performance that exhibits the impersonator's dedicated professionalism. So, even though Hindle's brawling and Wesner's pants-wearing were not always done onstage or to express a particular stage character, such behavior was nevertheless framed as part of the act (or as part of the work that went into making their acts great).

I propose that this mass press reception is largely based on the careful cross-identification methods male impersonators employed to maintain the notion that they were women performers whose jobs were to impersonate something they were not. Far from illustrating the permeability of gender roles, male impersonators actually traded on popular sentiments that gender was relatively fixed in relation to the body, as were race and socioeconomic status. Through the wording of photograph labels, advertisements, and public reports, impersonators provided constant and clear proof that they were women but virtually none that they were feminine or respectable ladies. Nevertheless, I argue that the public did largely perceive the most commercially successful impersonators as respectable ladies. First, impersonators' identities as middle-class White women made them eligible to fulfill cultural standards of respectability. Respectability, I argue, was then read from the absence of its appearance in the on- and offstage gendered aesthetics and behaviors of these performers. In other words, anything and everything masculine impersonators did could be taken as a professionally cultivated talent and thus a quality that necessarily contrasted to their authentic "non-performative" selves. In short, male impersonators cross-identified to publics as being respectable Victorian ladies specifically because impersonators *could* align with these standards *and also* continually presented themselves in ways that defied such standards.

This active cross-identification process can also be traced in how impersonators paired their masculine aesthetics with carefully feminine self-promotions. For instance, Hindle's and Wesner's advertising almost always foregrounds women's pronouns and identifiers such as "Miss," "Mrs.," and "actress."[46] The dogged use of these gendered textual cues does not appear to be standard practice for all women variety performers; some, for instance, identify themselves by their full names and without additional articles.[47] In addition to using gender-identifying language, impersonators also carefully contextualized their acts in these ads. At first, they favored terms that implied character impersonation such as "protean artist" or "character vocalist," but as their specialty spread, "male impersonator" became the standard label. Selwyn initially advertised herself as a *seriocomic performer*, a term that, according to Rodger, a range of women performers used to characterize the specialty of sentimental and lighthearted songs.[48] But, while a male impersonator might sing these songs, "seriocomic" does not directly indicate the specialty of gendered impersonation. Therefore, it is significant that Selwyn's advertising changed in the *Clipper* over several months and "seriocomic" was replaced with "character vocalist."[49]

There is a similar language switch in Hindle's advertising that, I suggest, demonstrates her active public cultivation of cross identification. Hindle's US debut was heavily preadvertised in trade papers, but early promotions do not clearly state her specialty of male impersonation (although her gender is indicated as she is called Miss Hindle or, slightly later, Mrs. Vivian). But shortly after her debut, Hindle's advertising started to include phrases clarifying that her specialization is illusions of men. One not-so-subtle *Clipper* advertisement announces that "Miss Hindle's" specialty is "wonderful comic impersonations of MEN AND MANNERS OF THE DAY."[50] The overarching theme in all of Hindle's advertising is that she is a master talent and a not-to-be-missed variety success. But another near-omnipresent message is that Hindle is a woman (a Miss) whose main talent is impersonating men and their manners. Based on the frequency and placement of these advertisements in entertainment and trade papers, I suggest that variety-going audiences had ample exposure to information about both Hindle's gender identity and the nature of her act as a gender illusion. Whereas identification performers visually and orally show audiences who the performer "actually" is during the act, here, a cross-identification process has already built awareness that the visual and oral material of the act opposes what the performer "actually" is.

I cannot poll variety audiences to quantify what they actually knew about Hindle before a performance, nor can I record exactly how they received Hindle's act in light of their knowledge base. However, in addition to the general knowledge we have about how publics thought of middle-class White women (which Hindle was), published performance reviews and op-ed pieces provide information about popular interpretations of her act. A review published in the *Clipper* describes Hindle's song set ("Pretty Jemima," "The Perambulator," "On a Seventh Street Car," and "Rackety Jack") as well as her respective characters ("a gent of the first water," "a gent in the army," "the Washington fop," and "a lively young swell").[51] The reviewer raves about her song execution and characters and offers only the criticism that Hindle annoyingly hums song interludes. The reviewer also remarks that "the lady" is of "medium stature" and "pleasing figure" and that "the Lingard style of business is the lady's *forte*."[52] So, in the context of praising Hindle's skillful execution of masculinity, the reviewer simultaneously articulates Hindle's offstage self as "the lady" who is in possession of a "pleasing figure." Based on publicity photos, I doubt the reviewer could see Hindle's figure beyond the cut of her boxy suit. Other accounts of Hindle's stage aesthetics support my interpretation: Hindle was not known to wear clothing that accentuated waist, hips, or breasts, and she also tended to stand in ways that made her appear straight, boxy, and broad. Thus, I believe the reviewer's reference to her pleasing figure is simply a type of description liberally applied. The reviewer also carefully mentions Hindle's talent at "the Lingard style." William Lingard was a well-known variety performer who specialized in quick-change female impersonations; in referencing Lingard, this reviewer connects Hindle's masculine stage work with that of a well-known gender illusionist. Thus, Hindle's masculine stage presentation is characterized as enjoyable specifically because the reviewer never forgets there is a lady under the masculine illusion (even if there is no outward sign of it). Hindle's advertising was written and paid for by her management and her, but it is unlikely she had control over these reviews. Thus, reviews evidence popular impact, or what some in the general public saw when they watched male impersonations and what they thought of its performers.

Some scholars have proposed that this knowledge paradigm—that audiences were well versed on impersonators' offstage gender identities—functioned as a vehicle for audiences' sexual desire. Vicinus and Rodger suggest that heterosexual men liked male impersonation because it created space to entertain fantasies about the unseen-but-known body of the woman under the act. Rodger supports this interpretation by referencing the convention of the quick change: male impersonators changed costumes between each song in stage wings or behind opaque screens. Rodger believes that these quick changes reminded heterosexual men that a feminine body existed just underneath the layer of easily removed men's clothing.[53] While this may have been true in some cases, it does not align with how male impersonation was originally crafted as a vehicle to help women avoid sexual objectification and harassment. Furthermore, Hindle and Wesner were always quite masculine both onstage and in other public settings (i.e., not especially feminine under the act). In fact, this is why Anthony Slide argues that popular knowledge of impersonators' gender was used by men with same-sex desires to safely express tastes for masculinity under the guise of sexual woman gazing.[54] So one scholarly camp argues that impersonators were publicly contextualized as women so that men could heterosexually gaze at them, and the other proposes that impersonators were publicly contextualized as women so that men could homosexually gaze at them. But neither interpretation credits impersonators with what they intended and tried to communicate via their identities and their acts or presumes that the popular effect was primarily connected to this process. And these interpretations do not mesh with the body of evidence that demonstrates how meticulously impersonators formed readable contrasts between their so-called illusionary gender expressions and their presumably respectable selves. Framing male impersonation as a cultivated process of cross identification recognizes the agency of performers in having intents and enacting methods, and it also credits commercially successful impersonators with cultivating a type of popular impact that resulted in lasting commercial success.

In theory, an impersonator could have methodically disclosed certain identities to trigger a response of desiring sexual gazes to increase her profit and popularity. However, cross identification is more than just how an actor can clue in audiences to the nature of her unseeable but desirable body. Rather, I suggest it is a method of projecting sentiments of hegemonic identity compliance onto bent actions. Hindle and Wesner wore men's attire onstage, of course, but both also wore similar clothing in their day-to-day lives. Wesner's *New York Times* obituary casually remarks, "Throughout her life Miss Wesner has preferred man's apparel."[55] Although wearing men's clothing was considered strange and even illegal in some areas, I have found no record of Hindle or Wesner ever being legally cited or even socially censured for this. Hindle and Wesner also had overt romantic relationships with women, and when newspapers reported on these romance scandals, articles focused on the scandal part (a physical fight, an accusation of theft, a court case) rather than the nature of the relationship itself. Hindle actually wrote a series of poems for the *Clipper* that explicitly names a woman as the object of the writer's romantic desire. For many of Hindle's contemporaries, such overt same-sex sexual expressions would have marked them as disreputable or engaging in illegal behavior. In a decade or so, such acts would also evidence a pathological identity. And yet, Hindle published these poems at the height of her popularity and seemingly without personal repercussion.[56] The context of cross identification not only protected her from social or legal blowback; it actually encouraged the public to read respectability into these acts of cultural deviance.

Through a contemporary lens, it is hard to comprehend how such overt sexual and gender deviation could have been interpreted as compliant Victorian respectability. In fact, most contemporary scholarship advances a much different claim: that male impersonators were already accepted as people who bent gender, so mass publics also accepted other types of deviation from them. This position leads to the conclusion that male impersonation created the space for women who desired to bend gender and sexual rules to be accepted. But there is another way to see this. I have no doubt that Hindle's and Wesner's positions as popular entertainers as well as their race and socioeconomic status shielded them from the harshest of cultural criticisms and legal punishments. But variety was not such an idolized genre that its performers could do whatever they wanted and still retain their popularity and reputations. Male impersonators with commercially successful careers traded on their cross identification; only when their gender pronouns, gender specializations, and gender identities in contrast to their masculine practices were firmly embedded in the public consciousness could they then count on receiving personal leniency in gender or sexual matters. That is to say, only by first developing a clear context of respectability around them—including in their adherence to gender, race, and socioeconomic precepts—could male impersonators craft a commercially successful gender-bending product. And only successful performers were given leniency from Victorian precepts—due, I propose, to the presumption of their inherent conformity established by their acts. In this regard, any personal space male impersonators had in their lives is an indication not of the progressive impact of these acts but rather of the fact that these acts *did not* create any lasting breakage in hegemonic identity systems.

To support my position, I offer up one final Hindle story. On June 6, 1886, Hindle legally married her dresser, Annie Ryan. According to news accounts, Hindle was in Grand Rapids, Michigan, for a performance engagement. After one night's show, Hindle found a minister to conduct a wedding ceremony for her and Ryan. The minister later implied that he thought Hindle was the man in the wedding party. There is no evidence I am aware of that Hindle was medically assigned male at birth, had so-called male reproductive organs or genitals, or was an intersex person. Moreover, Hindle always used women's pronouns and titles in her promotion materials and had also legally married at least one man before. Therefore, the minister's perception that Hindle was a man was very likely based on Hindle's clothing (she was supposedly still in stage costume), perhaps her behavior, and also certainly because she identified herself to the minister as "Charles Hindle." Aside from the fuzzy details of this particular wedding story, I have come across no other example where Hindle personally claimed to be a man. So, I surmise that Hindle's dress, proffered name, and whatever else she told the minister that night were not necessarily indicative of her assigned or desired gender identity but rather a means to obtain a legal marriage. Hindle was living in a time and location that allowed legal marriage only between men and women. "Annie Hindle" could not very well marry "Annie Ryan," and, besides, "Annie Hindle" was still technically married to Charles Vivian. In the major cities where Hindle most often lived and worked (i.e., *not* Grand Rapids), the information about her being a woman who dressed in men's clothing and sometimes had intimate relationships with women circulated more prominently. But in Grand Rapids, Hindle's presentation, name identification, and desire to marry a woman seem to have been enough to convince a minister to conduct a marriage. And this minister's ardent convictions—paired with his press statements—were the beginning of Hindle's end.

Hindle and Ryan's marriage was first reported locally but was quickly reproduced in city and national papers such as the *Clipper, Sun,* and *National Police Gazette.* These bigger, more cosmopolitan papers could have made a joke out of the minister: a person who could not tell a male impersonator from a man. They could also have commended Hindle for producing an impersonation so skilled that she could fool a minister into conducting a marriage ceremony. Instead papers used the minister's position as their jumping-off point to call into question Hindle's sex identity. Headlines read: "An Unexpected Marriage—One Woman Marries Another—Is She He?" and "Since the marriage of Annie Hindle to her maid the question arises, 'Is she he?'"[57] These reports also mention Hindle making a supposed post-marriage "confession" that she was really a man.[58] Hindle's masculinity—so often publicly praised as the exemplar of her skill at appearing as what she was not—was now suddenly proof of her secret identity. Newspapers claimed that Hindle had defrauded variety audiences by billing herself as a woman who played men. She was, they professed, merely a man who played men, just one more seriocomic in the variety bucket.

Even reminders about Hindle's first marriage to Charles Vivian did not reverse the growing popular belief that she was a man who had been passing as a woman to make a living as a male impersonator.[59] The immediate consequence was that Hindle had trouble filling her venues and was disengaged from future bookings. When she could get work, it was infrequent and at small, seedy spaces, the end result being that Hindle went into semiretirement.[60] A reporter describing his encounter with Hindle several years after the scandal claimed: "It was immaterial to her, [Hindle] said, rather naïvely, whether the reporter addressed her as 'Sir' or 'Madam.' Either term, she added, was acceptable."[61] The author's depiction of Hindle here—without a care about how she was addressed—might have sold papers, but I see it as little matching Hindle's realities. Hindle's billing and advertising loudly identified her as "madam"; her financial success was based on a cultivated public awareness that a "madam" was always under the act; her career took a nosedive when the public was no longer sure she was that "madam." The author implies that people who assume gender designation is immaterial are "rather naïve." I think Hindle would entirely agree.

Hindle's performances absolutely bent identity norms, and they were, unequivocally, gender-bending acts. Yet, this designation is just one element of the larger story of male impersonation. It is critical to move past initial classifications of drag acts to also investigate how exactly such acts bend and to what specific ends. Hindle walked, talked, and acted like a middle-class White man—so much so that this illusion could fool an audience, could even fool a minister. And yet, no one was actually fooled (well, perhaps the minister) because Hindle clearly contextualized her masculinity as an act that opposed her respectable woman self. If Hindle was indeed "the original male impersonator, the model from which all others copy their feeble imitations," then her cross-identification process was also likely a model that other impersonations drew on.[62] In this regard, I suggest it was unlikely that any successful male impersonation act created a progressive cultural disruption; these acts could surely bend gender rules but did not, nor were they intended to, challenge or expand macro-Victorian identity precepts. The hard irony in Hindle's story is that, as a woman, she often deviated from the gender and sexual rules her cross-identification act ultimately upheld. When she was widely thought to be a man, her men's dress and marriage to a woman should have marked her as a conforming Victorian subject. Yet, when she was assumed to be such, she could no longer maintain her cross-identification process and thus her career success.

TILLEY'S VAUDEVILLE PROCESS

Maggie Weston was a rather middling male impersonator who was successful enough to remain in the business but lacked the mass appeal of Hindle or Wesner. Weston did have one thing going for her, though: foresight into the changing cultural climate of the late nineteenth century. Instead of bragging about her flawless impersonations of men, Weston's advertising declares that the most commendable thing "about Miss Weston's singing male character songs [is that] she never forgets for a moment (though dressed as a man) that she is a lady."[63] Unlike most other variety impersonators' *Clipper* advertisements, Weston's publicity focuses on what might seem to be a performance flaw: she will see herself as a "lady" (and, by extension, her audience will see her as such) during her masculine act. While Hindle was called a lady, she was also contextualized as having the talent to conceal this identity onstage. I have found no review or advertisement that characterizes Hindle as the type of lady whose ladylike predilections are evident in her stage performance. Weston's perspective toward her stage act would not necessarily make her a variety star. But it could very well have made her a vaudevillian one.

Despite vaudeville's emphasis on showcasing only the most respectable of variety entertainments, there was still a place for male impersonators. Like their variety predecessors, vaudevillian impersonators performed a song-and-dance set with costume changes between numbers. They still dressed in detailed men's fashions, they still advertised heavily in trade publications as talented gender illusionists, and the swell character still dominated their repertoires. But gone were the flawlessly mimetic presentations: vaudevillian impersonators' suits slightly hugged their hips and waist, performers sang in higher registers, and songs about drinking and womanizing were now delivered in third person.[64] Vaudeville impersonators' engagements with offstage publicity forums shifted, too. In addition to clearly identifying as women performers in advertising, impersonators also took pains to continually demonstrate to the public that they were feminine, domestic, soft, and heterosexually inclined. The epitome of this particular identification process was Vesta Tilley.

Cross-identification techniques enabled variety performers to be masculine within the presumptive framework that they were true women under it all, even (especially) if this could not be seen or heard. Due in great part to the popularization of sexology literature as well as news stories about gender and sexual scandals, the late nineteenth-century US public had a slightly different set of presumptions. The relationship between assigned sex and "natural" Victorian gender expression remained strong, including for the middle-class White women who practiced male impersonation. And, yet, one was no longer automatically presumed to flow from the other. Widely circulated stories about "sapphic slasher" and "gender invert" figures depicted women who had been assigned female at birth but did not possess or demonstrate natural feminine predilections or a draw toward heterosexuality.[65] Carroll Smith-Rosenberg asserts that a mid-nineteenth-century public would probably not have assumed women performers were dressing as men to display their personal sexual or gender natures. However, she attributes a particular shift in this mass perception to the popularization of a late nineteenth-century trope called the masculine (or mannish) woman.[66] This mannish woman was a woman who was definitely not a man but nevertheless had an unnatural alignment with masculinity. These women were characterized as not only engaging in disreputable or unlawful gender behavior but also exhibiting a dangerous and pathological identity.

To avoid being implicated, I suggest, vaudevillian impersonators took active steps to identify themselves not just as women but also as women who could never be comfortably masculine, onstage or off. In his 1912 reflective book, *From Theatre to Music Hall*, W. R. Titterton describes one of his "Woman's Movement" acquaintances who "wore a high stiff collar that sawed her neck, and the most atrocious of baggy knickerbockers! She was a horror to look upon. I found it difficult—in spite of my careful upbringing—to refrain from profanity."[67] Depicted by Titterton as decidedly unfeminine in clothing and presentation, this woman inspires both his "horror" and "profanity." Yet, Titterton invokes this figure in contrast to Vesta Tilley, whom he describes as follows: "A dapper young man in an exquisite purple holiday costume strolls from the wings, leaning on his bending cane. He comes to the centre of the footlights, and poses with crossed legs and staring monocle, the features deliciously quizzical and inane. It is a perfect picture—perfect in color and composition, the quintessence of seaside dandyism; but for a subtle hint of womanly waist and curving hips you might fancy it indeed a round-faced boy."[68]

Of note in this passage is, first, that Tilley's menswear delights Titterton rather than inspiring his horror and profanity. Second, Titterton refers to Tilley with men's pronouns, which add to his claim that she created a "perfect picture" of a man (so much so that she can be called "he"). Third, Titterton keenly takes note of Tilley's "womanly waist and curving hips," apparently in spite of her spot-on men's clothing and perfect replication of masculinity. Titterton concludes his characterization of Tilley, whom he refers to as "my lady," by proclaiming that he would give anything to keep her "swaggering in [her] trimly fitting clothes across the London boards."[69]

At the turn of the century, White women wearing men's clothing (knickerbockers) and desiring inclusion in masculine social roles (voting) were often characterized as horrors and abominations: physically female but unnaturally mannish in political, social, and sexual inclination. Reducing or dehumanizing women by characterizing them as not womanly enough had long been a primary means of excluding Black and working-class White women from the channel of limited power that true womanhood provided. Now such tactics were also engaged to separate progressive middle-class White women from their previous access to social respectability. Despite this, Titterton makes clear that vaudevillian impersonators were still thought of as true ladies. So how did vaudevillian impersonators encourage this particular identification? One popular method was to shift their stage presentations away from mimesis through the appearance of the performing body. Unlike variety stars, vaudevillian impersonators rarely cut their hair into short men's styles, instead using wigs or pulling their long hair under hats that could be removed at the show's end. While songs continued to focus on drinking, partying, and womanizing, they were often sung in third person so that the performer was not physically representing boorish actions but merely describing them. According to Rodger, many vaudevillian impersonators also used higher singing registers to signal their femininity.[70] Costume choices, verbal techniques, and singing styles were methods for male impersonators to reveal the feminine personae they wished to make fully identifiable even while they played men.

Beyond these basic performance methods, the more successful vaudevillian impersonators drew from a larger bag of tricks for helping the public remember what they "really were." For example, Tilley's popularity and economic success were intimately tied with how she performed images of men that never concealed her ladylike capacities. Rodger and Slide both ask why Tilley, whose routine lacked either Hindle's realism or the overt sexualization of Christmas pantomime principal boys, was so massively popular. I suggest that Tilley drew audiences not because she could pass as a man or even because she was all that sexually titillating but specifically because she could be overtly rather than presumptively read as a "lady" who was mimicking men's behavior. In her memoir, *Recollections of Vesta Tilley*, Tilley claims that her appeal was her skill at "character studies": the enactment of stereotypical modes of dress, coiffure, and what she calls men's "business" such as lighting cigarettes, puffing cigars, or straightening ties.[71] Hindle had been called a *lady*, too, a term that identified her as a respectable woman performer. But by the turn of the century, this title does not appear as frequently attached to just any middle-class White woman and certainly not to masculine ones. So, when Titterton and other reviewers call Tilley a "lady," I see them alluding to both her class status (her husband was eventually knighted) and her well-known genteel femininity that was not hidden by but rather displayed alongside her character studies.

According to Tilley's memoir, she wore highly realistic men's fashions and, to emphasize the supposedly authentic nature of her clothing, painstakingly padded and bound her curvy body to fit into standard men's cuts.[72] Titterton certainly praises Tilley for her well-constructed men's costumes, but he also clearly comments on a fit that showed "a subtle hint of womanly waist and curving hips."[73] Perhaps Titterton was straining to see Tilley's shape underneath her costume; after all, Hindle's reviewer also commented on her "pleasing figure." But, whereas Hindle's publicity photos do not support her reviewer's claim, Tilley's images do. One popular photo captures Tilley in a dark suit and tie, cream-colored vest, boots, and fedora. She stands at full length with her hands in her pants pockets, looking casually to one side with her eyebrows slightly raised. At first glance, her costume and persona suggest a well-to-do yet bored gentleman character, but scrutiny reveals some of Tilley's more calculated performance methods. For instance, Tilley leans slightly onto her right leg so that her trousers tug against the curve of her hip and thighs. This starkly contrasts with how variety performers posed in careful sitting positions or with their boxy suits floating around their bodies. Tilley's stance is accentuated by her very common body tableau of pulling the sides of her unbuttoned jacket or overcoat behind her forearms to tuck her hands into the trouser pockets (see fig. 2.2). This body language is likely a bit of her masculine "business." But, in Hindle's and Wesner's photographs, their jackets either drape over their middles or are securely buttoned. Tilley, who is already standing in a way that highlights her legs, has now pulled her men's clothing away from the curves of her upper body.

In publicity photographs, most variety impersonators transmitted their masculine characterization as a form of gender passability, and realism was highly prioritized in their aesthetic. Tilley's images are more layered. Her presentation is not overtly feminine or sexualized, she does appear to be accurately presenting menswear, and she is clearly evoking a recognizable man persona. And yet, Tilley does not look masculine in the way variety impersonators did. In fact, some pictures of Hindle and Wesner are fully visually readable as images of men (this is why many photos are titled with performers' names and gendered titles). But even though Tilley presents in masculine clothing and persona, I can read her in these images as a woman performer. Based on comments she makes in her memoir, I suggest that Tilley would conclude that this "not passable man but not overtly feminine" aesthetic was due to her own natural character. That is to say, Tilley would frame her inherent feminine predilections as easy to control but impossible (and undesirable) to conceal. In the words of Tilley herself, "I leave just enough of the woman in my impersonation to keep my work clean and make it remembered."[74]

Many of Tilley's performance reviews also demonstrate the effectiveness of her identification methods. For instance, James Agate concludes his favorable description of Tilley's act by declaring that she is "master of her characters, she was mistress of herself."[75] Certainly any actor would be happy to hear they have mastered their character. Tilley performed only man characters, so Agate's assessment commends her skill at this. Yet, mingled with Agate's praise for her masculine performance is his mention of Tilley's public offstage identity or her status as "mistress of herself." This odd turn of phrase clearly speaks to how Tilley's gender-bending success is connected to her remaining visibly in control—being "mistress"—of her own womanly self. As I have argued, many of the effects of a given gender-bending act can be traced to the performer's cultivated methods and their overarching intents. Thus, I suggest that these reviews reflect a preferred reading of Tilley and her management's intended messages. While some of Hindle's reviews mention her figure or ladylike qualities, I have no evidence that Hindle encouraged a feminized interpretation of her body, only that she crafted a clear articulation

Fig. 2.2. Vesta Tilley as "Algy." *Courtesy of the Music Division of the New York Public Library Digital Collections.*

of herself as a respectable woman. In contrast, there are many instances where Tilley actively encourages the public to see her as a "mistress," lady, or otherwise feminine subject. For instance, when Tilley was a child performer, her father-manager Harry Ball had billed her ambiguously as the "Pocket Sims Reeves" and "The Great Little Tilley."[76] When Tilley reached puberty, her advertising switched (see fig. 2.3) to titles such Miss Vesta Tilley, Lady Tilley, and, after her marriage, Lady De Frece.[77] Tilley biographer Sara Maitland argues that this language change was a mode of identifying her as not just a woman performer but also a very feminine woman. In fact, Maitland praises the "wisdom of Tilley's London manager who insisted" that she be identified via these pronouns and titles "lest there be any doubt or confusion about her 'real' or 'natural' gender."[78]

Tilley backed her textual gender narrative with a flurry of feminine publicity photographs. In addition to photos depicting themselves in various stage personae, vaudevillian impersonators often posed for images that supposedly captured their offstage, lived realities. Most images tend toward elaborately feminine dresses, jewelry, and hair updos. These pictures appear with some frequency alongside impersonators' persona shots in literature such as George Odell's *Annals of the New York Stage* series. Odell's fourteenth volume features three photographs that were used in the promotion of male impersonator Bessie Bonehill's debut on November 4, 1889. In the first image, Bonehill wears a dark tweed suit and bowler hat and clutches a walking stick. In the second, she is in full tuxedo with top hat, standing with her feet apart and hands in her pockets. The third is a portrait of Bonehill in a low-necked dress with puffed sleeves. She wears a necklace, a watch pinned to her chest, and an elaborate updo.[79] Similarly, in Tilley's non–stage persona photographs (many are reprinted in her memoir), she wears lace, pearls, or fur and has her hair styled into a bouffant updo or covered by big feminine hats. As justification for these elaborate presentations, Maitland explains that Tilley "demonstrated her love of feminine frills, and particularly for jewelry, whenever possible."[80] Tilley's memoir also includes photos in which she leans lovingly into her husband, as well as purportedly candid shots of her volunteering at charity events and playing with children. Whether a real love or a calculated expression, her penchant for the culturally feminine is clearly evident in these images. However, almost no part of Tilley's actual life resembled the image of true womanhood she cuts in these photos. Tilley held down a full-time career that required her to constantly travel away from her home, she was the primary wage earner for her entire family, and

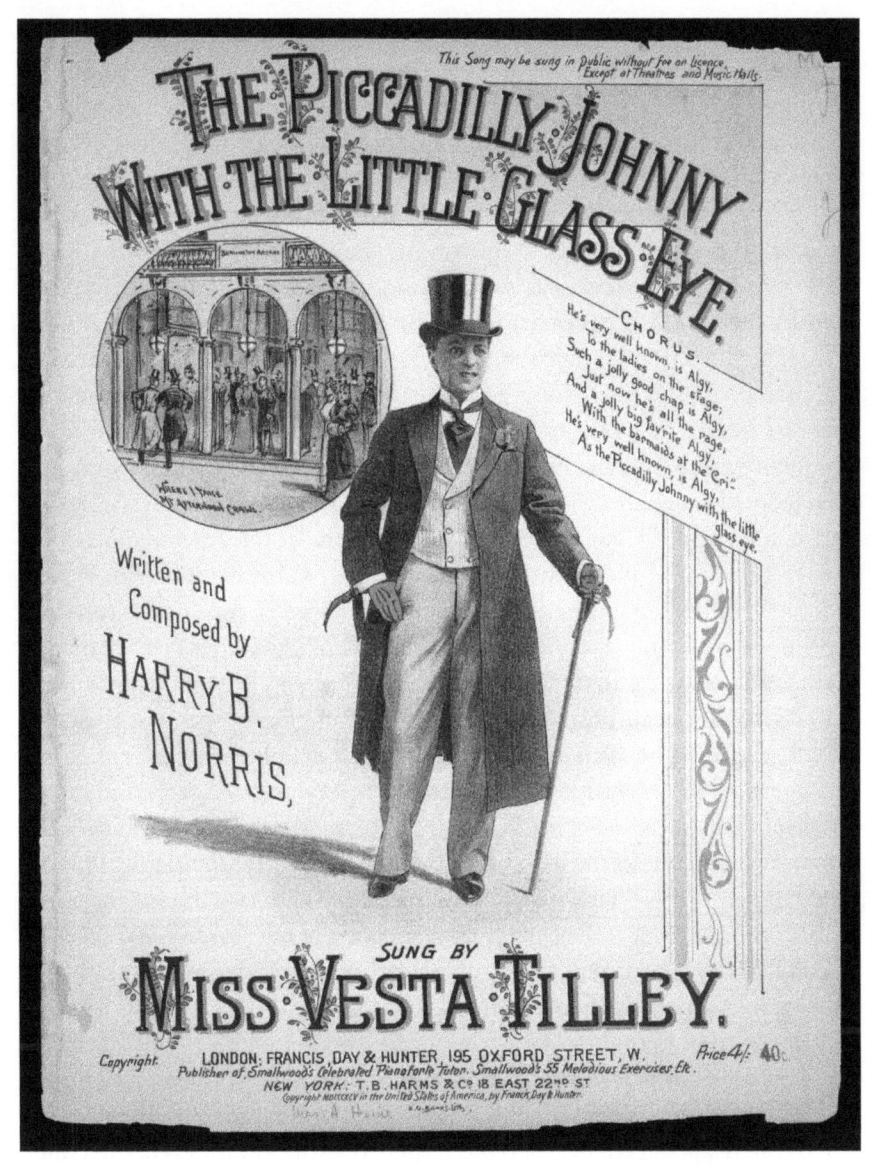

Fig. 2.3. "Miss" Vesta Tilley as "the Piccadilly Johnny with the little glass eye."
Courtesy of the Music Division of the New York Public Library Digital Collections.

she never had children. Despite these realities, Tilley remained a "true and perfect woman who, despite her career on the stage, was interested only in her home and husband"—at least in the popular cultural imagination.[81]

Tilley also disseminated her ultrafeminine public persona via a newer convention called the celebrity interview. Trade and gossip papers had always reported on impersonators, but variety performers interacted with these sources primarily to promote upcoming shows or publicize their unique skills rather than disseminate private information. At the end of the nineteenth century, though, celebrity interviews had grown into a popular news feature, and reporters sought out celebrities to narrate or respond to personal stories about themselves. Some celebrities (Tilley among them) even penned these stories for the press, thereby fully controlling their personal narrative. Frequent topics for vaudevillian impersonators were romantic interest in men (contextualized as the desire for marriage and family), domestic desires and habits, and dislike for women "professionals, reformers, and educators."[82] Prime examples of this personal celebrity narrative appear in Tilley's memoir; although published at the end of her career, it repeats the tone and sentiment (and often even the exact wording) of her earlier celebrity statements and essays. As always, Tilley uses her job as a male impersonator as the fulcrum for her feminine identification. For example, she spends a great deal of time detailing her attention to accuracy and detail when performing her onstage masculine "business." One passage in her memoir extols the lengths she went to make her stage wig look like a natural short haircut because "I had long wavy hair, one of the few things that female vanity would not allow me to sacrifice."[83] This anecdote supplies the public with two important pieces of information. First, Tilley has great dedication to her masculine stagecraft. Second, Tilley is a woman with high partiality to long feminine hair, which she simply cannot sacrifice for this stagecraft.

Tilley also used these forums to make known her politically conservative position on mannish women and "family values." She wrote a piece on the subject for the *Pittsburgh Gazette Home Journal* in 1904, and an almost identical narrative appears in her memoir. Explicating the key difference between women who sometimes wear "knickerbockers" and women who are actually gender degenerates, Tilley suggests that the derogatory term *mannish woman* should be extended beyond the realm of medically diagnosed gender inverts to also identify women with political interests or desires for social independence. Her logic is that while all women are technically capable of working and living in masculine public spheres, women who do so would no longer be feminine because that is "not a woman's job, in my opinion, and [women] would be much better employed in looking after their homes and families."[84] Tilley then very cleverly suggests that women who wear pants from time to time are not mannish women per se, as long as their other interests and behaviors exemplify feminine domesticity.

The careful development and deployment of this feminine identification in both her onstage practice and her public persona made Tilley a very rich and very famous gender-bending performer. It also aided her by building an ideological barrier between her and the same-sex sexual deviance ascribed to mannish women and gender inverts. In *Psychopathia Sexualis*, Krafft-Ebing declares that female inversion is rampant "in opera singers and actresses, who appear in male attire on the stage by preference."[85] He also proposes that feminine ladies can be duped into same-sex relationships with gender inverts who present as dashing masculine figures. Relatedly, the *Sun* notes how male impersonators would often receive "mash notes" (love notes) and romantic gifts from their fan base of women.[86] Even though vaudevillian impersonators were framed as recipients rather than instigators of these attentions, such incidents, combined with impersonators' masculine stage presentations, brought them dangerously close to public perceptions of sexual deviance. Tilley directly addresses this in essays recounting romantic attentions she received from both men and women. She even hyperbolically describes her husband, Walter De Frece, as one of those pathetic, love-stricken fans who followed her from show to show, giving her gifts and requesting private meetings. While her story teases De Frece for these gestures, she also frames them as eventually swaying her into dating and later marrying him.[87] Tilley does not deny receiving similar attentions from women fans but takes these gestures—as opposed to those of De Frece—as frivolous, childish, and misplaced.[88] She recalls a story about a woman who purchased front-row seats to her shows, sent her flowers, and made many requests for private meetings. Tilley's disapproval of this woman is palpable as she recounts her appropriate response to these inappropriate attentions. As her story goes, Tilley finally agreed to the meeting request but first "took off my wig, undid all my little plaits and left my hair in a fuzzy bush without even bothering to put a comb through it, partially removed my makeup, and smothered my face with cream [. . .]. I then threw round me the wrapper which I kept for making up only."[89] In emphasizing how she removed all elements of masculinity from her body and presented her most raw and basic (feminine) self, Tilley's narrative dodges any culpability for encouraging this same-sex attention. Tilley then writes: "I let her have a good look and then said: 'There, now you see what you have been following round for so long. Perhaps that will cure you!'"[90]

Aside from Tilley's telling of it, I have no proof that this incident actually happened. But Tilley did not write essays, pose for photos, or give celebrity interviews just to disseminate cold, hard truths; everything she put into the public domain added to her persona as a true woman, which she, then, figuratively and literally, banked on. Therefore, I suggest that this story be read allegorically as a scenario that highlights important details about Tilley's identification process. The first is her ability to quickly remove masculinity. Unlike variety impersonators who lived in their masculine looks, Tilley easily shatters her stage presentation by applying cold cream and undoing braids. The second is that Tilley removes her masculinity *before* she meets the fan so that she is not to blame for even unintentionally duping this woman, as the removal of the masculine persona yields a feminine appearance under whatever dashing figure she cut onstage. The final detail is Tilley's "cure": her feminine self is the reality check to her fan, demonstrating that women like Tilley would never welcome the romantic attentions of women. While this story is short, it offers up the critical message that Tilley is an inherently feminine woman and thus has socially appropriate reactions to same-sex situations that sometimes happen because of, but are never encouraged by, her male impersonation career.

Tilley's vignette ends with the fan's excited response of "I know you have only made yourself look like that on purpose, and I love the real you more than ever!"[91] I read this ending as Tilley's roundabout way of, once again, emphasizing her skill at performance. That is, her stage business is so detailed that this fan has become convinced that this representation is "the real" Tilley. Undoubtedly, this ending is also Tilley's way of casting the fan as delusional. Nevertheless, it is a strange way to end, because in effect the fan is characterizing Tilley's femininity as a public gender performance. And so it was. Tilley always publicly appeared feminine (even when playing men), enamored with domesticity and repulsed by the romantic attentions of women. But Tilley, along with her publicity team, made herself into this public image by transforming her from a working-class child mimic named Matilda Powles to the glamorous and genteel Lady De Frece. And Tilley did this by cultivating a strong identification image all the while wearing men's clothing and singing, "Girls, if you'd like to love a solider, you can all love me!"[92]

GENDER-BENDING'S AFTEREFFECTS

Male impersonation is crucial to the history of gender-bending, and the parsing I have done in this chapter demonstrates many ways this practice was a significant vehicle for women performers. Not all gender-bending shatters identity categories, and not all bent acts result in lasting queer impact. This is neither a requirement of the genre nor one I wish to impose on it. However, the bentness of male impersonation has largely been theorized as a catalyst for progressive cultural spaces and sentiment. Certainly, any time an actor presents a queer version of identity, their action walks the line of cultural disruption. Relatedly, audiences are empowered to decode performances as queerly as they choose, even if such a reading does not sync with the performer's expressed intents. But this queering of identity was absolutely not the intent of the most successful impersonators. So, while this outcome might be reflected in some audience members' interpretations or experiences, it cannot be a universal conclusion about these acts.

A traditional gender-bending rubric that evidences progressiveness via the basic readability of sex-gender disjunction will easily support the conclusion that male impersonation was wholly disruptive. This is why we have a body of well-researched and well-written scholarship that casts male impersonators as empowered gender nonconformists, out-and-proud lesbians, or people who changed the Victorian gender and sexual game. I do not contest that Hindle's life was atypical and that—while her success lasted—she enjoyed certain cultural liberties. Likewise, as much as Tilley extolled the virtues of home and domesticity, she did not personally follow her own precepts. But these performers received such personal leeway not because their bending led to a loosening of cultural rules but, instead, because of their intentional efforts to shore such rules up. Victorian standards for women were racist and classist, and so Hindle's and Tilley's lives could, first, only be achieved by non–working-class White performers. Second, these lived freedoms did not unequivocally extend to other middle-class White women and, as is evident with Hindle, did not extend past performers' immediate commercial popularity. The bulk of middle-class White gender or political reformers were still branded as deviant women, and Hindle and Tilley could easily have been contextualized similarly as dangerous models of gender or sexual progressivism. And yet, they were not. Therefore, Hindle's and Tilley's careers are testaments to how well performers built separation between their bending and other actions that were actually progressive. Successful impersonators did constant work to foreground and transmit their natural alignment with, conformity to, and support of Victorian identity models. Acknowledging this fact leads to a more holistic accounting of the aftereffects of male impersonation.

My conclusions—divergent from the main body of literature on this practice—should not cast these acts as better or worse forms of bending but simply as more complicated ones than scholars have recognized. Such a nuanced reading is beneficial in that it shows diversity among bending practices while avoiding painting gender-bending's impacts with a broad brush. This is, in fact, my only chapter that scrutinizes practices specifically designed and deployed for popular commercial consumption. Other chapters detail gender-bending acts that are sometimes performed for money or career success. Yet, the performers in El Teatro Campesino or those who put on local drag king events are primarily invested in identity politics, civil rights, or community affiliation and only secondarily focused on funding this work. This was not true for performers who took up male impersonation specifically because the money and opportunities were better than in ballet, olio, and circus acts. While some male impersonators did lead unconventional types of lives, performers seeking money and job security could not afford to alienate the ticket-buying general public. In this regard, male impersonation shares a key commonality with the most popular and commercial forms of contemporary drag: performers will necessarily cultivate an identification or cross-identification process so that their work reifies the least controversial beliefs of the most people.

NOTES

1. "Variety Halls," *Clipper* (New York), December 16, 1876.
2. "Amusements," *Clipper* (New York), August 1, 1868.
3. Quoted in De Frece, *Recollections of Vesta Tilley*, 188. A good deal of information about Tilley comes from her own autobiography, which she published under her married name, Lady De Frece, and many of these stories and quotes cannot be verified by other sources. While Tilley's accounts may or may not be true, they clearly reflect her most common and successful public modes of self-promotion and advancement.
4. Ibid., 129.
5. Indeed, the queer butch and drag king acts I explore in chapters 4 and 5 are sometimes called male impersonations in popular and scholarly literature.

6. In terms of both audience and performer composition, variety and vaudeville constituted predominantly White entertainment genres. Black performers worked in entertainment circles facilitated by the Theatre Owner's Booking Association (TOBA), also sometimes called the Chitlin' Circuit or Black vaudeville.

7. Vicinus, "Turn-of-the-Century Male Impersonation," 187; Aston, "Male Impersonation in the Music Hall," 248.

8. Vicinus, "Turn-of-the-Century Male Impersonation," 187. See also Aston, "Male Impersonation in the Music Hall," 248.

9. Examples of the first are Senelick's *Changing Room*, Aston's "Male Impersonation in the Music Hall," and drag practitioner DiFranco's *Art of Drag Kinging*.

10. Duggan, *Sapphic Slashers*, 144–148; Vicinus, "Turn-of-the-Century Male Impersonation," 187–190.

11. Rodger, *Champagne Charlie and Pretty Jemima*, 87.

12. Muñoz, *Disidentifications*, 7.

13. Welter, "Cult of True Womanhood," 151.

14. Tasker and Negra, *Interrogating Postfeminism*, 3.

15. Crenshaw, "Mapping the Margins," 1244–1245.

16. Rodger, *Champagne Charlie and Pretty Jemima*, 72–73.

17. An olio performer was a comic singer or dancer who performed during scene changes or between the acts of a play. Their primary role was to occupy and entertain the cheaper ticket holders in "the pit" (the standing space below the apron) who were assumed to be rowdy and uncouth. Many olio performers transitioned from these positions into variety and vaudeville.

18. Rodger, *Champagne Charlie and Pretty Jemima*, 13; Zellers, "Cradle of Variety," 582.

19. Zellers, "Cradle of Variety," 580–582.

20. Rodger, *Champagne Charlie and Pretty Jemima*, 17. Other women may have been in these spaces to enjoy a drink, a smoke, or a show. However, little exists in the archives about their presence, likely because documentation would have marked them as disreputable.

21. "Amusements," *Clipper* (New York), October 24, 1868.

22. Rodger, *Champagne Charlie and Pretty Jemima*, 17.

23. "Amusements," *Clipper* (New York), September 16, 1876.

24. For example, see Rodger, "He Isn't a Marrying Man," 112; Senelick, *Changing Room*, 329.

25. Rodger, "He Isn't a Marrying Man," 112.

26. For more examples, see Welter's "Cult of True Womanhood."

27. Giddings, *When and Where I Enter*, 86.

28. "Amusements," *Clipper* (New York), October 24, 1868.

29. Vaudeville's popularity declined with the rise of cinema in the late 1920s.
30. Royle, "Vaudeville Theatre," 487.
31. Ibid.
32. Smith-Rosenberg, *Disorderly Conduct*, 270.
33. Krafft-Ebing, *Psychopathia Sexualis*. Inversion theories were based on a specific sexual system that assumed there were only two sexes, and that they each had innate correlations to cultural gender roles and heterosexual desires.
34. The phrase "masculine women" was immortalized in a 1925 song by Edgar Leslie (lyrics) and James V. Monaco (music) aptly titled "Masculine Women! Feminine Men!" I also reference this song lyric in the title to this chapter.
35. "Amusements," *Clipper* (New York), September 16, 1876.
36. "Stranger Than Fiction," *Sun* (New York), December 27, 1891.
37. Ibid.
38. "City Summary," *Clipper* (New York), May 30, 1874.
39. "Music Halls," *Clipper* (New York), December 19, 1868.
40. Senelick, *Changing Room*, 333; see also figure 2.1, side by side photographs of Ella Wesner and Louise Rott.
41. See Odell's *Annals of the New York Stage*, vols. 8 and 9, for images of Blanche Selwyn and J. H. Selwyn, whom I suspect might have been married for a time.
42. Rodger, *Champagne Charlie and Pretty Jemima*, 128. Their marriage was reported in the press to be short lived and physically abusive. See "Music Halls," *Clipper* (New York), September 26, 1868, and "Stranger Than Fiction," *Sun* (New York), December 27, 1891.
43. "Annie's Indignant Hands," *National Police Gazette*, January 3, 1880; "Stranger Than Fiction," *Sun* (New York), December 27, 1891.
44. This quote is referring to Wesner. "City Summary," *Clipper* (New York), August 6, 1870.
45. Press accounts that are critical of male impersonators tend to center on scandals associated with public and legal feuds.
46. For example, see "Amusements," *Clipper* (New York), September 5, 1868; "Amusements," *Clipper* (New York), October 24, 1868.
47. For example, see "Amusements," *Clipper* (New York), October 17, 1868.
48. Rodger, "North American Variety and Vaudeville Stage," 78.
49. "Amusements," *Clipper* (New York), August 26, 1876.
50. "Amusements," *Clipper* (New York), October 24, 1868.
51. "Music Halls," *Clipper* (New York), December 19, 1868.
52. Ibid.
53. Rodger, "He Isn't a Marrying Man," 123.
54. Slide, *Encyclopedia of Vaudeville*, 332.
55. "Ella Wesner Lies in Man's Garb," *New York Times*, November 14, 1917.
56. Hindle's poems appear in the *Clipper* from 1870 to 1873 and then again from 1878 to 1879.

57. "One Woman Marries Another—Is She He?" *Clipper* (New York), June 12, 1886; "Stage Whispers," *National Police Gazette*, July 3, 1886.

58. I am much indebted to Rodger's detailed examination of local newspaper archives for details of this story beyond what is printed in Hindle's obituary in the *Sun*. A reporter from the *Telegram-Herald* confronted the wedding party as they were celebrating the marriage at a restaurant and badgered Hindle to publicly say she was a man. When Hindle refused, the reporter followed them back to their hotel and stayed until two in the morning. In what appears to be an attempt to get the reporter to leave, Hindle did declare (the only direct time I have seen) that she was a man ("He Isn't a Marrying Man," 117).

59. The *National Police Gazette* claimed "Annie Hindle (?) or Charles Hindle (?)" married Charles Vivian without him knowing that she was a man. Yet, when "he discovered her sex [to be male] he wanted to masquerade with her but not having such a feminine appearance failed to make a success" ("Stage Whispers," August 21, 1886). Although Vivian is portrayed here as a fool and perhaps some type of deviant, he also comes off as an unwitting victim of Hindle's gender fraud.

60. Hindle's story has a less tragic end than others. She had been careful with her earnings and was financially capable of supporting herself and Ryan with only the sporadic work. They lived in a New Jersey home Hindle purchased.

61. This piece is actually an obituary for Hindle, in which the reporter recounts meeting Hindle at the funeral for her wife, Annie Ryan. "Stranger Than Fiction," *Sun* (New York), December 27, 1891.

62. "Amusements," *Clipper*, September 16, 1876.

63. "Amusements," *Clipper*, August 26, 1876.

64. Rodger, "He Isn't a Marrying Man," 124.

65. *Sapphic slasher* is a term Duggan uses in her book of that title.

66. Smith-Rosenberg, *Disorderly Conduct*, image gallery pages C and D.

67. Titterton, *From Theatre to Music Hall*, 145.

68. Ibid., 147.

69. Ibid., 145.

70. Rodger, "He Isn't a Marrying Man," 123.

71. De Frece, *Recollections of Vesta Tilley*, 129.

72. In fact, Tilley claimed her outfits were so trendy that they often became the next big thing in middle- and upper-class men's circles (Maitland, *Vesta Tilley*, 122).

73. Titterton, *From Theatre to Music Hall*, 147.

74. Quoted in Vicinus, "Turn-of-the-Century Male Impersonation," 189.

75. Quoted in Slide, *Encyclopedia of Vaudeville*, 501.

76. Maitland, *Vesta Tilley*, 19; De Frece, *Recollections of Vesta Tilley*, 23, 46.

77. De Frece, *Recollections of Vesta Tilley*, 46.

78. Maitland, *Vesta Tilley*, 88.

79. Odell, *Annals of the New York Stage*, 355.

80. Maitland, *Vesta Tilley*, 73.

81. Rodger, "North American Variety and Vaudeville Stage," 289.
82. Smith-Rosenberg, "Discourses of Sexuality and Subjectivity," 272.
83. De Frece, *Recollections of Vesta Tilley*, 148.
84. Ibid., 73.
85. Krafft-Ebing, *Psychopathia Sexualis*, 398.
86. "Stranger Than Fiction," *Sun* (New York), December 27, 1891.
87. There is more than one perspective on how the couple met and finally began to date: De Frece's father owned a theater house that employed Tilley.
88. De Frece, *Recollections of Vesta Tilley*, 234–235.
89. Ibid.
90. Ibid., 235.
91. Ibid.
92. Ibid., 137.

THREE

Mythical, "Sexless" Characters
Identity Borders in El Teatro Campesino

IN 1965, LEAFLETS were distributed to the agricultural workers in Delano, California, proposing they convey work grievances and express their "future hopes" through a "bi-lingual community farm workers' theatre project." Printed in neat typewriter letters was the project's overarching message: "If you can sing, dance, walk, march, hold a picket sign, play a guitar or harmonica or any other instrument, you can participate!"[1] For the first two years, El Teatro Campesino (the farm workers' theater) performed skits and songs about farm worker abuse as well as the benefits of unions and *huelgas* (strikes).[2] These *actos* (productions) evoked the historical Mexican *carpa* (variety show) format: they entertained and educated through animated physicality, bawdy and satirical material, and stock characters. A handful of early organizers ran the theater project, but local laborers filled out the shows and protests. As El Teatro Campesino expanded in geographic scope beyond Delano, actos began to incorporate *indigenismo* (indigenous legacies) and Chicanismo (the expression of Chicanx culture and art), Mexican *mitos* (myths), and Mayan, Aztec, and Catholic iconography.[3] In a time during which being "American" meant assimilating to middle-class White appearances and values, these shows were particularly culturally radical. Consequently, El Teatro Campesino became one of the most recognizable arms of *el Movimiento* (the Chicanx civil rights movement).

This chapter details complex issues surrounding *teatristas* (women troupe members) of El Teatro Campesino during the 1970s and 1980s as well as their complex methods of navigating these issues.[4] Specifically, I explore how teatristas developed a gender-bending performance process that revised rather than fully accepted or fully abandoned their layered racial-gendered positions. Breaking from convention, I begin this chapter not by describing those specific gender-bending practices but by instead detailing the history of El Teatro Campesino. This is not intended to privilege the troupe over its performers but rather to highlight a specific context where a revisionary identification gender-bending process would work well. Practitioners of revisionary bending are not generally interested in fully disavowing or fully reimagining personal or institutionally defined identities, even if they might be channels for marginalization or oppression. Teatristas proudly identified as Chicana and Latina and had valid reasons for working within El Teatro Campesino. And yet, el Movimiento and El Teatro Campesino have been characterized as organizing models that maintained gender and sexual hierarchies. This chapter investigates why teatristas so often took on gender-bending projects, what such practices looked like, and how these women altered their bent practices as necessary. I argue that revisionary gender-bending was a critical method of empowerment: a necessary action if they were to continue as members of these organizations without wholly acquiescing to unwanted sexual and gender positions.

Although these complex gender-bending practices were personally and politically fulfilling to the troupe's performers, they have been only very tangentially discussed. One reason has to do with the manner of historicizing el Movimiento organizations and another with the scholarship on gender and sexual issues within el Movimiento. El Teatro Campesino has become famously associated with both narratives. First, Teatro Campesino is often framed as accomplishing critical activist and cultural work such as unionizing agricultural workers, educating populations about race-based injustices, and expressing Chicanx pride. Theater scholarship generally frames Teatro Campesino as an exemplar of how theater projects can effectively instigate social transformation. The other narrative comes from feminist cultural scholarship during the 1980s and 1990s that critiques Teatro Campesino, often pointing to its work and figurehead Luis Valdez, for upholding racialized forms of sexism and heterosexism. In addition to this fairly intense historical debate, there has also been contention in the form of legal proceedings, physical altercations, the closing off of public access to Teatro Campesino archival material, and continued silencing of feminist cultural perspectives.[5] So, to be explicit, I am principally interested in why teatristas gravitated toward gender-bending practices and how they constructed and deployed them. When discussed at all, this topic is often overshadowed by debates about group dynamic or used as evidence that teatristas were either subaltern subjects or completely empowered troupe players.[6] Neither perspective captures the complicated, layered performances they developed or the intersectional reasons why they crafted these particular representations. Exploring the messy context around Teatro Campesino is critical for fully understanding the intents, methods, and goals of this revisionary process. Such contextualization is not a vilification or canonization of Luis Valdez, the troupe, or its accomplishments. Instead, my archival exploration illuminates something else entirely: that this revisionary process grew from and supported the plurality of Chicanahood, or what Gloria Anzaldúa terms *mestiza consciousness*.[7]

Here is an example of both the layered complexity of these gender-bending practices and how they were shaped by the teatristas' social and troupe positions. One of the main claims of sexism in El Teatro Campesino is that teatristas had to perform as subjugated, pathetic, and abused women. A core member of Teatro Campesino from 1973 to 1980, Diane Rodriguez explains that "the roles for women, they were always somehow victimized because that's how it was seen in the society, do you know what I'm saying? So they weren't that much fun to play."[8] Characters such as Gila in *La pastorela*, Pelada Rasquachi in *La carpa de los rasquachis*, and Vera in *El fin del mundo* are victims of sexual and physical assault as well as cultural oppression. In one of the earliest versions of *La carpa de los rasquachis* in the archives, Pelada Rasquachi is described thus: "In marrying El Pelado Rasquachi she suffers a double oppression: she is oppressed as a farm worker and also as a woman. She suffers at the hands of her husband who works out his oppression by mistreating her."[9] This character embodies some of Chicanas' multiple and specific oppressions; representing them onstage can be a good method of illuminating the relationship between gendered abuse and racialized social injustice. However, core troupe member Socorro Valdez (hereafter referred to in this chapter as "Valdez") angrily describes these as women who *"aguantaban todo"* (put up with everything) and Rodriguez offers, "There have been very few roles in Teatro Campesino that I have thoroughly enjoyed."[10] So, while these characters highlighted the intersecting matrix of Chicanas' oppressions, teatristas have made exceedingly clear that this was boring, embarrassing, and unfulfilling work for them.

But here is the other end of it. Rodriguez says:

> The two roles that I enjoyed the most have been Satanás and La Muerte. They've been basically androgynous roles. I haven't enjoyed the women roles at all.... I've played the mother, the girlfriend ... the standards. [...] What has been fun is the opportunity to play that male/female role like Satanás ... oh, it's wonderful, it's freedom. Like Satanás or La Muerte in *La Carpa*. It was a wonderful, wonderful piece. And the roles of Satanás or Muerte are wonderful because you can do everything.... As far as the women and as far as the repertory goes. [...] The female roles have been weak. The nonfemale roles I've played have not been weak. These nonfemale roles—well, they stand out.[11]

Rodriguez is describing her joy in playing roles she terms *androgynous, male/female,* and *nonfemale*. In another interview, she characterizes these as "roles that are neither man nor woman."[12] Valdez also often played what she calls "sexless" characters such as *calaveras* (skeletons).[13] There are archival records of Yolanda Parra and Olivia Chumacero performing as San Miguel (St. Michael), Angela Cruz as Satanás (Satan), and Stephanie Buswell and Vicki Oswald as diablos (devils). Similar to Rodriguez's statement, in almost every primary interview I have found, teatristas describe their passion for creating and playing these roles.[14]

Despite being versed in the history of both US theater and El Teatro Campesino, I was quite surprised when I discovered so much archival material on teatristas performing or talking about these characters. My preferred term for them is Valdez's *sexless*, which I see as particularly apt for characterizing both the context of these characters and also their bent quality. Sexless characters can be gendered, as Valdez was as a masculine calavera in *El fin del mundo*. But even if a particular sexless character is performed in a gendered way, all sexless characters are nonhuman and thus lack the biological markers medically used to assign sex. In this regard, the offstage sex and gender identity of an actor does not represent any meaningful point of contrast to or collusion with a sexless character. Women were not selected to play these parts because they were women and the characters were women. Likewise, women were not selected to play these gender-bending parts because they were women and the characters were men. In fact, because these characters have a sexless base, there appears to have been a relative lack of gender-consciousness in their assignment. Men and women members performed sexless characters, and these roles appear to have been enjoyable and important to them. But, while sexless parts constituted a range of performance options and possibilities for all performers, they were especially important to teatristas who felt limited by "female and only female" parts.[15] Teatristas have said they were unhappy with their acting opportunities in Teatro Campesino, and many scholars argue that this should have compelled them to break with the troupe. But it is too simple to say either that teatristas were oppressed by their acting opportunities and should have left or that their continued work with the troupe meant they were happy. Such conclusions cannot acknowledge the complexity of Chicanas' cultural and political positions nor the impact a revisionary identification gender-bending process can have on them.

When sexless characters are mentioned in published histories of Teatro Campesino, they are most often used to demonstrate the troupe's communal, actor-driven model of producing role types and performance pieces or to show the troupe's commitment to indigenismo and Chicanismo. Perhaps unsurprisingly, they are neither framed as a teatrista-driven innovation nor as acts of gender-bending. The work I illustrate in this chapter will not fit snugly inside the canonical definition of gender-bending. Teatristas identified as women, and sexless characters were not men or male characters, even if they expressed masculinity. Moreover, some sexless roles expressed femininity while others had no gender affiliation at all. What is important, though, is that teatristas called these roles "nonfemale" because—whether masculine, feminine, or genderless—they lacked a key identity designation that the performers personally embodied. In this regard, sexless characters were fundamentally bent from a significant aspect of the performers' lived selves. Furthermore, it is telling that teatristas discursively separated these roles from the gendered ideological contexts and representational structures that informed both their lives and the women roles in the troupe's repertoire. Thus, by classifying these acts as gender-bending, I identify and explore them as a form of bent identity expression that manifests in the formation of readable contrast between teatristas' own well-known racial-gendered positions and a lack of such embodied positionality in the characters.

Certain forms of gender-bending can be effective methods of revising particular assumptions attached to the known subjectivity of the performer. Identification and cross-identification processes enable actors to express their normative identities so as to appear to the audience that they blend with cultural hegemony. In contrast, a revisionary identification process expresses what Muñoz summarizes as "various accounts of tactical identification together."[16] In other words, teatristas' audiences could visually, aurally, and ideologically identify them as Chicana women. This mode of identification was not closed off or shut down by the gender-bending performance; rather, the performance acted as a channel to revise how teatristas' identifications could define their stage actions. The act did not invite audience members to decode the success of the sexless role via its contrast or alignment with the identification they had made about the actor. Instead, audience members were encouraged by specific performance and advertising methods to separate their clear knowledge about the actors' identities from the impact the stage product could have. Sexless characters were always necessarily bent away from actors' lived subjectivities, but, in effect, the lived subjectivity of the actor was presented as having little bearing on how skillfully accomplished the sexlessness of the character was. This particular bending methodology—a revision of how the offstage self could impute meaning to the performance—was successfully employed by teatristas to navigate conflicting positions and allegiances.

I term Teatro Campesino teatristas' particular revisionary bending process a *mestiza* practice. I build this from Anzaldúa's mestiza consciousness, an ideological model for how Chicanas embody discrete locations, ethnicities, and genders and also live within pluralistic, conflicting identities.[17] Anzaldúa defines a mestiza as a Spanish, indigenous, Mexican, and/or US American woman who embodies particular racial, cultural, sexual, colonized, socioeconomic, gender, and border identities. Yvonne Yarbro-Bejarano adds that Chicanas' lived experiences are not singular but rather formed from "multiple determinants—gender, class, sexuality and contradictory membership in competing cultures and racial identities."[18] According to Anzaldúa, a mestiza does not reject or abandon any aspect of her contradictory and overlapping history because all is integral to her contemporary self. In fact, this selfhood allows Chicanas to have a delineated sociocultural identity and flexibility within as well as the ability to permeate the borders of said identity. Moya Lloyd proposes that "whether real or metaphorical [these borders] may, but do not have to, confine the mestiza. She can move across them, refusing to be contained by them."[19]

El Teatro Campesino was a very important artistic extension of the Chicano civil rights movement, and the troupe also encouraged or at least enabled sexist and colorist governance and role-assigning practices. I bring this up not to condemn or celebrate Teatro Campesino but to set the stage for how particular interests and contexts encourage the development of revisionary identification practices. Instead of always accepting undesirable or sexist positions or completely leaving the troupe (and, by extension, the movement), teatristas revised their position: they engaged with a performance practice that allowed them to exist within their particular bounded identities and also have relatively unbounded opportunities for creative performance expression. Like male impersonators, teatristas used the forum of gender-bending to mobilize personal freedoms and occupational opportunities. But, while successful impersonators strategically identified themselves with the hegemony via their acts, teatristas detached their public identities from the effect their acts might have while highlighting how their identities were the very reason for producing these acts in the first place.

To illustrate the work of teatristas and the dynamic of Teatro Campesino, I draw on historical narratives by theater scholars, cultural critics, and feminist scholars; primary materials published by Luis Valdez and the Teatro Campesino organization; televised interviews with troupe members; and a plethora of primary archival documents, including performance and candid photos, flyers and other advertising materials, playbills, internal troupe documents, drawings, and taped interviews. Before these archives were restricted, theater and feminist scholars used them to support various conflicting and contentious claims about the troupe. My purpose in using these archives in tandem with this academic work is not to take a side but rather to develop a holistic picture of practices and processes. In forming this picture, I also reference unpublished outlines, drafts, and scripts in the archives. Many of Teatro Campesino's productions were eventually transcribed (archived) as more formal scripts, some of which were later published. However, my knowledge of the troupe and my exploration of the archives lead me to believe that most of the troupe's early and midperiod work was not equivalent to a formally scripted production. Internal paperwork demonstrates that many Teatro Campesino skits and shows were mapped out loosely as plot and character outlines before a formal rehearsal process. However, to the best of my research, the dialogue that appears in early and midperiod archival scripts was not prewritten and then repeated verbatim by troupe members. Instead, I suggest the completed scripts capture a product that was developed by individual performers and their collective work in workshops. Because of Teatro Campesino's specific and unique process, I suggest sexless characters are more akin to the model of the actor-driven act than to the dictated cross-casting convention. A deeper understanding of how these practices were developed builds a more complete picture of teatristas' contributions to the genre of gender-bending.

CONTEXT AND CONFLICT

Teatro Campesino's early productions comprised educational skits, short stories, songs, and music. Actos were intentionally based in an "oral tradition, not a print culture or 'script' tradition" so they could be accessible to people who could not speak English or read.[20] This format lent itself to collaboration as performers developed characters and plot details that reflected their own talents as well as ideas borne from their physical and verbal improvisations. Rodriguez explains that "the Teatro Campesino style is not what a lot of people can do, either: the movement, the body... making the spine come alive."[21] While some of roles such as the *esquirol* (scab) were well-known stock characters, stories about them were "brought to life" by actors physically interpreting what they "*individually* know and feel."[22] As Broyles-González surmises, "To play a role or character [...] meant literally to create a character by improvising it to life, bringing it to life virtually from scratch."[23] After Teatro Campesino established residency in San Juan Bautista, California, around 1971, archival records show that a core group of members including Olivia Chumacero, Joe Delgado, Phil Esparza, Andres Gutierrez, Diane Rodriguez, Luis Valdez, and Lupe Valdez were responsible for creating and implementing troupe projects. Dubbed mitos (myths), midperiod productions reflect various members' interests in Chicanx and Latinx identity and culture, Chicanismo, indigenismo, religious iconography, urban labor, the Vietnam War and draft, and socioeconomic disparity. It is clear from this evidence that early and midperiod work was built collectively. However, media coverage and formal histories overwhelmingly name Luis Valdez as the "father" of this work, in what Broyles-González refers to as "great-man conceptual [framing]."[24] Luis Valdez was one of the key founders of the troupe and served as its commercial and organizational figurehead for a significant time. But Broyles-González argues that his framing as the troupe's auteur has led to the historicization of Teatro Campesino as "the life and times of Luis Valdez."[25]

After growing in recognition and popularity during the 1970s, Teatro Campesino toured around the United States and in Italy and Germany. But despite its widespread cultural influence, Teatro Campesino's funding declined in the 1980s, and many core members had to leave San Juan Bautista for work. During this later period, Luis Valdez transitioned the Teatro Campesino brand into mainstream ventures such as Broadway and film versions of the troupe's play *Zoot Suit*, the publication of scripts, and more commercial productions such as *Corridos*. At this later point, Luis Valdez did become almost singularly responsible for what Teatro Campesino was. The high-profile ventures in this later period do not fully reflect the actor-driven and collaborative style of early and midperiod work. Nevertheless, the late period generally sets the tone for popular news coverage and scholarly and popular histories of the troupe. For example, Jorge Huerta characterizes Luis Valdez as the troupe's figurehead, especially in terms of its efforts to artistically extend the Chicanx labor and cultural pride movement. Moreover, he attributes the overall impact of Teatro Campesino not primarily to its actor-generated performances but to published or recorded sociopolitical content such as in *Zoot Suit*.[26] Broyles-González suggests that this type of coverage occludes serious internal issues of sexism, colorism, and heterosexism by popularizing only positive, Luis Valdez–adjacent parts of the story.[27]

No doubt internal troupe issues were complex and multisided, and parts of them will forever remain undisclosed. But what is clear, even to outsiders like myself, is that Teatro Campesino, like most other US and Latin American revolutionary movements of this period, built its unification by promulgating ideas about a collective primary identification. El Movimiento fortified its allegiances via the concept of *La Raza*, or the belief that all Chicanx and Latinx people were a community united in their racial difference and ethnic distinctness. Ellie D. Hernández notes that "the very act of self-identifying as Chicana/o [was a] political act necessary to the formation of a definitive Chicana/o literary, cultural, and political voice."[28] But, while a unitary racial identification can serve as the basis for significant political protest and cultural development, this type of identity politics has been linked to serious gender stratification and unchecked beliefs about a natural "sexual division of labor."[29] For example, while Chicanas and Latinas were not denied the right to participate in el Movimiento, they were often expected to prioritize household, family, and childcare obligations, even within their activist choices. Helen Chavez is a good example: she combined child and spouse caretaking with her role in the United Farm Workers (UFW) by doing the part-time, at-home labor of keeping the books. And while I have no evidence that Chavez was unhappy with this arrangement, Dolores Huerta's displeasure at being expected to occupy a similar position within the UFW is well documented.[30] Hernández surmises that, although el Movimiento was organized around racial liberation, it "did not liberate [women] from the kitchen or other menial duties associated with liberation-style politics."[31] Likewise, Yarbro-Bejarano notes that if Chicanas' contributions "exceeded domestic tasks [...] they were generally not credited for these ideas and labor."[32] And when Huerta pushed for a more active and visible leadership role in the UFW, she was publicly criticized for abandoning her familial responsibilities, acting unfeminine, and "selfishly" imposing her own gender priorities.[33] Diana Taylor argues that any protest organization or movement that presents a unified racial front will find it "much easier [. . .] to recognize the racism directed at them than the sexism that exists both outside and within its boundaries."[34]

Unsurprisingly, some feminist cultural scholars have characterized El Teatro Campesino—a very visible arm of el Movimiento—similarly, as perpetuating racial solidarity at the expense of addressing its own gender and sexual inequalities. This is supported in statements where teatristas talk about their frustration with how they were treated both in the larger cultural context of the United States and within Teatro Campesino. In addition to arguing that Teatro Campesino's troupe structure was sexist, feminist scholars also argue that the way the group has been historicized is sexist. A common academic project in the late 1970s and 1980s was to critically question the positioning of canonical histories and the organization of knowledges in a given field, and feminist humanities and social sciences scholars especially questioned narratives that centralized White Western men's stories and contributions. It was in this fashion that Broyles-González proposed that the popular narrative on Teatro Campesino erroneously presented a "linear vision" in which Luis Valdez was the "'great man' directing anonymous masses of actors."[35]

To help frame Teatro Campesino in a way that also included teatristas, Broyles-González conducted an eighteen-month research residency with Teatro Campesino in San Juan Bautista.[36] By collecting new interviews with troupe members (including Luis Valdez), sorting through archival material, and observing rehearsals and performances, Broyles-González saw what she refers to as a "whole new history" of the troupe.[37] Teatro Nacional de Aztlán, or TENAZ, was an umbrella term for many Chicanx theater or performance art troupes operating in the United States during the 1960s and the 1970s. Like Yarbro-Bejarano's work on other TENAZ troupes, Broyles-González's narrative did not singularly revolve around documenting the actions or work of one figurehead. Instead, Broyles-González paid "careful attention to women's [verbalization of their] experiences" in creating a more holistic and multidimensional account.[38] Yarbro-Bejarano similarly drew on the feminist research method of collecting women's testimonies to create such a "collective and experiential" account of TENAZ performance actions and outcomes.[39]

But Yarbro-Bejarano also suggests that this testimony can be organized and shaped by traditional academic textual and cultural analysis. In effect, these scholars were developing new troupe narratives by foregrounding women's stories but also using these statements as evidentiary support for the "theory we construct and for any categories of analysis we apply."[40] Specifically, teatrista testimony was used by Broyles-González not only to create a more holistic account of Teatro Campesino but also to support her larger cultural critique that gender hierarchies were being institutionalized and maintained even among minority-rights groups.

Drawing from teatristas' own words and stories, Broyles-González parses a deeply embedded sexism within Teatro Campesino, which she implies prevented teatristas from achieving the same respect, equal rights, or power that Chicano men were gaining from el Movimiento.[41] For instance, she writes: "Performance was one of the most powerful organizing and consciousness-raising tools of El Movimiento. Yet, gender and sexuality consciousness tended to be underdeveloped in the teatro movement of that era. Virtually all teatros were male-led and male-dominated."[42] While I have certainly heard recordings and read transcripts in the archives in which teatristas express displeasure with Teatro Campesino, it is worth noting that many teatristas had a good measure of leadership power. Lupe Valdez served on Teatro Campesino's board as early as 1968.[43] Socorro Valdez directed the 1977 and 1979 productions of *Las cuatro apariciones de la Virgen de Guadalupe* and the 1978 productions of *La pastorela* and *El fin del mundo*.[44] Olivia Chumacero assistant-directed 1978's *Las cuatro apariciones de la Virgen de Guadalupe* and was also listed on Teatro Campesino's board of directors.[45] Yolanda Parra was not only the technical director and light designer for several productions but was also a musician and choral director for the 1979 *Las cuatro apariciones de la Virgen de Guadalupe*.[46] And in almost every program between 1977 and 1980, Diane Rodriguez is listed as the costume designer. In this regard, teatristas clearly did have some authority in the management and creative path of many productions.

When Broyles-González says that Teatro Campesino was deeply sexist, I believe she is primarily (although not only) referring to casting practices and acting opportunities. She writes: "Those male-led teatros, which typically featured both men and women, represented gender relations only inadvertently and to the detriment of women. Although politically progressive in some ways, acting ensembles—such as the famed Teatro Campesino or Teatro de la Esparza—focused their attention on relations of economic class, race, and culture. A sustained consideration of gender was viewed as threatening, and it was dismissed as divisive to the issue."[47] Teatristas do talk about having to perform embarrassing, pathetic, and one-dimensional characters primarily designed as "wife/mother/lover."[48] There were also issues with casting decisions that factored in teatristas' light or dark skin shades as well as beliefs that some teatristas were more fit to play "good girl" or "bad girl" characters.[49] Teatristas likewise expressed displeasure with having to stop playing roles and contributing to shows when Teatro Campesino went on tour because of a lack of childcare and child-friendly traveling accommodations.[50] Added to all this is the fact that Broyles-González's critique of Teatro Campesino's casting and acting opportunities was not taken well by Luis Valdez or some of her academic peers, who, she claims, tried to prevent it from being published because they felt it was derisive to *la causa* (the Chicanx civil rights cause).[51]

Broyles-González's work highlights some crucial sexism issues that should and must be part of the Teatro Campesino story. The fact that she does so with teatristas' own words is important, too, because it gives agency and central positionality to the subjects of discussion. However, virtually every time I encountered an archival document in which teatristas expressed their unhappiness with sexist casting and acting opportunities, I also found them expressing happiness with their opportunities to play mythical, sexless roles. And although Broyles-González likely had access to roughly the same set of archival materials I used, not everyone else did.[52] The Teatro Campesino archives (1965–1988) are currently housed by the California Ethnic and Multicultural Archives (CEMA) at the University of California, Santa Barbara (UCSB) Library. After the archives were closed to the general public in the early 1980s (in the wake of Broyles-González's research residency), Teatro Campesino archivist Andres V. Gutierrez wrote that "the formal relationship we are establishing with the University [UCSB] will provide for the preservation of the Archives and the increased availability of the collection for legitimate scholarly research."[53] That process took roughly thirty more years, with the archives opening for general public scholarly access in late 2009. Researchers working after Broyles-González's residency with the troupe but before the period I accessed the archives (2009–2010) very likely did not get to see all the primary source material in which teatristas explain why they joined Teatro Campesino and what roles they took on to fulfill that goal. And they very likely never encountered the scores of unpublished documents illuminating teatristas' complex gender-bending work as calaveras, diablos, and other mythical characters.

The archival insights I gleaned about teatristas' performance innovations are not fully present in the canonical troupe histories, but neither are they comprehensively addressed in feminist histories and critiques. I know Broyles-González encountered some of the same archival materials because they are mentioned in many of her published works, even if they are only directly analyzed in one section of *El Teatro Campesino: Theater in the Chicano Movement*. Intriguingly, in the notes section of the draft of this book manuscript (also held by CEMA because she was a professor at UCSB while completing this book), she has handwritten this: "Rather than elaborate further [on teatristas' contributions] in the context of the present book, I have decided to continue in the context of another book."[54] I gather from this note that Broyles-González decided to primarily focus her book around developing an alternative Teatro Campesino history, one that both was inclusive and documented its sexism and sexist academic canonization. This was an important and necessary project, to be sure, but that second necessary project on teatristas' performance innovations never materialized. And without that second half of the story, the overarching narrative of the troupe becomes about teatristas' sociopolitical limitations rather than their methods of claiming agency, living plurality, and growing as artists. So, while they were at first relatively invisible in the history of Teatro Campesino, teatristas have now been historically misconstrued as powerless and wholly oppressed figures of a patriarchal structure. My own characterization certainly acknowledges the sexist structures teatristas operated within, but I center my analysis on that second half of the story: instances where teatristas actively revised positions of marginality or powerlessness via gender-bending practices.

BENDING INTENT

Most scholarship builds its assertions about TENAZ's troupe dynamics and performance efficacy primarily from scripted materials and only secondarily from close readings of what actors were doing onstage. This is partly because of the ephemerality of performance repertoires (shows only run for so long) as well as the necessity of archiving and using archival materials to spread information about TENAZ to larger publics. In fact, centralizing the printed script in performance analysis (rather than working through various forms of perhaps poorly cataloged and likely ever-changing performance actions) is a standard approach in theater studies scholarship. And while much feminist scholarship on TENAZ integrates oral testimony, Yarbro-Bejarano's and Broyles-González's work also necessarily engages with field-standard, text-centered script-analysis practices. I do not mean to disparage this method or these scholars' use of it generally; on the contrary, I also use some script analysis in this chapter to compare what has been written down and archived with what might have been performed. But I mention the heavy use of script analysis in scholarship on Teatro Campesino to reemphasize that, while sexless roles might have been outlined or recorded at certain points, their dialogue, characterization, and movement were likely not pre-scripted or set in stone. The vast archive of Teatro Campesino scripts should not be taken as evidence that these roles lacked space for actors to wield autonomy over their product. Just the opposite: actors have articulated their very specific intents with these roles, and it is my position that they had had near-unilateral agency over their methods of expression.

Early and midperiod Teatro Campesino work does not generally appear to align with the traditional Western theater production framework where a script is written by a playwright; a director makes authoritative, key choices; actors memorize the script and work within the director's vision; and the play is produced on a stage in front of a non–physically participating audience. My archival research suggests that there is not a singular, definitive preformed script for any one acto or mito produced between 1965 and 1980. Rather, in any one archival file for a story such as *El fin del mundo*, there are a dozen varied script versions. Along with these complete scripts, there are also poems, songs, drawings, working drafts, and outlines that seem to have guided or reflected the story's theme and tone. This is why archived complete scripts represent just one version of a story that could be (and was) actualized in many different ways. Furthermore, it is unclear to what extent complete scripts do or do not reflect actors' improvisation work, group discussions, input from core members and other show producers, the workshopping that was key to the Teatro Campesino process, and whatever else was going on to build a particular show run. Details such as dialogue, setting, tone, or characterization could very well change from actor to actor, performance to performance, and production to production. Therefore, scripts must be contextualized as one way the company expressed a story, or perhaps as a single recorder's interpretation after a particular production run.

With that said, the scripts do give insight into what general themes and character types were heavily favored by the troupe as well as what ideologies or assumptions were frequently attached to them. In this regard, scripts clearly document some of teatristas' specific performance limitations and obstacles, even if they do not offer evidence about negotiated performance opportunities or revisionary methods of enacting roles. To highlight this divergence, I return to those scholarly assertions that teatristas were systematically marginalized in the troupe by their limited range of acting opportunities. Broyles-González evidences this claim with the fact that Teatro Campesino scripts mainly depict women as auxiliary characters with satellite identities such as *la madre, la abuela, la hermana,* and *la esposa/novia* (the mother, the grandmother, the sister, and the wife/girlfriend) and stereotypical designations of *la virgen* (the innocent maiden) or *la malinche* (the harlot).[55] Broyles-González concludes that these characters could only ever represent a "single dimension" of Chicana subjectivity—one that was pejoratively defined by powerlessness and victimization—and so marginalized the women who had to embody them.[56]

I understand why these characters would frustrate both Broyles-González and the teatristas who spoke about them to her. In a published version of one of the earliest actos, *Las dos caras del patroncito* (The Two Faces of the Farm Boss), the only woman is the silent, unnamed, bikini-clad wife of the White farm boss—a status symbol the esquirol "acquires" when he takes over the patroncito's job.[57] In a 1976 script of *La pastorela* (The Shepherd's Play) from in the archives, "Gila" is the only named woman character. She is forced into marriage by her father but then spurned by her would-be husband when she does not spend enough time preparing food. Later, when a *hermitanio* (hermit) attempts to molest her, her family justifies his actions as a product of "spells" and not sexual violence. Even sacrosanct parts such as La Virgen in *La Virgen de Tepeyac* were, according to Rodriguez, "asexual and iconistic" woman characters "that suffered from an 'I'm too divine to be human' complex."[58] Like Broyles-González, teatristas were clearly frustrated by some of these character types. Not every single woman in Teatro Campesino stories was passive or pejoratively stereotypical, but because teatristas performed all woman characters, they invariably played all the marginalized, victimized, or abused ones.[59]

However, it is my position that we cannot holistically gauge teatristas' performance opportunities by looking only at woman characters that appear in archived stories or scripts. Let me elaborate on this with an accounting of the 1977 production of *La pastorela*. A straightforward examination of the *La pastorela* script connected to this production run certainly demonstrates sexism in its characterizations. Gila is the only named woman character, and she is not even that central: when present at all, she is either the object of unwanted sexual attentions or else passively cooking and being ordered around. Rodriguez, who played Gila in the 1977 production, describes this role as "not huge or large or of much depth."[60] But, while Gila may be the only woman character, she was not the only character played by a woman. The quick plot of *La pastorela* is that Satanás is sent by Luzbel (Lucifer) to prevent some *pastores* (shepherds) from reaching the birthplace of Jesus. Satanás speaks riddles, dances, sings, turns the pastores into sheep, and entices them with money and women. When these activities are ineffective, Satanás calls on Luzbel's help; upon hearing the pastores' prayers, God sends his top soldier, San Miguel, to stop Luzbel, Satanás, and their diablo minions. The program for the winter production of *La pastorela* at the *Fiestas Navideñas* festival in San Juan Bautista lists Socorro Valdez (Cruz) as Satanás, Olivia Chumacero as San Miguel, and Stephanie Buswell and Vickie Oswald as diablos. Although all background pastores are identified as men, five are played by teatristas.[61] Because Gila is a woman character, a teatrista—Rodriguez—did have to play this role. But rather than having only this character to embody, teatristas could also take on the scheming Satanás, evil diablos, or heroic San Miguel. And as Rodriguez, Valdez, and Chumacero continually reiterate, even the most coveted woman role "wasn't as fun as the [other] roles we did play."[62]

When it came to sexless parts, a gender-indiscriminate casting practice appears to have been fairly standard, even for masculine roles such as San Miguel. That is to say, these roles were filled without primary consideration for how the actor's offstage gender would or would not align with the character. My assertion is based on an internal casting sheet I discovered in the archives, which was used to plan the winter 1980 production of *La pastorela*. Each part is listed down the left side of the sheet, and, to the right of each part, there are fillable boxes for "first choice," "second choice," and "third choice." Names have been scribbled into these boxes to help the casting director(s) remember the preferred choices for a given part. Written as "first choice" for Satanás is "Angela" (I believe this is Angela Cruz), and "second choice" is "Ernesto Heradez" [sic]. This casting note demonstrates how Satanás might be played by either a woman or a man actor, and Angela appears to have bested Ernesto this time. Likewise, in the "Angel" category, the first choice for San Gabriel (St. Gabriel) is an actor named "Rogelio" and first choice for San Miguel is "Yolanda" (probably Yolanda Parra). While both angel roles are grouped into a single box (denoting a similar genre of character), one is presumably going to be played by a man actor and the other by a woman actor.[63] The lead human parts in both the 1977 and 1980 productions were cast

Fig. 3.1. Teatro Campesino performers as calaveras; image from the *American Perspectives* broadcast on Teatro Campesino productions.

with attention to how the gender of the actor aligned with the gender of the character (Rodriguez played Gila), but sexless and background characters did not follow this model.

There are numerous archival examples of teatristas taking on these types of roles beyond *La pastorela*. For instance, in one amazing picture, a teatrista I believe is Diane Rodriguez plays Luzbel, blowing thick smoke out of her nostrils and down over a sinister goatee.[64] The most commonly performed sexless roles I found evidence of were calaveras. Images depict teatristas descending onstage en masse wearing full-body skeleton costumes, masks, and skullcaps (see fig. 3.1). There are many photographs of Valdez as a machismo-dripping *pachuco* calavera in *El fin del mundo* (The End of the World).[65] In images from *La carpa de los rasquachis* (The Traveling Show of the Oppressed), Valdez is on her hands and knees with tongue wagging out, playing a calavera who is acting like a dog.[66] Prevalent in Mexican myths and cultural celebrations, calaveras are skeleton or skull-like apparitions that symbolize a spiritual connection between the world of the living and the world of the dead or the unknown. Those in the Americas might associate calaveras with *El Día de los Muertos* (The Day of the Dead) celebrations, or maybe the artwork of José Guadalupe Posada. In a 1976 interview for the talk show *Catch 2*, Teatro Campesino member Phil Esparza says: "Each and every one of us has a calavera inside. And so when you reach that point, skin color, nationality, it doesn't make any difference because we are all calaveras inside."[67] As in Posada's drawings, the calaveras in Teatro Campesino productions might have masculine and feminine gender signifiers layered over their forms (e.g., they might wear a dress or a bandana). Yet, calaveras remain fundamentally sexless, mythical, and nonliving beings. Humans have skeletons, but calaveras lack humans' identity components such as race or gender. Instead, what primarily defines a calavera is its "common denominator" skeletal structure: a set of bones that all humans share underneath their unique living structures. In this regard, calaveras are both not distinctly human and a "universal symbol" of baseline humanity.[68]

Because of their universal yet not human quality, calaveras were something of a "blank slate" for actors to create and develop their own ideas about characterization, including in terms of racial and gender signification. Sentiments about calavera characters having baseline neutrality are reflected in various production records of *El fin del mundo*. In the archival manuscript attached to the 1980 production, Reymundo "Mundo" Mata purposefully overdoses on drugs to enter the world of the "unliving" and search for his pregnant girlfriend, Vera. Mundo meets several calaveras who were once people he knew in the world of the living but are losing their gender, sex, and race identities as they settle into calaveras. These calaveras look and behave like humans in some respects but are not subject to the same cultural rules that shape human identification practices. For example, this particular script describes a scene where a calavera sex worker named Chata, upon securing a client, "goes on stripping until she is down to the bone."[69] I assume this line is recording how Chata removed layers of clothing to visually reveal the actor's skeleton leotard underneath. Chata is a feminine calavera, and, in fact, Mundo recognizes her as a former woman he knew in the world of the living. Yet, Chata does not possess the medical markers of a female body: when she takes off her feminine clothing, underneath lies the "common denominator" skeletal structure rather than specific genitals or secondary sex characteristics. So, although calaveras such as Chata can look and act in a gendered way, these characters' expressions are not assumed to be reflecting the human equivalent of sex identity.

Teatro Campesino actors performed calaveras in masculine, feminine, androgynous, genderless, or sometimes multiply gendered and ungendered ways. Pairing production and candid images in the archives to actor statements about their favorite roles suggests that these parts were highly enjoyable for all. But for teatristas who did not care for other gendered performance duties (playing human woman parts), these roles offered something beyond enjoyment. Building and creatively embodying sexless characters effectively revised the parameters of teatristas' own performance limits and obligations. In playing these characters, teatristas did not hide their gender identities from the audience (most calavera costumes were quite formfitting, and teatristas' names are clearly marked in programs). So, technically, a Teatro Campesino audience had many ways to identify these performers as women and many opportunities to factor their cultural beliefs about Chicanas into their interpretations of the sexless characters. In fact, this is exactly parallel to what male impersonators encouraged their audiences to do. But in the context of a revisionary gender-bending process, the expression of the character—whatever that might be—is not meaningfully informed by the personal identity of the actor. That is to say, there is no embodied equivalence between the live human performer—in terms of gender, sex, or race—and a mythical figure that possesses none of these. Thus, I argue that a revisionary process encourages audiences to apprehend the queer identity quality of the character separately from any specific meaning gleaned from the discrete identity of the performer, while also understanding that this act is fundamentally bent from all actors' lived selves. In the next section, I illustrate how exactly teatristas discouraged audiences from making identification or cross-identification connections and instead invited them to frame the teatristas' personal identities as significant to Teatro Campesino's overarching purpose.

SEXLESS MASCULINITY

A revisionary iteration of gender-bending frees actors from having to produce performances that directly reflect or comment on their lived identities. This empowers them to physically perform characters in expansive and unbounded ways. Teatristas like Socorro Valdez routinely built and enacted masculine mythical characters, and I have found no evidence that this common casting practice was overtly contested or questioned within the troupe. In offering an explanation for why she so frequently took on these roles, Valdez told Broyles-González that "those characters of men needed to be played. But unfortunately the men in the group at the time were not capable or free or whatever the problem was."[70] This statement is ambiguous in terms of what exact roles she was playing and why, but it does illustrate how Valdez was often in charge of performing roles that "needed to be played," regardless of whether those roles were masculine.[71] Moreover, it is important to note that I found no evidence in the archive of Valdez performing main characters that were human men. So, although it might have happened, I see her statement as primarily referring to the mythical, sexless characters she played where she layered masculine attributes onto them.[72]

Archived scripts, outlines, and notes document many popular iterations of the *El fin del mundo* story line, and, in addition, there are copious performance, publicity, and candid photographs of particular productions. Because I have not located a video or sound recording of *El fin del mundo*, these items are essential in illustrating how teatristas enacted the gender-bending quality of "sexless masculinity." For instance, many performance stills and posed shots from the 1980 production depict Valdez as the main calavera character, the masculine Huesos (Bones). Huesos was a gang leader who was killed during a robbery. Now in the world of the dead, he retains some of his former human attitudes and characteristics but is slowly losing them as he settles into calavera life. Huesos looks primarily like all other skeleton characters in that he lacks organs, muscles, and skin. This effect is largely accomplished through Valdez's makeup and costume treatments. For example, her base costume is a light-colored leotard with a full-size skeleton image painted on top. While human skeletal structures are often medically sexed based on shape and size, the bones painted on Valdez's costume are too simple to convey this type of classification. Furthermore, Valdez's entire face and neck are defined in white and black makeup that mimics a generic human skull. But while Huesos is a sexless calavera, he is also a masculine character that some scripts allude to as not having been dead long enough to lose all aspects of his former self. Thus, layered on top of Huesos's neutral calavera are some culturally masculine signifiers. For instance, while he wears no shirt to cover his skeletal ribs, he does wear zoot suit–style high-waisted, baggy trousers with wide suspenders (in some images, a pack of cigarettes is tucked under one of his suspender straps). Above his skull face is a shock of dark hair styled into a large pompadour, and Huesos also wears a wide bandana across his brow, pulled down over his eyebrows and ears. So Huesos presents many aspects of readable gendered machismo, but these gendered elements are symbols layered over his clear calavera frame.

Many of these images are production stills, thus offering insight into Valdez's methods of performatively expressing sexless masculinity. In one image,

Valdez-as-Huesos is engaged in an intense conversation with Mundo, the protagonist. Although Valdez's face is covered in black and white makeup and her forehead is obscured by the bandana, her eyes are perceptibly tense and fixed. She also has her hands deeply thrust into her pockets as she slouches into a concave shape. Her hands-in-pockets, forward-slouch posture forms the stereotypical pachuco tableau—a physicality that is visually identifiable not only as masculine but also as a known iteration of racialized masculinity.[73] Valdez clearly transmits her characterization of threatening physical toughness—a plausible expression from a former gang leader—in every image I saw. Yet, if one looks beyond the layers of machismo and calavera, Valdez's own small and curvy body is clearly evident. Annie Hindle's broad and stout body contributed to her overall masculine aesthetic. Contrastingly, in scenes where Valdez stands next to Marco Rodriguez, the actor playing Mundo for this production, Valdez barely reaches to the bottom of his chin (although the pompadour does give her a few inches). Moreover, although Rodriguez is a slim person, Valdez's own arms and frame appear significantly thinner than his. And, frankly, Valdez's tight leotard does little to obscure her other physical body features. In historical examples where women posed as men in public and performance settings, secondary sex characteristics such as breasts and hips were pointedly concealed by loose clothing, binding, or padding. Hindle wore boxy, buttoned-up suits, and Tilley said she padded herself to create a more masculine shape. But Valdez's base skeleton costume is not boxy in the least, and I see no indication that her body is padded. Thus, it would be easy to classify Valdez's body as a stereotypical woman's body—thus Valdez as a woman performer—if an audience member desired to make such a classification. This is why, unlike identification and cross-identification practices, Valdez's masculine characterization demonstrates a revisionary identification: audiences can fully identify her but do not need to in order to apprehend the queerness of her characterization.

Let me elaborate on this point with a story from Broyles-González's own ethnography. After watching *El fin del mundo*, she explains, "How astonished I was to discover backstage after the performance that the extraordinary Huesos was played by a woman."[74] Perhaps Broyles-González was shocked to see a woman actor backstage because the masculine stage illusion projected by Huesos had been so complete. This is, in fact, what a traditional gender-bending discourse would lead us to conclude about her statement. But even just from viewing production images, it is quite clear that a woman played this part. In fact, I found this example because I had been going through archival images looking for women with readable bodies playing nonwomen roles. But, unlike me, Broyles-González was not specifically scouting for evidence of women's alternative performance practices. She was just watching *El fin del mundo,* enjoying the characterization, and taking in the show's various messages. Even if Valdez's personal gender identity were readable onstage (and I suspect it was), it appears to have mattered little in the overall success of her characterization. Thus, I suggest the reason Broyles-González did not notice a woman playing Huesos was that this particular information was largely irrelevant to the purpose of the production and the successful enaction of the character.

From what I have gathered in the archives, women actors generally played women characters, men actors played men characters, and all actors played sexless characters. Thus, all mythical, sexless characterizations were bent from actors' fundamental positionality of being real humans with some form of assigned sex identity. If mythical and sexless characterizations are foundationally bent roles, then Valdez's skill at this form of bending should be gauged by how well she accomplished the otherworldly effect of being mythical and sexless. In the story above, Broyles-González labels the Huesos performance "extraordinary" before she discovers a woman did it. This tells me that the novelty of Valdez's act was not just that a woman was able to do masculinity but that a human was able to do a nongendered, nonraced, and nonsexed characterization so well. Although Huesos is a masculine calavera, his masculinity cannot—is not intended to—impart key information about his fundamental or core self; underneath the masculine pompadour, baggy trousers, and bandana, Huesos must be identifiable first and foremost as a collection of bones that belongs to the world of the dead. Awareness of Valdez's personal gender would have added little to the impression of how well she was accomplishing this otherworldly characterization. Thus, a revisionary identification process does not prevent an audience from decoding and classifying the performing body, but neither does the success of the characterization pivot on whether the actor has or has not concealed their own specific embodied identities. Such a notion complicates presumptions that audiences cannot appreciate staged queerness or bentness without using the actor's available identity as their fulcrum for understanding it.[75]

I have described one type of revisionary gender-bending process: when performance actions shift how lived identities may meaningfully inform the actor's bent product. In this case, the only meaningful contrast between the acting body and the character is the actor's status of being a live person in contrast to the mythical and sexless nature of the character. In the case of Teatro Campesino, I have no doubt that Valdez's own racial-gendered identity was extremely important to her personal subjectivity, her position in el Movimiento and Teatro Campesino, and her reasons for taking on sexless roles. And yet, while fundamental to her and her actions, those particular identity details do not inform the overall impact of her sexless performance nor even primarily explain why her act is a bent one. In effect, Valdez inhabits a dualism, a mestiza consciousness, by living her subjectivity and allowing it to impel her work while also not having to allow it to define her work methods and products.

GENDERLESSNESS

In addition to sexless masculinity, it is also common to find archival records of performances where mythical characters lack gender signifiers. Teatristas performed as genderless calaveras in *La carpa de los rasquachis* (1976, 1978) and *El fin del mundo* (1980); as gender-indistinct diablos and Satanás in *La pastorela* (1977, 1980); as La Muerte (Death) in *La carpa de los rasquachis* (1976, 1978); and as Diablo in *Corridos* (1970s). A good example of genderless mythical characterization is Valdez's rendition of Calavera for the 1978 European tour of *La carpa de los rasquachis*. The main villains of the story, Calavera and Diablo, play many of the secondary characters that interact with the protagonists. At various points in the narrative, Calavera morphs into a nurse, border smuggler, welfare worker, server, funeral director, dog, mayor, and undercover cop.[76] In spite of these enactments, Calavera generally retains its underlying inhuman skeleton appearance and always morphs back into its primary identity between characters. As with Huesos, Calavera has no human equivalent of a sex or race identity. Thus, Valdez's costume is similar in that it comprises a neutral leotard and leggings with a simple skeletal structure printed down the front. But, unlike with Huesos, most of Valdez's face is concealed under a skull-shaped headpiece that extends over her head and down to her mouth. Her chin is painted black and highlighted with long white teeth.

Huesos was a masculine pachuco calavera slowly losing his ties to his previous living racial-gendered identity. In contrast, Calavera knows how to play with gender but seems to have no material connection, past or present, to human identification. Thus, Huesos and Calavera represent different approaches to the sexless role, but neither characterization trades on Valdez's own embodied identities to impart the impression of sexless inhumanity. Several images from *La carpa de los rasquachis* depict Valdez on her knees, hands flopping in the air and head tilted quizzically to the side.[77] In the scene represented, protagonist Jesus Pelado Rasquachi is employed as a dog walker and so Calavera has morphed into Babushka, a bad dog he must care for. Valdez's skeleton mask does not allow for much expression around the eyes, forehead, cheeks, and nose, but her slightly smiling mouth and wagging tongue read strongly as doglike. As with Huesos, Valdez's short, thin, and curvy body is still quite visible to the audience. However, her particular enactment of this character revises what meanings are being most strongly communicated by her body. For example, several images show dog-Calavera Valdez sandwiched between two other actors. To her right stands Babushka's wealthy owner, played by Diane Rodriguez in a feathered hat, cat-eyed glasses, and a long fur coat, striking a demure yet snooty stance while holding Babushka's leash on the tip of her finger. To her left is the actor playing Rasquachi, taking a wide-legged stance and sporting a thick black moustache, flannel shirt, and trucker hat. Both actors are playing up racial-gendered stereotypes of particular men and women. On its knees between this hegemonically feminine woman and this classically masculine campesino, Calavera looks even more inhuman and alien, despite the fact that a human woman is playing it.

Valdez shares a gender identity with Rodriguez, and Rodriguez was clearly cast in her role because a woman was needed to play this woman character. Even if Rodriguez were asked to play this role because of her acting talent (and I have no doubt she was), she was also asked to play it because, as a woman, she was assumed to either naturally embody this woman character's identity or at least be more suited to creating and expressing it onstage. I have described how some teatristas objected to having to take on undesirable woman parts merely because they were woman performers. However, if a man actor had played this woman character, I argue that audiences would still factor his body into their overall interpretations of the character. That is, they would have seen his man self as a gestus-like indictment of the character, a means of mocking or parodying her as grotesquely gendered. Thus, whether a woman actor or man actor played the role, audiences would still have drawn on their knowledge of the performer's offstage gender identity to enrich their interpretation of the character.

I do not intend to imply here that women cannot also bend or denormalize femininity via their performance of it. In chapter 5, I document a type of gender-bending I call female-femmeing that is intended to do just that. However, I argue that a standard identification gender-bending process—the process attached to the most popularly known forms of commercial bending—encourages audiences to assume that all bodies fit into hegemonic categories of gender when not performing a bent gender act. In this model, Rodriguez plays a woman character because she is a woman actor. If she were bending, she would play the part of the man on her left, the campesino. And yet, kneeling between the woman playing a woman and the man playing a man is Valdez, a woman playing neither a woman nor a man nor a human nor even a real animal. The performance of such an inhuman, mythical, genderless figure presents a queer stage picture of nonidentity, a stark contrast to the cisgender identities of the characters surrounding it as well as to the embodied identity of its performer. This constitutes a revisionary form of bending because the audience is aware of Valdez's personal identities and could mobilize this information at any time to try to understand the significance of the character. Despite Broyles-González's testimony that she did not know Valdez played Huesos in *El fin del mundo*, I argue that a general audience's lack of knowledge about core Teatro Campesino members cannot be assumed. Valdez was known for playing characters such as these, and she has a rather distinct, small body. In addition, programs naming the actor playing each character accompanied many performances. But if and when audiences identified Calavera as Valdez, there was still no useful comparison to be made between her known personal statuses and the inhuman, animalistic, morphing, and devious figure she was expressing. In contrast to the seeming correlation between Rodriguez's gender and the hyperfeminine character she portrayed, Valdez's personal identities could not further support or refute audiences' impressions of Calavera's character.

For Valdez, this type of both/and mestiza practice allowed her to ground herself in her racial-gendered connections with her teatro colleagues and audience members and also enact Calavera without the weight of this identity predetermining her performance. Valdez was, in essence, free to do as she pleased. This freedom is most evident in images that capture Calavera being its own evil self during one-on-one interactions with Diablo. In one photo, Valdez is extending her hands in the air and, with one leg pointed toward the audience and the other bent, moving into a deep and sweeping bow. Another photo depicts Valdez tensed, knees bent, and hands poised to strike out. She directly faces the audience, and the black empty hollows of her eyes create a striking contrast to the white mask and fully open mouth.[78] These photos illustrate Valdez's full range of body movement in forming her characterization: Calavera crouches, points its legs, shapes its body into an "S," extends its arms, and menacingly thrusts its chin forward. During all of this movement, Valdez's formfitting leotard does not conceal the shape of her body at all. Yet, if Calavera's costume were loose or accompanied by, say, a heavy cloak, Valdez would not be as able to create such elaborate and interesting physical characterizations. Her practice neither clearly identifies nor clearly hides these readable embodied identities but rather revises their usefulness and meanings.

Role types such as these appear to have been an ever-present aspect of Teatro Campesino's repertoire, for several reasons. First, mythical characters were an extension of Chicanismo: familiar Latin American and Chicanx icons of power, spirituality, and culture. As Rodriguez explains, calaveras are a "universal symbol" of strength and historical legacy that "our race is not afraid of."[79] Second, these parts enabled distinct bodies to temporarily free themselves from the cultural implications of their own identifications and create stunning performances with meaningful impact. Emma Pérez proposes that women of Color must fight toward a "decolonial imaginary," where they can experience, theorize, and take pride in their own specificity and legacy apart from a Western binary or singularity.[80] In this regard, Valdez's body and cultural identity do not disappear beneath her act; rather, the context and methods of her performance revise what such positionality can mean within the play's narrative.

REVISIONARY GROWTH

I have put forth a case for why teatristas so often played sexless parts: the revisionary gender-bending process embedded in these roles enabled them to expand their acting opportunities without hiding or disavowing their racial-gendered identities. And yet, I do not wish to imply that teatristas had these opportunities solely because of Teatro Campesino's leadership or benevolence or that a revisionary bending system was already in place before teatristas began to take an active part in it. Teatristas continually supported, cultivated, and expanded these roles, and this commitment, I suggest, is key to their presence and longevity. Teatro Campesino members occasionally appeared on local talk or news television shows to promote the troupe's upcoming work. During an interview on Monterey's *Nine AM Morning Show*, Olivia Chumacero discusses the 1980 production of *El fin del mundo* and also

Fig. 3.2. Right: Olivia Chumacero models her La Flaca costume on the *Nine AM Morning Show*.

models the calavera costume she wears in the production (see fig. 3.2). Chumacero's costume is similar to that of Huesos: a light-colored leotard with a simple skeleton shape painted down the front. Chumacero is not in stage makeup during her morning show appearance, but several candid snapshots in the archives reveal that Chumacero painted her full face like a skull with black-rimmed eyes, white and black defined features, and two rows of long skeletal teeth.[81] During her morning show interview, Chumacero wears her hair in two braids, but, for the actual production, her hair was pulled up and back.

Chumacero's calavera character, which she identifies on the morning show as "La Flaca," does not have the clear layer of gender signifiers that other calaveras such as Huesos have. I was, therefore, surprised that in some archived scripts of *El fin del mundo*—including one marked as "first/revised" draft and attached to the 1980 production—La Flaca is stereotypically feminine and heteronormative: she is passive, wears dresses, and responds positively to the sexual attentions of masculine characters (both calavera and human). Flaca and her friend Calaca enter this script's story line when they are "picked up" by "guys" on their way to a dance. Flaca and Calaca flirt and dance with these masculine characters and, when sexually advanced upon by them, assert their appropriately chaste femininity by saying they are "family girls."[82] It is hard to gauge where these specific details fall in the timeline of the show's production. They could have been part of an original outline or draft written by one or several core members. In this case, La Flaca's final characterization and dialogue would have been subject to Chumacero's own individual interpretation and workshopping. Alternately, this script might be recording one particular show or an amalgamation of a particular production run. So, while it could evidence Chumacero's personal performance choices, I find the former possibility (a base she built on or away from) most likely because of the script's label of "first/revised" draft. Luckily for me, I have a much more definitive way of knowing what Chumacero's personal characterization of La Flaca was besides just guessing at script time lines. I can reference Chumacero's own words.

In her conversation with Lillian Rojas, host of the *Nine AM Morning Show*, Chumacero explains that many sexless characters have distinct personality characteristics. Chumacero announces that her character is named La Flaca because the character's bones are thin (as exemplified by thinly painted bones on her leotard). La Flaca is a Spanish title with a grammatically feminine ending (*a* versus *o*). So, a logical assumption from this character's name might be that La Flaca, if not female, is at least a feminine creature. This assumption would align with La Flaca's scripted characterization. However, during the interview, Chumacero translates her own character's name not as "the thin woman or girl" or even "the thin feminine character" but instead as "the thin one."[83] Even though script details and grammar indicators seem to mark La Flaca as a feminine calavera, Chumacero's own verbal interpretation is the first and best indicator of the intents and methods she employed in her performance. Some calaveras in *El fin del mundo* did have clear gender and race displays (like Huesos), but Chumacero's verbal translation of her character, her costume, and her presentation do not similarly indicate gender. Chumacero could have enacted this character in an identifiably gendered way, of course, and perhaps that makes more sense to the story outlined in the draft. However, Chumacero's explanation and presentation makes her intentionality clear: she has chosen this character's identity to be neutral or genderless.

In addition to claiming creative license over the characterization of sexless parts, teatristas also encouraged and perhaps even instigated critical shifts in the style of costume of such characters. Broyles-González's own discussion of teatristas performing as calaveras is grounded in her assertion that the requisite costume was artistically and physically stifling (and race-masking). I agree with this assessment to an extent. The Calavera mask worn by Valdez in the 1978 production of *La carpa de los rasquachis* likely did limit her ability to act with her entire face. But Valdez's Huesos costume and Chumacero's La Flaca costume for the 1980 production of *El fin del mundo* did not employ masks. Instead, both actors painted a skull pattern over their otherwise totally exposed faces. In her *Morning Show* interview, Chumacero holds up one of the molded calavera masks and explains: "But now we don't use the mask; we have makeup. And it's very interesting because you can use your entire face for your expressions. It's really interesting. Before we went from half-mask, half calavera mask, and the lower part was makeup. And now we do the entire face and it's just great." In response to Chumacero's explanation, Rojas surmises that "now you get to use the whole body."[84] Rojas is absolutely right. While both mask and makeup communicate the inhuman essence of a calavera, makeup yields a distinct advantage in terms of physical characterization.

I have no incontrovertible proof of who exactly instigated this particular costume transition, but I do have a strong guess backed by archival evidence. Teatristas contributed to many of the technical aspects of productions as directors, assistant directors, choreographers, lighting designers, technical directors, music designers, musicians, and costume designers. In fact, almost every program between 1977 and 1980 lists Diane Rodriguez as show costumer or costume designer. During the *Morning Show* interview, Chumacero says, "We have a costume lady in our company. Her name's Diane Rodriguez and usually she's the one that gets everything together and makes it."[85] It is a fair assumption that Rodriguez—herself a performer of sexless roles—had a good measure of influence in the decision to shift from the masks worn in 1978 to the makeup used later for these parts. This particular costume evolution demonstrates teatristas' clear intentionality, investment in the revisionary gender-bending process, and commitment to maintaining a mestiza consciousness.

NOTHING REJECTED, NOTHING ABANDONED

The few texts that mention the mythical, sexless roles do not examine them as acts of gender-bending. Indeed, these performances are very different from the canonical notion of what gender-bending looks like or accomplishes. However, during the celebration for the reopening of the Teatro Campesino archives at UCSB, one of my professors—referring to my very early research on the topic—asked Diane Rodriguez about her "gender-bending" performances with the troupe, and she knew exactly what type of work that term referred to. When teatristas designed and enacted sexless mythical characters, they were absolutely bending boundaries of identity, albeit via a less recognizable revisionary process that allowed them to live in and also move around personal identity-based positions. Unlike male impersonators, teatristas were not designing their acts for the highest financial gain. Instead, they were looking for ways to contribute to el Movimiento that were also personally enjoyable and fulfilling. Whether playing Gila or Huesos or Calavera, teatristas always remained Chicana performers and thus remained within the stratified cultural contexts that impelled them to take and develop these roles in the first place. But teatristas also effectively mobilized their performance positions within Teatro Campesino to accomplish their goals, and they did so without irrevocably altering their personal and cultural subjectivities.

So, what is the macrocultural impact—if any—of a bending technique that creates space for the performers while not necessarily changing larger meanings attached to their identities but disallows such meanings from fully determining their sociopolitical work? In 1983, Rodriguez likened her relationship with Teatro Campesino to a traditional Western marriage structure. While not totally egalitarian, "it's not like someone is dictating to us that we must be here. [. . .] Rather, we all have our own input and we all want to be here because we can contribute."[86] Rodriguez's marriage analogy acknowledges how racial-gendered inequality is the embedded norm in many institutions, and it also clearly speaks to why she did not just divorce herself from Teatro Campesino. Rodriguez believed in la causa and wanted to contribute to it via her work with Teatro Campesino, even if her position in this process was not a totally egalitarian one. Eleven years earlier, Chumacero told Cecelia Trujillo about the significant internal troupe conflicts but also explained "a sense of good feeling there, that something was being accomplished."[87] Again, the sentiment is that Teatro Campesino's structure was not ideal but that participation was more beneficial than not for her and her cause. Rodriguez says that she and the other teatristas "could have walked away, but we stayed because we believed we were moving a community to self-empowerment through art."[88] Without denying that their specific identities as Chicana women were used by those in power to force them into some unhappy positions, these women instead chose to focus on how their identities inspired their own innovative contributions and encouraged them to maintain loyalty to la causa. A revisionary theory of bending makes room for the performing Chicana body to carry this dual or mestiza signification: the body remains socially marked for specific and important reasons, but the implications of such marks can be revised at politically significant moments via specific bent practices.

The complexity and uniqueness in teatristas' drag process is that, as Anzaldúa would put it, "nothing [is] rejected, nothing abandoned."[89] Of the many archival photos of the 1978 tour of *La carpa de los rasquachis*, one that really stands out is a postperformance cast shot in which the members are lined up in three rows, casually smiling or leaning against each other. Most have already changed into street clothes, but a few are wearing costume pieces or stage makeup. Socorro Valdez is front and center, crouched on her knee, still wearing her skeleton mask and leotard, still fully characterizing Calavera. The only major differences between this image and her show look is that she has thrown on a pair of pants and removed her performance gloves, which are tucked into her waistband. What appears to be a large, sparkling ring is visible on the third finger of her left hand.[90] When I first stumbled across this archival image, I found the combination of Valdez's inhuman characterization with this traditional marker of marriage a bit jarring. But it actually rather poetically characterizes Valdez's dual embodiment. The visibility of the ring triggers a reading of her body that was not encouraged during her performance, and I began thinking about Valdez's traditionalism, domesticity, or buy-in to mythic frameworks of love and romance. But, of course, Valdez was already subject to and implicated in gendered and racialized expectations regarding marriage, children, and domesticity; these did not change or dissolve just because she got to play sexless creatures. By not hiding her ring in this picture, she demonstrates how cultural beliefs and expectations are deeply inscribed onto her and her body. And yet, she is still performing the inhuman heck out of Calavera. She looks nothing like the other women in the photo, but she is just like them. She is also inhuman Calavera. She is both.

The efficacy of a revisionary bending process may be, then, that it forms a viable ideological space for further questioning identity, or at least allowing that identities can and should be mobilized when politically (not just commercially) useful. Reflecting on her eagerness to play sexless characters, Valdez says it was her way of "aborting the fact that I was female and only female."[91] Broyles-González uses this statement to support her overarching claim that teatristas were limited by Teatro Campesino's sexist standards and expectations. In other words, it was so terrible to be a woman in this troupe that Valdez wanted to abort her own woman identity. And I think that, in part, Valdez is speaking to this point. Because of their gender, teatristas were often pigeonholed into embodying negative figurations of Chicanahood. But, equally important in Valdez's statement is her context that, in order to "abort" her singular gender identity, she took on and performed sexless roles. As I have argued, the gender-bending process employed by Valdez allowed her both to be an identifiable Chicana troupe member and not to be held to *just* these singular standards of performance. So, I argue that this statement indicates Valdez's desire to abort not her woman identity but rather a singular identity and to move toward embodying a politically useful and mobilizable mestiza dualism. It would not be appropriate to apply a mestiza framework to non-Chicana or non-Latina figures or expressions, even if they practiced a revisionary form of gender-bending. But, in this case, "mestiza consciousness" aptly articulates the intent, process, and macroideological impacts of teatristas' work: their actions neither supported nor rejected their identities but rather successfully reconfigured how those identities could order their political contributions. In working toward la causa through established artistic outlets, many teatristas did find their voices or contributions marginalized. However, in both choosing and transforming performance practices, teatristas built a space apart from, "among," and also "between" the implications of their assigned and lived identities.[92] This is not an ideological space that all people could use or would even find useful, but it did help teatristas "move across [identities], refusing to be contained by them."[93]

Let me finish by returning to the 1978 production of *La carpa de los rasquachis*, in which Valdez played Calavera. There is also a main woman role in the story—Pelada Rasquachi. Both Calavera and Pelada illustrate difficulties faced by migrant and working-class Latinx and Chicanx laborers, and thus both contribute to the production's central message advocating labor organizing. In theory, Valdez could have played the part of Pelada to communicate the same ideological themes she did playing Calavera. Furthermore, Pelada's abhorrent racial-gendered mistreatment by US institutions is likely something Valdez could identify with personally. But, while Valdez might have had to live some aspects of Pelada's life, Valdez did not have to singularly live them as Pelada does. In the cast photo, where she is still performing Calavera, Valdez is living within her intersectional reality and also inhabiting a character that exists independently from those realities. Whether she takes on the role of Pelada or Calavera, the production's message remains the same. Whether she plays Pelada or Calavera, she will still be treated like Pelada from time to time in her real life. In playing Calavera, she is not stepping away from being a woman like Pelada but rather stepping away from being *only* a woman like Pelada, from being "female and only female." Her gender-bending work demonstrates her awareness and embodiment of physical identity borders, her active intent to move across those borders, and her tolerance for the ambiguity and duality of being both. Thus, I conclude that this particular iteration of revisionary identification gender-bending does not fundamentally alter gender and racial oppression frameworks, but it can grow a mestiza space, a place where nothing has to be rejected and, likewise, nothing has to be abandoned.

NOTES

1. Both the English and Spanish versions of this flyer were away on loan during my residency at the archives. The excerpts quoted here are from a selection of archival material published by the Teatro Campesino organization in 1985 (Teatro Campesino, *Teatro Campesino*, 7).

2. While *campesino* means "rural person or country peasant," the translation of El Teatro Campesino as "the farm workers' theater" is a common one. I have decided to use Chicanx and Latinx to identify mixed groups of people rather than categorizing mixed groups under the masculine formation (Chicano, Latino) or an ending that reinforces the gender binary (a/o or @). People and groups that clearly identify as men or women are categorized with the ending that suits their personal identification (e.g., Chicana).

3. More specifically, Chicanismo and indigenismo emphasize the connection between Chicanx and Latinx people and culture and Mexican, Spanish, and indigenous religious and historical legacies. This work also promotes pride in contemporary Chicanx and Latinx cultural practices. *Chicano* was initially a pejorative term for the children of Mexican immigrants but was reappropriated in the 1960s to convey cultural pride, ethnic respect, and political affiliation among Mexican immigrants, mestizos, and US citizens with familial or historical connections to Mexico.

4. According to Spanish linguist Ariel Schindewolf, *teatrista* could technically be considered a gender-neutral term for theater person, but Broyles-González uses this word specifically for women performers, likely because of the term's linguistically feminine ending. I use it only for women performers and mainly to name those working with El Teatro Campesino. Schindewolf, personal communication with the author, June 2, 2011.

5. Following Broyles-González's ethnographic and archival work on the troupe and subsequent scholarship that heavily criticized the troupe and Luis Valdez for perpetuating sexist organizational structures and casting practices, the Teatro Campesino archives were closed to general public and scholarly use; access was granted only rarely, on a case-by-case basis and with express consent from the troupe. When, in the late 1980s, the archives were moved from Teatro Campesino's main offices to the California Ethnic and Multicultural Archives (CEMA) at the University of California, Santa Barbara (UCSB), I suspect they were intended to be opened for general use. I have been told that students threw tomatoes at Luis Valdez and called him a sellout during the welcoming event. The archives were then not made accessible for general public use until late 2009. In 2010, UCSB hosted a conference to mark this public reopening. As a graduate student at UCSB, I submitted my early work on teatristas' gender-bending practices, facilitated by the newly opened archives, and it was accepted. I then received a personal phone call over winter break because organizers were concerned my paper would be negatively received by Luis Valdez, the keynote speaker, and I was asked to rewrite or reorganize it. A few years later, I submitted this work to a midlevel Latin American-focused scholarly journal, and it was turned down without peer review by an editor who commented that this topic had already been discussed ad nauseam. There is virtually no published work on teatristas' gender-bending practices, so I assume the editor was referring to the larger debate about whether Teatro Campesino was a sexist organization. This article was later published in *Gender and History*.

6. Broyles-González's body of scholarship on the troupe, the article "Out of the Fringe? Out of the Closet" by Maria Marrero, and my own work are the only scholarly sources I am aware of that focus on these practices in more than a very tangential, evidentiary way.

7. Anzaldúa, *Borderlands/La Frontera*, 77–91.

8. Rodriguez, interview with Paulina Sahugan, CEMA 5 S9.

9. This quote can be found in the character description list of the 1973 *La carpa de los rasquachis* in CEMA 5 S1 B13 F5: II.

10. Valdez, quoted in Broyles-González, *Teatro Campesino*, 140; Rodriguez, quoted in Broyles-González, "Living Legacy of Chicana Performers," 50. Because of my primary focus on teatristas, in this chapter, I refer to Socorro Valdez as "Valdez" and her brother Luis Valdez as well as Lupe Valdez by full name.

11. Rodriguez, quoted in Broyles-González, "Living Legacy of Chicana Performers," 50.

12. Rodriguez interview, *Catch 2*, CEMA 5 S5.

13. Valdez, quoted in Broyles-González, *Teatro Campesino*, 149. *Calavera* technically means "skull" but is commonly used to mean "skeleton," and many examples in the archives and in scholarly work translate the word in this way.

14. For example, see Marrero, "Out of the Fringe?"; Broyles-González, *Teatro Campesino*; and Rodriguez, interview with Paulina Sahugan, CEMA 5 S9.
15. Valdez, quoted in Broyles-González, *Teatro Campesino*, 150.
16. Muñoz, *Disidentifications*, 26.
17. Anzaldúa, *Borderlands/La Frontera*, 77.
18. Yarbro-Bejarano, "Gloria Anzaldúa's *Borderlands/La Frontera*," 11.
19. Lloyd, *Beyond Identity Politics*, 48.
20. Teatro Campesino, *Teatro Campesino*, 49.
21. Rodriguez, quoted in Broyles-González, "Living Legacy of Chicana Performers," 48.
22. Teatro Campesino, *Teatro Campesino*, 4.
23. Broyles-González, *Teatro Campesino*, 150.
24. Ibid., 130.
25. Ibid., 150.
26. Broyles-González writes that "Huerta's perspective on the history of El Teatro Campesino has become something of an official version, shared by countless researchers" (*Teatro Campesino*, 130). In addition to Huerta's history in *Chicano Theater: Themes and Forms*, see Cárdenas de Dwyer's essay, "Development of Chicano Drama and Luis Valdez's Actos," in *Modern Chicana Writers*, as well as *Voices of Aztlán: Chicano Literature of Today*, edited by Harth and Baldwin.
27. Broyles-González, *Teatro Campesino*, 130.
28. Hernández, *Postnationalism in Chicana/o Literature and Culture*, 23.
29. Rose, "Traditional and Nontraditional Patterns," 26.
30. Ibid. UFW leaders commonly assigned the group's women members gender-stereotypical positions such as secretarial work and childcare.
31. Hernández, *Postnationalism in Chicana/o Literature and Culture*, 57–58.
32. Yarbro-Bejarano, "Female Subject in Chicano Theatre," 390.
33. Rose, "Traditional and Nontraditional Patterns," 28–29.
34. Taylor, *Archive and the Repertoire*, 5.
35. Ibid., 132.
36. Broyles-González does not explicitly state the dates of her research residency, but based on the dates of interviews she conducted in San Juan Bautista, I believe it was late 1982 to 1983.
37. Broyles-González, "Living Legacy of Chicana Performers," 47.
38. Broyles-González, *Teatro Campesino*, 134–135.
39. Yarbro-Bejarano, "Chicanas' Experience in Collective Theatre," 45.
40. Broyles-González, *Teatro Campesino*, 134–135.
41. Broyles-González, "Living Legacy of Chicana Performers," 47.
42. Broyles-González, "Foreword," xv.
43. Teatro Campesino, *Teatro Campesino*, 45

44. This evidence can be found in CEMA 5 S14 B9 F3; CEMA 5 S14 B10 F23; CEMA 5 S14 B10 F5; and CEMA 5 S14 B9 F17.
45. The program is in CEMA 5 S14 B10 F5, and the 1976 script is in CEMA 5 S1 B22 F2; Teatro Campesino, *Teatro Campesino*, 47.
46. CEMA 5 S14 B10 F23.
47. Broyles-González, "Foreword," xv.
48. Broyles-González, *Teatro Campesino*, 144.
49. Ibid., 152.
50. For a description of Olivia Chumacero's struggles in this area, see Broyles-González, *Teatro Campesino*, 147.
51. Broyles-González contends that two conference talks she gave on Teatro Campesino were prevented from timely publication. Broyles-González also claims that Luis Valdez "went as far as to contact my publishers and threaten them" if he were not allowed editorial control over her book ("Powers of Women's Words," 120). When she and her publishers refused, she says, he withdrew permission for the use of the interviews she had conducted with him in San Juan Bautista and worked with Teatro Campesino to restrict future general public access to the archives.
52. The archives Broyles-González examined in San Juan Bautista would have lacked at least six years of future material (1983–1988) that the current archives hold. In addition, CEMA archivists have organized and labeled many of these materials.
53. The key word here is "legitimate" research, implying that Broyles-González's presented and published work on the troupe was not considered by some in the Teatro Campesino organization to be a legitimate use of the archives. Teatro Campesino, *Teatro Campesino*, 44.
54. Broyles-González, *Teatro Campesino: Four Cardinal Points*, manuscript draft in CEMA 97 B1: 62.
55. Translations my own.
56. Broyles-González, *Teatro Campesino*, 135–136.
57. This particular script is in a small collection of Teatro Campesino actos published in 1971 under Luis Valdez's name (Valdez and El Teatro Campesino, *Actos*).
58. Rodriguez, quoted in Marrero, "Out of the Fringe?" 134.
59. Men may have played woman parts, especially in the early actos before women began to steadily perform with the troupe. However, I have found no evidence of such casting practices in the archives. If they happened, they were likely rare.
60. Rodriguez, interview by Paulina Sahugan, CEMA 5 S9.
61. This program is in CEMA 5 S14 B9 F3. Some other interesting casting for this production: Luis Valdez played Luzbel.

62. Rodriguez, quoted in Marrero, "Out of the Fringe?" 134.
63. Casting sheet, CEMA 5 S1 B22 F5.
64. CEMA 5 S6 B39 F1 #10.
65. *Pachuco* does not have a direct English equivalent but might be generalized as a young man who participates in urban street gangs.
66. *Carpa* literally means "tent," but in this case, it refers to traveling tent shows or plays. In the glossary of the 1973 production, *rasquachis* are the oppressed, characterized by having a poor, crude, and short lifestyle. See CEMA 5 S1 B13 F5.
67. Esparza interview, *Catch 2*, CEMA 5 S5.
68. Rodriguez interview, *Catch 2*, CEMA 5 S5.
69. *El fin del mundo*, 21. CEMA 5, S1 B18 F2.
70. Valdez, quoted in Broyles-González, *Teatro Campesino*, 149.
71. Ibid.
72. Broyles-González claims that Valdez did play nonmythical man characters, but, aside from a few instances of teatristas performing as background men, the closest evidence I could find was of teatristas playing mythical characters with masculine gender characteristics.
73. This body stance is also iconically depicted by Edward James Olmos performing as El Pachuco in the stage and film versions of Teatro Campesino's *Zoot Suit*. For examples of Valdez's characterization, see these photographs: CEMA 5 S6 B8 F5 #59; CEMA 5 S6 B8 F6 #70A; CEMA 5 S6 B9 F1 #75; and CEMA 5 S6 B9 F1 #76.
74. Broyles-González, *Teatro Campesino*, 129.
75. See Meyer's analysis of the *I Dream of Jeannie* drag number in "Unveiling the Word" (70–72).
76. Diablo morphs into a farm owner, a farmer, a car salesman, an undertaker, a campaign manager, a border patrolman, and Louie Rasquachi's girlfriend.
77. CEMA 5 S6 B12 F4 #18.
78. These images can be found in CEMA 5 S6 B12 F3 #5; CEMA 5 S6 B12 F3 #10; and CEMA 5 S6 B12 F3 #15.
79. Rodriguez interview, *Catch 2*, CEMA 5 S5.
80. Pérez, *Decolonial Imaginary*, xvi.
81. For example, see CEMA 5 S6 B8 F3 #7. This photo is not a performance still but rather depicts some social event that likely occurred directly before or after the show.
82. *El fin del mundo*, CEMA 5 S1 B18 F2.
83. Chumacero interview, *Nine AM Morning Show*, CEMA 5 S5.
84. Rojas, *Nine AM Morning Show*, CEMA 5 S5.
85. Chumacero interview, *Nine AM Morning Show*, CEMA 5 S5.
86. Rodriguez, quoted in Broyles-González, "Living Legacy of Chicana Performers," 51.

87. Chumacero interview, by Cecelia Trujillo, CEMA 5 S9.
88. Rodriguez, quoted in Marrero, "Out of the Fringe?" 134.
89. Anzaldúa, *Borderlands/La Frontera*, 79.
90. This image is in CEMA 5 S6 B12 F3 #3.
91. Valdez, quoted in Broyles-González, *Teatro Campesino*, 150.
92. Moraga and Anzaldúa, *This Bridge Called My Back*, 232.
93. Lloyd, *Beyond Identity Politics*, 48.

FOUR

The "First Punch" at Stonewall

Counteridentification Butch Acts

A LOW, RICH voice projects over a packed, anticipatory audience to introduce the show's cast and announce the opening number.[1] Later, the person who owns this voice appears onstage in a dark suit—or perhaps a tuxedo or a white Navy uniform. The actor has a loose jacket but snug pants and a hairstyle that is very short and styled into a flattop that tapers down the forehead in a widow's peak. This slim, handsomely masculine figure is Stormé DeLarverie, the master of ceremonies for the Jewel Box Revue, a popular song-and-dance show featuring "twenty-five men and one girl."[2] The twenty-five are dazzling, showgirl-style female impersonators, and the one is DeLarverie. What audiences associate with DeLarverie's aesthetic changes depending on where the Jewel Box is performing that night. At popular gay clubs, audiences might assume DeLarverie is "family": a sexually queer, genderqueer, or trans person. If the show is at the Apollo or a locale connected to the historical Theater Owners' Booking Association (TOBA) circuit, audiences might associate DeLarverie's act with the expressive female masculinity popularized by some Black women blues performers. But when performing for a majority non-Black and nongay crowd, DeLarverie could be seen as something else. Esther Newton recounts trying to pick out the "girl" among the twenty-five female impersonators, and, according to Newton, there were "general gasps of wonder that greeted Stormé's revelation of her gender at the finale."[3] I interpret the gasps as implying that audience members had not considered that DeLarverie could be the "girl" because they had not considered that DeLarverie could be gender-bending. Instead, they took DeLarverie for what DeLarverie appeared to be, a cisgender, heterosexual man. Until DeLarverie showed them differently.

This chapter explores the masculine stage expressions of Black performers who publicly identified in various queer ways, sometimes by adopting terms such as *B.D. woman, bulldagger, bulldyker, bulldykin' woman,* or *butch* and sometimes by rejecting cisgender and heterosexual identity labels. Woman-identified or non-man-identified Black musicians doing various queer forms of masculinity onstage was a common enough occurrence in Black entertainment venues during the first decades of the twentieth century.[4] This same performance style continued, although less frequently, into the 1950s and 1960s via Black performers working in gay-themed or mafia-owned nightclubs or with racially integrated drag troupes. These performers acted in readably, often stereotypically, masculine ways both onstage and in other public settings. However, none of the performers I discuss in this chapter publicly identified or "passed" as men. Rather, I argue that their slick masculine aesthetic was an expression of queer butchness: a performative masculinity that acted as a public signifier of their noncisgender alignment and queer sexual desire.

My first project in this chapter is to document how these performers created a stage aesthetic that was very masculine but would not be interpreted as a male impersonation. This stage methodology was informed by performers' lived masculinities as well as their specific intent to build queer community, or at least advertise their availability for romantic encounters with women. I explore this particular gender-bending process via performers working during the first three decades of the twentieth century in TOBA venues (also sometimes referred to as the Chitlin' Circuit, Black Theater Circuit, and Black Vaudeville Circuit), in blues and jazz clubs in Harlem's entertainment district, and in racially integrated spaces called "black and tans."[5] I specifically highlight the work of Stormé DeLarverie, even though DeLarverie's popularity peaked decades after this period. Bailey argues that performances from this early period by women "dressed in more 'boyish' or masculine fashion" became a performance norm for "Black LGBT cultures." Thus, later queer performances like DeLarverie's are demonstrative of how earlier methods became "an integral part of the social fabric of Black LGBT communities."[6] The later time context of the 1950s and 1960s and DeLarverie's connection to a popular national touring revue also mean more archival documents and primary recorded interviews exist to illustrate the performance style and lived identity of people who enacted this bending. Connecting DeLarverie's midcentury work to earlier Black theater acts reveals a more detailed picture of queer butch intents and methods.

My second project is to document some of the micro- and macroimpacts produced by this form of bending. I again turn to DeLarverie to illustrate this because DeLarverie is known for supposedly swinging the "first punch" during the 1969 Stonewall Rebellion.[7] Other butch performers—Gladys Bentley and Blackie Dennis, for instance—used their stage work to communicate about their own gender and sexual queerness (and romantic availability) to the audience. However, I argue that DeLarverie's involvement at Stonewall, historicized as a key gay civil rights event, strongly evidences that DeLarverie's aesthetic was intended to be read as neither a cisgender expression nor a male impersonation but rather a public expression of queer, nonman butchness. DeLarverie's public identification as a queer person by police during the rebellion is proof that although DeLarverie had the skill to pass as a man (or as a heterosexual and cisgender male impersonator), DeLarverie's gender-bending was a counteridentification. The counteridentification process aligns the bent aspect of the identity expression with a minoritarian group identity by presenting the performer or persona as readably queer rather than cisgender or heterosexual.

I give primary focus to DeLarverie in this chapter for one more important reason: DeLarverie is routinely classified as a male impersonator.[8] Although I suggest that this is an inappropriate term for naming and defining queer butch acts, it is easy enough to guess why it was, and remains, so often used with DeLarverie. First, there was a lack of varied and detailed gender-bending terminology in the midcentury—a drag language insufficiency that continues today. Second, I demonstrated in chapter 2 how male impersonation originated within particular forums available only to respectable White women performers. The term can certainly be extended to other types of gender-bending that foreground an identification or cross-identification process. However, I argue that DeLarverie is called a male impersonator most often because the basic drag discourse formula remains unquestioned. That is, DeLarverie publicly identified as not-man (the Jewel Box identified DeLarverie as a "girl," although DeLarverie did not publicly follow suit), and DeLarverie presented masculinity onstage. Pairing a cultural framework that assumes people are cisgender with the standard gender-bending definition leads to the conclusion that a "girl" expressing masculinity is impersonating a man because masculinity is the purview of men. In this regard, the title of male impersonator implies that DeLarverie's masculine act was mimetic, following the well-known format of variety and vaudevillian women performing temporarily as men characters.

Referring to DeLarverie as a male impersonator shifts this term into a universal definer for all forms of masculine expression that are done by people who are not men. But this term was originally introduced to identify a performer who had specific large-scale commercial goals, not to describe all forms of bending that express a masculine aesthetic. Calling DeLarverie a male impersonator gets the job done, if the job is to define DeLarverie as a gender-bending performer of masculinity. But this particular discursive shortcut also presumes that cisgender and heterosexual masculinity is the default expression of men's bodies. This displaces the centrality of DeLarverie's own performative intents and goals and also obscures DeLarverie's lived identity. I argue that DeLarverie was not a girl playing at masculinity or impersonating a man, as male impersonators said they were doing. Just the opposite: DeLarverie was cultivating a readable form of masculinity onstage that was similar (although not identical) to DeLarverie's own personal queer butchness. In other words, both stage and personal masculinities were intended to be a clear and present sign of gender nonconformity rather than cisgender replication or alignment. Male impersonators intended their masculine acts to be read as skillful illusions that starkly contrasted to their own natural womanhood. But DeLarverie's act was intended to express a form of masculinity that comfortably fit with a nonman body: a butch counteridentification that would attract women's sexual attentions and align DeLarverie with queerness.

The connection between DeLarverie's act and historical male impersonations not only disregards their divergence in intents and goals but also implies a troubling progress narrative. Framing DeLarverie's work as a continuation of male impersonation ignores key differences in methodology, issues of access (who could perform these acts), and macroimpacts (which bodies could trigger certain mass public reactions or commercial opportunities). Male impersonation was the act of a respectable White woman seeking individual commercial gain by performing to White Victorian audiences. Contemporaneous performers such as Gladys Bentley, Gertrude "Ma" Rainey, Bessie Smith, Josephine Baker, and Ethel Waters, however, were not allowed in male impersonation forums. These women were blues and jazz singers, musicians, and dancers who sometimes performed in men's dress clothing and sometimes performed songs about aggressively pursuing romantic and sexual scenarios with women. This entertainment appealed to people across racial and socioeconomic statuses, but it was grounded in Black culture, sentiments, and community. And, unlike the commercial White male impersonation occurring at roughly the same time, these masculine acts were not designed to reveal the feminine woman or respectable lady under the stage persona. Just the opposite: they demonstrated the performer's investment in being both personally and socially identified as queer. Vesta Tilley dressed as a dandy to sing "Girls, if you'd like to love a solider, you can all love me!" and Rainey dressed in a tuxedo to sing "I don't like no men."[9] The difference is that Rainey was not playing a heterosexual man onstage and a heterosexual lady elsewhere; her song and her presentation advertised her own personal interest in (and availability for) nonheterosexual romance and desire.

Instead of contextualizing DeLarverie and earlier performers with related racial and community contexts as male impersonators, I call their specific form of bending *queer butchness*. This term signifies key qualities of their particular stage aesthetics while also making room for a more nuanced investigation of performers' intents and the acts' macroimpacts. *Butch* broadly indicates a readable form of cultivated cultural masculinity. Sometimes the term is fitted to a man who expresses stereotyped masculinity (e.g., Butch Cassidy), but more colloquially, "a butch" names a masculine lesbian woman. Bailey extends this term to "a kind of catchall gender category for biological females that consists of FTM transgender men, masculine lesbians, aggressives, tomboys, studs, drag kings, and so on."[10] In this regard, "butch" contextualizes a person's masculinity as separate from their medical birth assignment. My addition of "queer" to butchness connects this type of masculinity to stage practices that express it in a readably queer way. In other words, the butchness displayed by performers onstage is intended to appear to the audience as a noncisgender identity expression.

In this regard, a queer butch performance might produce an idealized or even quotidian masculine look, but it will also serve to indicate that the performer does not have and is not producing a cisgender man's identity. In fact, I suggest that a well-deployed queer butch act will methodologically convey the ideological possibility that "nonman masculinity" can be both attractive and comfortable. My position here is informed partly by Robin Maltz's discussion of what she calls "stone butch realness," or the readability of highly masculine women. Maltz uses the term to create a division between masculine people who are, desire to be, or "pass" as men and people who are clearly and resolutely not men but also express a hegemonically "uncompromising" form of masculinity.[11] Not all performers of butch queerness personally identified as lesbians, women, or female; however, I have found no evidence that the performers I explore in this chapter personally identified as cismen or wanted to appear as such during or after their performances. Thus, I define queer butchness as a representation of hegemonic masculinity that is readable both as a performance and as done by someone who is not a cisman even if they are comfortable being masculine all the time. In a discussion about 1990s drag kinging styles, Halberstam defines "butch realness" as a genre of kinging done by women who are personally very masculine. Although these acts were huge crowd-pleasers at drag shows, Halberstam favored the kings who did humorous or exaggerated masculinities, which he calls "male mimicry" or "denaturalized masculinity."[12] In comparison, Halberstam argues, butch realness performers display the "authentic or unadorned and unperformed" masculinity of their lived identities.[13] Halberstam creates a categorical division between "walk-on[s]" at drag king shows who "could have easily passed as male" in public contexts and the gender-bending theater of drag king performers who do overtly constructed masculine acts.[14]

Queer butchness, I propose, names a cultivated theatrical act of masculinity that might be similar to but is not the same as the lived masculinity of its performers. Maltz and Halberstam describe butch performers who strutted, flexed, swaggered, and flirted their way across the stage. Bentley and DeLarverie performed their acts in tuxedos with top hats and tails. Such overt preening behavior and formal attire would be difficult to sustain in daily life. That is to say, a butch performer might be very masculine in the everyday and still present a theatrical slicked-down, dressed up, polished expression of masculinity when onstage. In this regard, I suggest that a masculine person can bend masculinity onstage even if not presenting it as blatantly denaturalized or humorous. I have argued that any analysis of gender-bending should focus on exploring the presentation of a queer identity relationship or the readable deconstruction of a normative one. A key aspect of queer butchness is that the masculinity presented onstage is not intended to read as a cisgender expression of self, or what Maltz terms the appearance of "unified body-gender."[15] Halberstam does define lived "female masculinity" as a decidedly queer identity that diverges from both cisgender and traditional transgender narratives of sex and gender synchronicity.[16] In a similar fashion, I argue that the "contradiction" of a readably nonmale body/nonman self capably and comfortably exuding hegemonic masculinity—whether quotidian or stylized—can constitute a queering of normative identity and thus is a salient form of gender-bending.[17]

In documenting the more expansive and self-determined gender system that orders ballroom culture, Bailey explains that queer people are not limited within ballroom spaces to only identify themselves with standard hegemonic dichotomies (cis/trans or gay/straight) and often choose to "reformulate sex, gender, and sexual knowledge" relationships to better suit them.[18] Building on this, I propose that queer butchness replicates many elements of masculinity that are ideologically positioned in contrast to lived womanhood, and it also queers the corollary that masculinity is the natural or comfortable purview of manhood only. Male impersonators presented masculinity as a construction doable by women while simultaneously identifying masculinity as owned by men and naturally contrasting to women. Queer butchness has the opposite effect. By doing masculinity, the nonman performer reveals that masculinity can have a strong, naturalized, and comfortable connection to nonmen. Whereas identification ideologically aligns the body and identity with majoritarian norms, these butch acts encourage audiences to see the performer as ultimately nonmajoritarian. Thus, I suggest queer butchness exemplifies what I refer to as the gender-bending process of counteridentification.

The attachment of the term *lesbian* to these historical butch performers is common, even though performers rarely used this term and some did not use other time-specific terms such as bulldyker, either.[19] I suggest that this sexual-identity assumption does not arise simply from their gender-bending jobs; it also reflects the success of their counteridentification intents and methods. Some have suggested that Gladys Bentley's stage act was an overt method of signaling her interest in same-sex sexual relationships.[20] This particular motive is less clear in DeLarverie's work; more evident is how DeLarverie's stage aesthetic was designed to display solidarity with the queer people DeLarverie considered "family." But, in both instances, a carefully deployed stage aesthetic worked to align the performers with queer identity. Jane Mansbridge argues that such public acts of counteridentification feed into oppositional consciousness, or the celebration and promotion of minoritarian pride. Such consciousness, she suggests, can then encourage "members of an oppressed group to [...] undermine, reform, or overthrow a system of human domination."[21] Public acts intended to identify the self with a marginalized or minority group could very well heighten the precarity of already vulnerable people. But Mansbridge also articulates their potential to start a larger process of revolting against hegemonic institutional structures.

Similarly, Cohen considers how the active, public life of a person socially marked as deviant can be a powerful form of defiance leading to organized resistance. Effective civil rights efforts are often depicted as large-scale rebellions, marches and protests, or other forms of traditional activism.[22]

However, Cohen suggests that the continued lived noncompliance of racially and sexually marginalized people can also develop into a rich form of political resistance. She references the lived defiance of unwed teen mothers of Color who are well aware of cultural expectations and, moreover, that complying might give them slightly more access to rights, benefits, or respect. Rather than framing these people as dysfunctional or social failures, Cohen sees their continued noncompliance as an active form of cultural defiance: while their choices may "not necessarily [be] made with explicitly political motives in mind, they do demonstrate that people will challenge established norms and rules and face negative consequences in pursuit of goals important to them."[23] In short, Cohen identifies the potential for resistant "oppositional politics" in microactions that consciously challenge dominant power structures, especially if people are aware that these actions will likely deny them "access to and protection from" state power.[24] In highlighting DeLarverie's performance practices and public image, I put two key items into dialogue. The first is DeLarverie's reputation for being able to cultivate a very hegemonic type of masculinity. The second is DeLarverie's targeting by the police on June 28, 1969, either because DeLarverie appeared to be a woman in men's clothing or because DeLarverie was identified as a gay man. Either way, I suggest that DeLarverie's queer identification was not an accident but a conscious choice to be counteridentified with the persecuted queer community that would begin the Stonewall Rebellion later that night.

A brief word about the gender and sexual identity terms employed in this chapter. In previous chapters, I had evidence such as pronoun and title usage that performers publicly identified as women. Furthermore, although some expressed same-sex desires, they did not publicly identify with terms such as *lesbian* or *homosexual* or time-specific words such as *gender invert* or *sapphic*. I can make neither claim for queer butchness performers. Early twentieth-century performers such as Bentley and Rainey identified as women possessing various sexual and romantic interests, including for women. The term *lesbian* as it is now popularly used was not commonly engaged until the mid-1920s, and, even then, it did not fully characterize these performers' broad sexual interests and gender expressions. Some performers called themselves B.D. women, bulldaggers, or bulldykers to reflect their sexual interests as well as their gender presentations or desired relationship roles. Other performers avoided these terms, instead making vague allusions to unnatural, nonnormative, or "between the sexes" interests and behaviors.[25] The issue becomes even more complicated with DeLarverie, who did not publicly declare a sexual and gender identity but was deeply invested in the New York queer community. To the best of my research, DeLarverie was assigned female at birth and visually presented as a ciswoman during the early part of DeLarverie's singing career. DeLarverie was also billed by the Jewel Box as "a girl" and as "Miss DeLarverie." However, when pressed to personally identify in the documentary *Stormé: The Lady of the Jewel Box*, DeLarverie instead asks to be known simply "as me." Because of this statement, I do not feel comfortable calling DeLarverie a lesbian (although there is evidence that DeLarverie had relationships with women). I am also uneasy using she/her pronouns, so I refer to DeLarverie in this chapter by name only. I do make the claim that DeLarverie was queer but, in this context, "queer" broadly marks DeLarverie as a person who did not fit majoritarian cisgender and heterosexual norms and also built a family with people who did clearly identify as gay and lesbian.

QUEER CULTURAL SPACE

My next step is to illustrate a unique genre of Black queer performance that has been subsumed and occluded under the label of the White commercial product of male impersonation. Bailey makes connections between the contemporary ballroom scene and Harlem Renaissance communities populated by Black entertainers in the first part of the twentieth century.[26] I similarly connect DeLarverie's midcentury queer butchness with the tone and aesthetic cultivated by blues and jazz artists and "Black vaudeville" performers such as Ma Rainey, Bessie Smith, Josephine Baker, Ethel Waters, and Gladys Bentley. These performers worked steadily from the 1910s to the 1930s in Harlem's entertainment district and venues along the TOBA circuit. White vaudevillian male impersonators did not generally work in these places. Thus, I suggest that people frequenting these spaces would be more familiar with the idea and aesthetic of queer butchness than the heteronormative identity play of male impersonators. With the exception of Bentley, the performers I name above wore men's attire as well as dresses, feathered headpieces, and heavy jewelry onstage. Records also show that many of these performers—Bentley included—publicly expressed heterosexual desire, married men, or had biological children. So, on one hand, these figures did not fully embody a lived stone butch stereotype, yet, on the other hand, their staged and lived gender and sexual expressions did not reflect the ladylike parameters of true womanhood. First and foremost, Black women could not really become true women in the eyes of White society. Paula Giddings notes that some middle-class Black women did attempt to live according to Victorian doctrines of piety and modesty, but this lived politics of respectability did not ensure they would regularly receive dignified treatment or respectable standing.[27] It was much more likely that Black women would be broadly painted by mass culture as unfeminine and hypersexual regardless of their class status or what they did to assimilate.

Although the White ideal of true womanhood was inaccessible for working-class and Black women, their individual respectability was still measured by hegemonic society against this rubric. Therefore, it is noteworthy that there was such a wide divergence between these respectability standards and the blue content of many Harlem Renaissance acts as well as the sexual interests and gendered expressions of their performers. Many blues and jazz musicians had overtly sexual stage acts and song lyrics; in addition to singing about sexual desire for men, Rainey, Bentley, and Smith also sang about their desires for women and their desire to dress in men's clothes to initiate these romances. There are also mentions of Bentley publicly flirting with women patrons during her shows at the Clam House and Ubangi Club. Bentley personally claimed to have married a woman, and secondhand statements suggest Ethel Waters and Josephine Baker also had public relationships with women.[28] Waters, Bentley, and Baker were photographed in what appears to be performance wear of full tuxedos and slicked-back hair. There are also rumors that Rainey posed or performed in a men's suit jacket, top hat, and tie.[29] In Bentley's case, the type of masculine stage presentation and dress that defined her acts was also a feature of her public persona.

Queer butchness is a stage expression that reads as masculine, but it is not a developed illusion of a man, not an androgynous mixture of men's and women's gender signifiers, and not an illusion cultivated to conceal an innate femininity. Rather, queer butchness performers cultivate a salient and recognizable form of masculine expression that is not normally associated with women's bodies and identities. The popular turn-of-the-century sexology theory of gender inversion assumed that a woman displaying "mannishness" (e.g., dressing in men's clothes or desiring women) actually wanted to be a man. As discussed in chapter 2, the term *mannish woman* was also applied to women who did not expressly desire to be men but failed to achieve the feminine standard of true womanhood. By virtue of their racial designation, Black women were already marked by White society as having feminine shortcomings and thus as more mannish or masculine women. There are obvious problems with the now-defunct theory of gender inversion and the racist context that defined true womanhood. However, my point is that Rainey, Smith,

Bentley, and others did not have to be completely hegemonically masculine in everything they did onstage to be contextualized as mannish. Relatedly, wearing dresses or devoting themselves to husband and home would not transform them into respectable "true women." So, even though these early entertainers did not always exude the hegemonic masculine aesthetic that characterized later queer butch acts, I nevertheless suggest that the distance between their self-presentations and actions and hegemonic femininity cast them as quite masculine.

Butch performers appeared in tuxedos and top hats, publicly sang about their sexual desire for women, and were bawdy, flirty, and aggressive onstage. I suggest that this type of masculinity was read by audiences not just as a stage persona but also as signaling the performer's interest in or alignment to "the life," what might now be referred to as the LGBT community. Maltz argues that masculine signifiers that perhaps "may have passed for real male" in mass public and commercial domains are often read differently in minoritarian locations (she references Greenwich Village) as butch "codes of virility and sexual dominance."[30] Relatedly, I argue that the cultural space where queer butchness occurred most often—in Harlem's entertainment district and along the TOBA—makes it much more likely that it would have been read as both a queer stage act and an expression of the entertainer's queerness. When Bentley headlined at Harlem's Clam House with her "deep, rumbling voice, closely cropped, greased down hair, and masculine clothes," the geographic context of the act allowed her to be seen differently than a male impersonator doing a masculine act at a vaudeville show.[31] So my presumption about audience interpretation here is based not only on circulating popular knowledges, such as the mannish woman, but also on the particular ideologies and aesthetics that were integral to Black entertainment spaces in this era. Harlem in the 1920s had a reputation for producing exciting and sexually explicit entertainment that could not be found in "respectable" venues or vaudeville houses. Black vaudeville TOBA performances were a little more buttoned-up than many headline acts in Harlem spaces like the Clam House, but still these shows were more raucous than their White vaudeville counterparts. I do not mean to imply that Harlem, TOBA, or other Black entertainment spaces were unilaterally accepting or "anything goes" atmospheres. However, I do suggest that these entertainment spaces were popularly understood as places that would cater to deviant or salacious interests, largely—in the eyes of White society at least—because of their connection to Black bodies and geographies. Thus, people in these spaces had less to lose than vaudevillians by being sexually explicit, presenting in queer ways, or otherwise diverging from Victorian ideals and norms.

White people certainly went into Harlem's entertainment district, and perhaps some also attended TOBA shows. However, the acts I describe here were done by Black performers and within Black community spaces. Thus, these performers knew the dominant knowledges and assumptions that would circulate among (and even attract) their specific audience base. Male impersonators took pains to publicly put their stage work and personal lives in line with middle-class White norms; any slip in this identification process meant financial and personal ruin. But Black women performers who were masculine or expressed same-sex desires actually had something to gain by being counteridentified with Harlem's racial-sexual minority community. Take, for instance, the financial success and personal gain of Gladys Bentley. Bentley was a talented piano player, singer, and lyricist, and she was also known for her dynamic stage presence, raunchy lyrics, and "unique" aesthetic presentations, such as "immaculate white full dress shirts with stiff collars, small bow ties and skirts, oxfords, short Eton jackets, and hair cut straight back."[32] While headlining Harlem's Ubangi Club, Bentley performed in a white tuxedo, top hat, and short, slicked hair, which James Wilson characterizes as oozing "masculine swagger and braggadocio."[33] She purportedly also openly flirted with women audience members during her act. Bentley's masculine presence was a performance inasmuch as it was not a mimetic reflection of her daily reality. But a key quality of queer butchness is that the cultivated masculine stage aesthetic is an act that echoes and intermingles with the queer lived reality of the performer. Primary sources mention Bentley wearing men's clothing pieces in public when not performing.[34] In addition, Bentley had several public romantic relationships with women and even married one. And Bentley was not only publicly accepted for this; she actually collected an exceedingly high salary of $125 per week plus tips at various locales during the 1920s and early 1930s.[35]

In a self-authored testimonial for *Ebony Magazine* published in 1952, Bentley articulates how her masculine stage presence was intended to align her with what she calls "unwomanly" gender and sexual inclinations. The article goes on to explain that after taking "female" hormones and finding a man romantic partner, Bentley was able to change herself and become "a woman again."[36] I found Bentley's partial attribution of her career success to her nonhegemonic gender and sexuality to be surprisingly open. In contrast, later parts of the testimonial—such as her description of the medical drug intervention and her effort to find joy in stereotypically gendered activities like cooking and bed making—read as if she were the victim of homosexual conversion therapy. Wilson has a different take on Bentley's testimonial: he suggests that her exposition of a "deviant" past coupled with her conversionesque narrative was a calculated career move. Her article, "I Am a Woman Again," was published decades after the Great Depression had effectively snuffed out the profitability of Harlem's entertainment district. During this economic downturn, Bentley moved across the country to Los Angeles but, even with the location change, could not garner a semblance of her former rates or bookings. In publicly confessing to a salacious past as well as detailing her reform, Wilson argues, Bentley was attempting to spark her career through the process of aligning herself with hegemonic cultural attitudes regarding gender and sexual behavior.[37]

Because I classify Bentley's act as queer butchness and not male impersonation, I am hesitant to call her an identification artist. Although Wilson's argument is about her offstage public performance of heteronormativity later in life, this line of argumentation might likewise imply that Bentley's earlier public persona was a similarly deployed moneymaking-through-targeted-audience-appeal process. Bentley absolutely did make money from her queer butchness, but to suggest that this was only (or even primarily) a marketing tool, one in which performers traded on queer aesthetics for financial success, is to remove it from the context wherein it was so successful. This type of gender-bending never took hold in White commercial entertainment contexts; rather, it was and continued to remain embedded in Black, queer, urban entertainment spaces. Without this particular context, queer butchness might very well have been read as a more standard form of identification bending or even perhaps as an act accomplished by a man actor. But I argue that, when enacted to its particular minoritarian audience, queer butchness was a visible counteralignment in terms of both stage picture and actor identification. And profit was just one ideal outcome of such an act.

As Bentley was making her 1950s public appeal to true womanhood, performers such as Stormé DeLarverie and Blackie Dennis were establishing reputations for their own queer butch acts. I do not have documentation that butch performers were steadily working throughout the 1930s and 1940s, but it is unlikely that this genre of performance completely dissolved only to reappear two decades later. Likewise, I assume there were more than just two performers—DeLarverie and Dennis—presenting such acts during the 1950s and 1960s, but there is scant documentation. While conducting research on drag queens for *Mother Camp: Female Impersonators in America* in the 1960s, Newton noted the absence of "drag butches" in the performance forums she frequented.[38] What exactly Newton meant by "drag butch" is unclear. She might have been referring to queer butchness performers or perhaps noting the absence of what would later become a small but vibrant drag king scene. Either way, Newton's point remains salient: she saw or knew of very few women performing masculine drag acts. Queer butchness most often occurred in urban, racial minority spaces, and the amount of extant information on these practices is relative to how popular and thus how widely visible individual performers became in that sphere and beyond it. Furthermore, the larger the performers' public profiles, the more likely that readily available archival records document their least controversial (i.e., most mass marketable) work. Nevertheless, there are some archives I can draw on to make this performance more visible and demonstrate its key cultural contributions.

Dennis and DeLarverie were performers with acts that showcased primarily their singing abilities but sometimes also their dancing and acting. The acts also involved them wearing high-end men's clothing pieces—tuxedos, suits—while behaving in a manner that would be commonly construed as heteromasculine (e.g., singing in lower vocal ranges and expressing desire for feminine women). Dennis worked mainly in mafia-owned New York clubs that were racially integrated and generally tolerant of nonmainstream sexual interests. DeLarverie worked mainly with the Jewel Box Revue, which had office and club spaces in Miami and New York but also toured nationally, including along the historical TOBA circuit and at gay-friendly bars. So, although there were exceptions to this rule, Dennis's and DeLarverie's work was predominantly done in queer, integrated, or Black performance spaces. Thus, I suggest these acts constituted a form of queer butchness that could easily be interpreted as such by the audiences frequenting these cultural spaces.

My characterization of these acts as queer butchness is based on more than just their geographic performance contexts and the location-specific knowledges of their audiences. Across the decades, butch realness acts have also shared key intents and methods. Whereas male impersonation was an overt expression of a cisgender identity and a mode of commercializing popular beliefs about women's normal capacities, queer butchness began and remained an expression of queerness and a mode of aligning the performer with various queered communities. Harlem Renaissance performances were commercial endeavors, to be sure, but these acts were not intended or deployed to present a conforming subject either onstage or off. Just the opposite: Bentley had a marked investment in cultivating a performance that would be interpreted as being done by a queer butch woman. This interpretation not only garnered financial rewards but also facilitated her romantic, familial, and community opportunities. In this latter regard, then, there is a strong alignment between the intents and methods of earlier queer butch acts and those performed in the 1950s and 1960s. DeLarverie performed in different spaces and to different audiences, but the intention was always to be read as a queer subject, and the effort to make sure that happened was always there, too.

My argument, then, is both that DeLarverie was intentionally performing queer butchness and that DeLarverie did this in ways that could reflect on DeLarverie's personal queer counteridentity. This is a complicated claim because the Jewel Box was a commercial organization and often downplayed its ties to gender and sexual queer cultures. Beginning in the 1930s, triggered by the Great Depression, there was a reduction in TOBA venues, a downswing in Harlem's entertainment district, and a shift toward more racially integrated entertainments. Thus, performers and troupes had to design shows to appeal to a variety of venues and audiences rather than just one niche market. Mara Dauphin explains that commercially inclined midcentury touring shows were often promoted broadly as "wholesome" family-friendly entertainments.[39] This was done by creating a false distinction between these shows' gender-bending practices and the near-identical practices that were part of queer culture, most explicitly through media marketing: marquees, advertisements, and program booklets. For example, the first page of every Jewel Box program announces that the theatrical practice of men playing women characters is traditionally gender normative—an "old mannish custom."[40] This appeal to history clearly ties the theatrical and skilled "female impersonation" accomplished by Jewel Box performers to "legitimate" vaudevillian theater practices or the "high-art" of cross casting done in Shakespeare's time.[41] This contextualization enabled the Jewel Box to maintain a tenuously acceptable mainstream reputation, which allowed it to tour to more places and avoid some of the worst instances of censure and violence. However, Dauphin also notes that many of the performers personally identified as gay or in various forms of gender transition.[42] Likewise, queer people repeatedly and enthusiastically attended these shows, and many Jewel Box performers became famous gay icons. Thus, the public facade of these shows does not necessarily match the realities of performers' lives, their stage work, or even the majority of their audiences' perceptions about the work. In fact, I argue that many Jewel Box performers were deeply invested in displaying queerness and building queer community solidarity.

THE COUNTERIDENTIFICATION PROCESS

DeLarverie's performance methods demonstrate not only an intent to craft a butch stage aesthetic but also an active desire for the act to be read as queer. According to publicity images as well as DeLarverie's personal biographic narrative, DeLarverie worked as a singer for various big bands prior to joining the Jewel Box Revue. During this time, DeLarverie went by the stage name Stormy Dale and wore longer hair, necklaces, and dresses with feather or lace trim when performing. In 1955, DeLarverie was encouraged to audition for the Jewel Box's master of ceremonies (MC) role. Although DeLarverie did not commonly dress in men's attire either to perform or in daily life, DeLarverie got a short haircut, landed the job, and held the position until 1969. Somewhere in this time frame, DeLarverie began dressing in articles of men's clothing offstage as well as on.[43]

The masculine MC role in the revue had been a staple long before DeLarverie joined. The Jewel Box was formed in the late 1930s when Danny Brown (joined later by Doc Benner) began to tour a group of "female impersonators," also referred to in some advertising as an "all male revue," to local Florida cities and sometimes Cleveland, Pittsburgh, and Detroit. Advertisements from 1935 to 1940 indicate that Brown himself played the tuxedo-clad MC. In 1939 or perhaps 1942, the Jewel Box settled into two nightclubs, both called Club Jewel Box, located in Miami and Tampa. In the mid- to late 1940s, the Jewel Box once again started touring, this time on a much larger national scale and to major cities such as Philadelphia, Milwaukee, Minneapolis, and Dallas.[44] As some point during the nightclub or national touring years, the MC part was taken over by "Miss Mickey Mercer" and possibly also "Miss Tommy Williams." The Jewel Box also started heavily employing the "twenty-five men and one girl" tagline. Both Mercer's and Williams's roles were advertised by pairing their masculine-presenting pictures with women's pronouns and titles and sometimes with the line "She's the HE."[45] Starting in 1955, the one and only masculine, tuxedo-clad MC for the Jewel Box Revue was "Miss Stormé DeLarverie."[46]

There are allusions to the Florida-based Jewel Box nightclubs being popular gay hangouts, or at least known gay-friendly spaces.[47] But, while touring nationally, the show attracted a variable audience base. The Jewel Box was a racially integrated troupe and played at some historical TOBA venues, where it presumably attracted a mixed-race audience. It also toured to well-known gay venues such as the Venetian Causeway Bar in Miami and likely attracted many sexually queer or genderqueer audience members at these spaces. Finally (and what I find most interesting), the Jewel Box sometimes played in theater spaces that primarily catered to a non-queer-identifying, White, "family entertainment" crowd. Unlike Bentley or even Dennis, DeLarverie had to build a queer butch act that could navigate this variant audience base.

Witnesses to the show have referred to DeLarverie as the "tuxedo-clad male" of the Jewel Box and a "Harry Belafonte" type.[48] I have not located video or sound records of DeLarverie's stage act, so, as in previous chapters, I rely on other performance records such as photographs and advertising materials from 1955 (when DeLarverie secured the Jewel Box job) onward.[49] The Jewel Box produced a series of keepsake program booklets, likely to give out or sell at shows. It also created a two-page handbill that simply listed the particular night's numbers and performers; in contrast, the program booklets are dozens of pages long, discuss historical theatrical cross-dressing, highlight featured performers, include large headshots and performance stills from popular numbers, and print the names and faces of the extended cast. All locations the Jewel Box had performed in "up to this printing" are listed in the back along with (positive) newspaper reviews and a game called "Boy Bernhardts," where readers match the "female impersonator" visage with the actor's out-of-makeup look. Twelve different booklets are held in the Queer Music Heritage Archives; among this collection, four have a full-page spread on DeLarverie that includes a short narrative and five posed images. Three performance stills of DeLarverie also appear in later pages. Five additional programs lack the full-page spread but still contain some of DeLarverie's headshots and performance stills.[50] Other useful sources on DeLarverie include an aftershow photo published in *Female Mimics* magazine and an image Diane Arbus created of DeLarverie for her "The Full Circle" photo project. I cannot say with certainty that DeLarverie is performing the Jewel Box MC character in either image, but DeLarverie is dressed and posed similarly. Moreover, because the latter photo was taken for a 1961 *Harper's Bazaar* feature, I assume DeLarverie was aware this image would be connected to the Jewel Box and DeLarverie's MC character.[51] A final source I draw from is DeLarverie's personal narrative recorded by Michelle Parkerson for the documentary *Stormé: The Lady of the Jewel Box*.

Some archived photographs of DeLarverie are close-ups of the head and shoulders, and others depict the entire body either carefully posed or in midperformance. In most of these images, DeLarverie's face is set in an unsmiling, serious expression with a furrowed brow and fixed gaze. DeLarverie is almost always dressed in a fitted, high-end suit. In Arbus's photo, for instance, DeLarverie wears a dark tailored suit, collared white shirt, thin tie, and men's ankle boots. Many program booklet images similarly depict DeLarverie wearing a traditional black or white-jacketed tuxedo and bow tie. In Parkerson's documentary, DeLarverie defines these costume choices as "loose" men's jackets paired with "skintight" pants. However, none of the suit jackets in these images look particularly loose, although many are long waisted. There are also two images that show DeLarverie wearing a white Navy dress uniform. These performance stills were likely taken during a part of the Jewel Box's show the handbill simply refers to as "sailors."[52] In all images from 1955 onward, DeLarverie's hair is short and close cropped, with a widow's peak. In the *Female Mimics* aftershow image, DeLarverie also sports a pencil mustache, a feature that is not present in any Jewel Box materials I reviewed.

In addition to putting together a recognizably masculine look for the MC role, DeLarverie elaborates on another much-utilized performance method: "What the boys [female impersonators] are adding, you have to take away. They're adding the hips, and the bust, and you're taking away; you're doing just the opposite, you're taking away from it. You're trying to compensate. In other words, your face doesn't match your body. But when you're onstage it looks that way."[53] Here DeLarverie articulates the intent to "take away," or methodically conceal body certain characteristics. The only means of doing this that DeLarverie articulates is wearing loose men's suit jackets, and it is unclear if DeLarverie also employed body padding or binding techniques. Whatever the methods DeLarverie used, the overall intent was to reduce the visibility of "feminine" body lines. However, I find it notable that in DeLarverie's explanation, building this less feminine shape is not framed as in the service of a male impersonation so much as it is an effort to make the body and face match. DeLarverie's "men's" haircut was a permanent feature, and DeLarverie's face generally looked somewhat butch, similar (although maybe not exactly the same) to the looks depicted in the images. So I argue that DeLarverie is articulating a method of putting together a nonfeminine physical look that aligns with DeLarverie's everyday butch face. The onstage body modification DeLarverie describes demonstrates DeLarverie's intent to make the body look less like a ciswoman and certainly more butch—but not necessarily more passably male.

Performance photos and DeLarverie's own statements also provide some detail about how DeLarverie's masculine MC persona was used within the revue show. As the master of ceremonies, DeLarverie verbally introduced the female impersonators and their numbers as well as the show's transitions. DeLarverie would also sing individual and group songs using a "low, rich voice" akin to a baritone.[54] Archival materials also indicate that DeLarverie would sometimes play bit parts in songs and skits. For instance, the handbill lists DeLarverie as both a sailor and a maharajah in separate numbers, and two program images depict DeLarverie in a Navy dress uniform.[55] I do not have a complete picture of what stage actions DeLarverie did when occupying these bit parts, but they appear to have been clearly connected to DeLarverie's MC role. In the sailor images, for example, DeLarverie is talking into a microphone and walking feminine performers to the front of the stage. Thus, I suggest that DeLarverie's ultimate purpose when occupying these bit parts was not to bring a man character to life but rather to serve as a visually masculine contrast to the feminine impersonators. Relatedly, DeLarverie often deployed this masculine stage aesthetic to create heterolooking romantic tableaux and duets with female impersonators. Karin A. Martin and Emily Kazyak's theory of "hetero-romance" attributes the entrenchment of heteronormativity to the constant visibility of idealized romantic cisman and ciswoman pairings.[56] DeLarverie formed similar tableaux with the feminine Jewel Box performers by holding their hands or linking eyes with them. In a picture printed in several program booklets, DeLarverie poses on a small staircase with featured performer Lynn Carter (see fig. 4.1). Their stance is like a modern prom photo in that DeLarverie is slightly behind and above and reaches forward to hold Carter's hand. Importantly, DeLarverie is also positioned on a higher stair step and so appears to be physically taller than Carter. Images like this and DeLarverie's onstage interactions with feminine performers cultivated a strong visual appearance of opposite-gender romantic interest or binary gendered coupling. Because of the mass cultural inundation of similar heteroromantic images, these tableaux served to make DeLarverie appear more masculine and performers like Carter more feminine.

In addition to introducing performers and numbers, singing songs, playing bit parts, and—according to DeLarverie—serving as stage manager, DeLarverie's MC roles included what Elizabeth Drorbaugh describes as building the show's "frame."[57] DeLarverie was to explicitly communicate to the audience that the Jewel Box Revue was not just a song-and-dance show

Fig. 4.1. Right to left: Stormé DeLarverie and Lynn Carter pose for a photo that would be used in promotional booklets for the Jewel Box Revue.

but centered in gender "illusion."[58] In addition to establishing this framing, Drorbaugh says, DeLarverie "ended that frame" by calling up the feminine performers to enact their stage reveals and by "taking one herself."[59] I have found no clear account of the terms, statements, or actions DeLarverie used to build or end these "frames" aside from a few mentions of Jewel Box performers taking reveals. The standard reveal is intended to make audiences aware that what appeared onstage does not represent the reality of the performer's own self. In the context of a gender-bending performance, reveals demonstrate a divergence between performed gender and offstage gender or assigned sex. My next chapter documents how some drag performers trade on the assumed purpose of the reveal to develop their disidentification practice: they reveal something "inauthentic" or unintelligible rather than an expected cisgender body. However, reveals are popularly conceptualized as illuminating the quotidian gendered reality of the performer in contrast to their stage act.

The program booklet itself functioned as a reveal for the Jewel Box performers including DeLarverie. Within the first few pages of several of the booklets, DeLarverie has a full-page spread of masculine, posed photos and this accompanying text: "Miss Storme De Laverie [sic] the only girl with the Jewel Box Revue has appeared as a female vocalist with many name bands. Audiences would not believe she was a girl due to her deep baritone voice."[60] Nevertheless, Drorbaugh says that DeLarverie also took a physical reveal onstage, and so does Newton, who recounts "the general gasps of wonder that greeted Stormé's revelation of her gender."[61] Newton says DeLarverie's reveal happened at "the finale" while Drorbaugh mentions particular songs, "The Surprise" or "Alaharajah's Dream," where it would take place.[62] DeLarverie alludes to removing a suit jacket onstage to show the "dirt" (i.e., to show an underlying body shape that seemingly conflicts with the gender being expressed), but it is not clear whether DeLarverie is talking about a personal technique employed with the Jewel Box or simply one that could be used by drag performers.[63] These details are evidence that DeLarverie likely did some form of physical stage reveal, which might have been a standard element of the show prior to DeLarverie's joining, or perhaps one requested by producers Doc and Danny. The point of DeLarverie's booklet spread seems explicitly to be naming DeLarverie as a gender-bending performer, which echoes Newton's earlier claim that some audience members might not have realized that DeLarverie's expression of masculinity could be part of a gender-bending performance. Moreover, given that the Jewel Box was advertised as featuring "25 men and one girl" and Newton describes trying to pick out "the girl" among the twenty-five showgirls, I suggest that DeLarverie's reveal was done to address any lingering audience confusion and also direct attention to DeLarverie as a skilled gender-bending performer.[64]

The most important question to me, however, is not why the reveal was used but rather what exactly the reveal was intended to reveal to a given audience. Not every audience member would have needed a clear visual directive—a reveal—to grasp that DeLarverie was something other than your average cisman actor. If the Jewel Box played to a queer crowd or a crowd familiar with Black women's performance traditions (as the troupe often did), many audience members would likely contextualize DeLarverie as a butch or at least presume DeLarverie's stage presentation was not strictly cisgender (i.e., a man playing a man character). Maltz is of a like mind, arguing, "Everyone who attended the performances most likely knew the impersonator was female."[65] While Newton and Drorbaugh do not say exactly *which* people were shocked at DeLarverie's reveal, I suggest it was likely those who lacked familiarity with particular marginalized knowledges such as cultural traditions of queer butchness and female masculinity. In other words, the "family-friendly" (heterosexual and/or White) audiences the Jewel Box sometimes played to might have been unfamiliar with the look of a masculine woman, or else assumed all women were cisgender presenting. Admittedly, DeLarverie's masculine styling, voice, and physical aesthetic had a bit more "realness" to it than earlier stage versions of queer butchness. I use "realness" in the ballroom sense of naming a quotidian cisgender and/or heterosexual performance aesthetic. Newton's and Drorbaugh's accounts suggest that DeLarverie's stage presence could be, at times, unreadable as queer to certain audience members. However, in the ballroom world, a winning realness act is "unclockable" not because it fools audiences into thinking the performer is heterosexual and cisgender but simply because the performer's known queerness is not visually or verbally evident in their performance.[66] Some ballroom performers even employ a "realness with a twist" action that visually reinforces the (correct) audience belief that neither they nor their acts are authentically heteronormative, even if they might appear as such for a time.

In a similar vein, any conclusion that DeLarverie was a nonqueer person or that the stage performance was that of a cisman would have been contrary to DeLarverie's own intents and goals. DeLarverie was invested in being seen as a queer, masculine, nonman, and many audience members understood this meaning from the space and context of the performance or other methods employed by DeLarverie or the show's advertising. For those who remained in the dark, DeLarverie's physical reveal functioned as a light switch (perhaps a floodlight). Toward the end of the Jewel Box's show, DeLarverie showed via song or perhaps the removal of clothing that DeLarverie was not a cisman actor but rather the gender-bending "girl" of the revue. While I do not have a full picture of DeLarverie's reveal, the available evidence leads me to believe that it did *not* include a disclosure of long flowing hair or a soprano voice or other highly feminine attributes. Nevertheless, this non-feminine reveal would still have effectively highlighted a disjunction between DeLarverie's performed stage identity (interpreted by some as a man's) and DeLarverie's real identity (clearly nonman but not a feminine ciswoman's either). In this regard, I see DeLarverie's continual engagement with the reveal as a critical part of the counteridentification gender-bending process: what DeLarverie really revealed was that "the girl" was still a pretty masculine figure.

Annie Hindle did not look or act particularly feminine under her male impersonation either, but Hindle's lived masculinity was publicly framed as part of her act rather than a real or authentic expression of her selfhood. DeLarverie's stage disclosure did the opposite work: it made uncontestably clear to audience members that DeLarverie was not a man and also not a hegemonic cisgender woman. Newton attributes audience "gasps of wonder" to their surprise at finding out DeLarverie was the girl. The supposition here is that audiences gasped because they did not realize "man-appearing" DeLarverie was a gender-bending performer. But I suggest that these gasps could also be connected to what exactly was revealed. If audience members happened to think DeLarverie was a heteronormative cisgender man, then it would be quite the revelation that DeLarverie was not only *not* a man *but also* that this nonman remained naturally and comfortably masculine. Thus, even if DeLarverie's stage persona could have visually passed as heterosexual and cisgender, it was not intended to, and DeLarverie took an active approach in making sure this was not the ultimate effect. It was this particular counteridentification—a commitment to being read not as a man and not as a hegemonic ciswoman but as a queer person—that multiplied DeLarverie's precarity during the Stonewall Rebellion.

COUNTERIDENTIFICATION AND ITS IMPACTS

I now turn to the potential impact of a counteridentification process, specifically how these bending intents and methods might suit the specific intersectional needs and concerns of performers and the marginalized communities they belong to. As I argued in previous chapters, gender-bending acts are necessarily responsive and influential to ideological and physical contexts beyond a singular performance, and even beyond the microspace of the theatrical event. For teatristas, a revisionary gender-bending process enabled them to live in their racial-gendered identities and support el Movimiento without being confined exclusively to pejorative narratives of Chicanahood. Similarly, for Bentley and DeLarverie, queer butchness was not only a popular stage aesthetic or profitable mode of performance; in embodying a slicked-back, dressed up, meticulously suave stage masculinity, these performers were also doing something that publicly declared their group association. For DeLarverie specifically, queer butchness was both a celebrated professional endeavor and a means of aligning with queer family, taking pride in a queer identity, and standing in solidarity with a persecuted queer community. Thus, close analysis of DeLarverie's Stonewall involvement in light of DeLarverie's stage practices illustrates the type of macro-oppositional politics that can follow from counteridentity acts intended to reveal queerness rather than transmit conformity.

DeLarverie presented as a masculine person who was not a man, and this type of gender variation has long been coded as the readable manifestation of an individual's same-sex desire.[67] Consequently, DeLarverie is called a lesbian in many scholarly histories, gay community publications, and news articles, a label that goes contrary to DeLarverie's own avoidance of such gender and sexual identification boxes—at least in public records.[68] The supposition that butchness means having same-sex interests was exactly the type of perception Bentley desired to cultivate—it helped her find romantic partners. But DeLarverie was less public with romantic relationships and sexual desires than Bentley was.[69] Thus, I suggest the constant referrals to DeLarverie as a lesbian are due to DeLarverie's masculinity in tandem with DeLarverie's public, familial relationship with homosexual and genderqueer people. For instance, Parkerson's documentary captures a lunch between DeLarverie and a former Jewel Box performer, Robin Rogers, during which both figures repeatedly declare that the Jewel Box cast and crew were a family unit.[70] After leaving the Jewel Box Revue, DeLarverie worked for many years as a bouncer at well-known lesbian bars in New York. In fact, William Yardley describes DeLarverie as "a self-appointed guardian of lesbians."[71] Apparently, DeLarverie acquired a gun permit and would travel "lower Seventh and Eighth Avenues and points between [. . .] patrolling the sidewalks and checking in at lesbian bars. She was on the lookout for what she called 'ugliness': any form of intolerance, bullying or abuse of her 'baby girls.'"[72] DeLarverie was also part of the Stonewall Veterans Association and frequently attended New York gay pride parades. So, although DeLarverie did not publicly or officially declare a particular gender or sexual identity, DeLarverie was nonetheless a visible member of the New York LGBT community and considered gay people to be queer family.

These details support my earlier claim that DeLarverie's reveal was intended as a counteridentification, or a guarantee that no audience member would leave thinking DeLarverie was a heterosexual cisman or even an undercover heterosexual ciswoman. Translated into a more contemporary catchphrase, DeLarverie's gender-bending counteridentity process was about being "out and proud," or publicly demonstrating identity pride via a public disclosure of personal queerness. I have found no account of DeLarverie receiving anything other than total audience adulation for "coming out" as a masculine nonman at the end of the show. Yet, as Butler notes, a readable embodied queerness will not necessarily receive the same positive response in a general public context as it might in a theatrical performance context.[73] This is exactly why Bailey argues that queer ballroom members of Color tend to deploy realness skills in homophobic, transphobic, or otherwise dangerous public spaces to appear "undifferentiated from the rest of the Black working-class people" around them.[74] This practice allows queer people to blend into the hegemonic background and, in effect, fool mass publics into leaving them the hell alone.

Bailey's articulation of realness as a useful public strategy of blending in does not mesh with the popular contemporary "out and proud" rhetoric. But Halberstam argues that this type of gay shame/gay pride model is most useful to people who will receive minimal censure for publicly displaying queerness.[75] That is, a person who is able to be "out and proud" likely also is in a physically safe community environment or possesses other powerful identities (such as socioeconomic status) that enable them to protect themselves. Conversely, queer people dealing with overlapping forms of oppression have to develop more complex self-care and success strategies than this basic form of public outness offers.[76] Moreover, in spaces where being "out and proud" might result in censure, violence, or death, not appearing queer is a means of surviving and even successfully gaming the system. Rather than framing these actions as identity shame, Bailey suggests they are forms of agency: a means of self-protection activated by people in a high state of precarity who have few other options for accessing institutional power.

DeLarverie was a person who lived adult life as a butch nonman, and, before that, DeLarverie grew up in Louisiana presenting as a ciswoman. DeLarverie was also a biracial person who remained of fairly low socio-economic status throughout life. Suffice it to say, DeLarverie belonged to multiple oppressed identity categories that resulted in unique obstacles and struggles, even before considering DeLarverie's public alignment with an LGBT community. In a time and place where people of Color, poor people, gay people, and gender-variant people faced constant censure and violence from both the public and institutions, such as the police, it hardly needs saying that DeLarverie lived a very precarious life. But like the subjects in Bailey's study, DeLarverie had a talent for doing hegemonic masculinity, and, to some people, DeLarverie was already unintentionally passing as a heterosexual cisman. Thus, it is plausible to argue that, confronted with a dangerously homophobic or transphobic public situation, DeLarverie might have been able to present as a conforming cisgender subject—at least for a short time. And yet, DeLarverie's actions during the Stonewall Rebellion reveal the opposite action.

There are several historical accounts of the now iconic Stonewall Rebellion, a multiday protest against police violence by members of New York's LGBT community. The event was largely unanticipated, and so it was not comprehensively documented by the press in real time. Thus, most holistic Stonewall narratives are actually cobbled together from the firsthand accounts of police and rebels, newspaper coverage of the event and its aftermath, and well-repeated stories among New York locals. These sources are layered and contradictory, and some parts of the most widely disseminated oral testimonies are now heavily questioned. With that said, this is how the story (often) goes: in the early hours of June 28, 1969, police raided the Stonewall Inn, a popular albeit shabby bar in Greenwich Village, New York. Homosexual, sexually queer, gender-variant, and transidentifying bar patrons were dragged out of the bar, physically assaulted, and arrested for a variety of reasons, most typically the illegality of certain sexual acts or gendered forms of dress. Police raids were not unusual at gay bars and bathhouses, and the Stonewall Inn had experienced them before. Nonetheless, these police attacks were terrifying and almost always violent.

The particular Stonewall story I am interested in continues like this: DeLarverie was in the thick of things and was being arrested for not complying with a New York statute regarding the amount of gendered clothing a person had to wear. That is, DeLarverie was identified as a woman who was dressed in men's clothing and not wearing enough articles of women's clothing. DeLarverie actively tried to resist the arrest, to get out of the handcuffs and out of police custody. Or the story might go like this: DeLarverie was coming back from a performance and still dressed in costume. Seeing the police raid, DeLarverie ran over to help Stonewall patrons, specifically a man who was lying on the ground after having been beaten. An annoyed police officer saw DeLarverie and said, "Move along, faggot."[77] DeLarverie did not move along and was placed under arrest. DeLarverie actively tried to resist the arrest, to get out of the handcuffs and out of police custody. Both stories end the same way: the police officer assaulted DeLarverie, and DeLarverie fought back by punching the police officer. The already agitated bar crowd exploded around DeLarverie's action, the situation escalated, and a large-scale rebellion began.

In the particular accounts I offer here, DeLarverie represents the "first punch" of Stonewall, or the prime catalyst for the increase of resistance that came to define the event. This narrative comes from Charles Kaiser's *The Gay Metropolis*, Patrick Hinds's "Uncovering the Stonewall Lesbian," and DeLarverie's own account recorded in *Stormé: The Lady of the Jewel Box*.[78] But other Stonewall narratives attribute this escalation to Sylvia Rivera, Marsha P. Johnson, or unknown transwomen who either escaped arrest or threw objects and yelled at police. Some narratives connect this moment to a White-identified but otherwise unknown butch lesbian. And, as is clear from my two DeLarverie accounts above, even among stories that directly name DeLarverie as the instigator, there are significant differences. I am not interested in proving any one particular historicization as the ultimate and unequivocal Stonewall story. Instead, I am intrigued by what recurring elements within these two DeLarverie stories say about DeLarverie's particular counteridentification process.

The first significant element is that police targeted DeLarverie at all. Certainly, DeLarverie was not the only victim of police violence, and perhaps any person within geographic proximity of the Stonewall Inn was subjected to similar dangers. No doubt the readability of DeLarverie's race made DeLarverie all the more susceptible to police targeting. And yet, both stories are explicit that the arrest was because DeLarverie had been identified as either a cross-dresser or a gay man. As previously discussed, some members of DeLarverie's more mainstream and privileged audiences did not question DeLarverie's masculinity because it rested so comfortably on DeLarverie's body. That is, some audiences did not know DeLarverie was a gender-bending performer because they did not notice DeLarverie was doing anything unusual. DeLarverie clearly did not like to pass as a heterosexual cisman, but I have no doubt that DeLarverie had the cultivated skill—built over fourteen years at four shows a day—to exude a type of masculinity that did not look all that queer. Because DeLarverie had this skill, it is important to give DeLarverie agency over any public reading of selfhood. I have already credited DeLarverie with actively using a stage reveal to make sure any unintentional cisgender man illusion was dissolved by the end of the show. Likewise, I also give DeLarverie credit for being spotted as queer by the police. If it were DeLarverie's intention to be seen as a queer subject, DeLarverie certainly knew how to make that happen—or not.

DeLarverie's stage reveal was perhaps executed by an oral declaration or the removal of a jacket. DeLarverie's public identity disclosure at Stonewall could have been accomplished through similar active methods: allowing police the time and proximity to scrutinize body shape, or perhaps verbally identifying as a member of the queer bar crowd. However, I suggest that DeLarverie's public "reveal" was probably not based on any explicit or overt action at all. Rather, it is likely that DeLarverie was read as a queer person because DeLarverie *did not* activate any particular external tropes associated with cisman heteronormativity that would have obscured DeLarverie's queerness. Onstage, DeLarverie did little to encourage a cisman reading, but, compared to the clear and overt "doneness" of the female impersonators, DeLarverie's masculinity blended into the background and thus seemed unremarkable in its normality. In contrast, as Bailey suggests, ballroom performers have to actively engage realness in nonballroom contexts to blend into the background. When contexts change, one must do more to be seen as less. Thus, when in geographic proximity to the Stonewall Inn and its queer patrons, DeLarverie would have had to do more to appear to be a cisgender, heterosexual bystander. DeLarverie could have done that but did not. Thus, I argue that the lack of doing was an active choice: DeLarverie's public counteridentification as a queer person was a direct result of DeLarverie's unwillingness to separate from the queer community by activating passing techniques.

In light of DeLarverie's stage commitment to transmitting queer counteridentification, it is not surprising that DeLarverie allowed this queer subjecthood to be seen at Stonewall. But the second significant element in this story, that DeLarverie's punch supposedly triggered an escalation into a larger-scale rebellion, builds on this point. DeLarverie's punch was not interpreted just as a singular act of queer self-survival but rather as the act of a queer person making an activist appeal for mass queer rebellion. Before discussing DeLarverie's action and its subsequent effects further, however, I must first make this point explicit: self-survival is an activist action in and of itself. As Leah Lakshmi Piepzna-Samarasinha argues, queer people of Color are disproportionately targeted when they participate in large, public forms of activism. Even when public rallies or marches are specifically protesting violence against queer people and people of Color, these people become the first and frequent foci of suppression and backlash. While Piepzna-Samarasinha does not necessarily write off these forms of protest, she does question the positioning of them as higher-value forms of activism, arguing that "a million different ways to fight," including semiprivate and microactivist actions, day-to-day survival, and self-care, must be not only valued but also seen as equally valuable activist practices.[79] Applying Piepzna-Samarasinha's arguments to Bailey's study suggests that public realness actions by ballroom members are both acts of agency and salient forms of activism because they preserve the lives of individual queer community members. In this same regard, DeLarverie's continued health and well-being—accomplished by actively unmarking the body as queer or even leaving this space of violence against queer people—would have been a valid form of queer activism. And yet, these actions would not have triggered the larger rebellion and visible movement that Stonewall has become known for.[80]

My argument is that DeLarverie's refusal to perform heteronormativity was an act of public counteridentification interpreted by those around DeLarverie as a call to queer oppositional consciousness. Oppositional consciousness theory frames certain civil rights movements as growing from individual and group acts of celebrating a shared marginalized identity as well as building a community that rejects shameful or pejorative narratives attached to that identity.[81] There is no question that DeLarverie was a joyful and proud member of the queer community. But, for DeLarverie, being queer did not mean publicly claiming a particular gender or sexual identity as much as it meant supporting and protecting queer people and developing what Rupp and Taylor call a "sense of we-ness" or a family-like collective with other queer people.[82] The narratives of DeLarverie at Stonewall highlight DeLarverie's dedication to the well-being of queer people (caring for a hurt gay man) and the celebration of queer community space (knowing about or being at the Stonewall Inn). Chela Sandoval suggests that when actions feed into an oppositional consciousness ideology, this process can inspire collective rebellion against oppressive systems.[83] In this regard, I suggest DeLarverie's disclosure of queer identity—in whatever active or actively nonactive form that took—was an act that directly fed a form of oppositional consciousness poised to trigger a larger queer rebellion.

I realize this argument attributes a large public rebellion to what I have essentially characterized as DeLarverie's choice not to actively assimilate. However, Cohen argues that living publicly as a social deviant is an act of defiance that can cultivate or inspire organized political resistance.[84] An individual's lived social deviance—embedded in the visibility of their non-institutionally supported choices—is not generally recognized as a political call to action. For example, an unmarried teenager of Color might not see becoming pregnant as an act of fighting against sexist and racist standards. Yet, Cohen suggests that an individual's unwillingness to correct or mold their life to those standards is, in fact, directly defying "established rules and norms."[85] People who become branded as social deviants usually start out with little institutional power or protection anyway; these people are keenly aware that continuing to resist—or continuing to fail to conform—will only compound the negative consequences they experience. So, if the teen in the example above refuses to marry or is even unwilling to be ashamed or unhappy about her pregnancy, she is not just living in her deviance but also exhibiting defiant behavior. When deviant people continue defiant behaviors—when they do not alter their actions even though doing so might keep them from punitive consequences—this functions as an act of "power, agency and resistance in the lives of largely marginalized people."[86] In this regard, Cohen identifies defiance in continued lived deviance, and she furthermore suggests that defiance can spark a form of political resistance that targets those structures that define what is deviant in the first place.

DeLarverie's staged acts of gender-bending counteridentification were not imbued with the same level of precarity as DeLarverie's counteridentification in the midst of a violent police raid. In fact, to the best of my research, DeLarverie's stage disclosure of a socially deviant queer butch identity was met with audience acceptance and joy. In this regard, DeLarverie's stage reveal may or may not have been defiant and may or may not have been an act of oppositional consciousness capable of igniting political resistance (although some gender-bending theatrical acts certainly have such potential). However, it was clearly a defiant act for DeLarverie to continue to appear queer in such a dangerous public context as the Stonewall police raid. Not all people that night had the option of physically conforming to hegemonic standards to avoid violent treatment, but DeLarverie did. And this is why DeLarverie's continued, public living of a queer identity in the context of violent police suppression was interpreted by those around DeLarverie as an act of defiance that had a politically resistant resonance.

In a strange parallel, DeLarverie's Stonewall story corresponds with Althusser's "little theoretical theatre." In Althusser's story, a pedestrian is hailed into existence (interpellated) by a police officer calling "Hey, you there!" After the pedestrian comprehends that he himself is within the terms of the hail (I am "you there"), he reacts based on how he understands his positionality within social ideology. If the pedestrian is another police officer, he might stop and have a friendly interaction. If the pedestrian is a criminal or perhaps just knows that members of his particular community are routinely subjected to unwarranted police violence, he might run or fight. When the officer tried to arrest DeLarverie for wearing men's clothes or tried to tell DeLarverie to "move along, faggot," DeLarverie was interpellated as a queer subject. Recognizing that the police officer had hailed DeLarverie into this social existence, DeLarverie chose the next act—to punch the officer—as a direct response to the positioning of that queer identity in the larger system. Punching the officer was an act of self-survival, to be sure. But it was also the reaction of an identified queer person resisting the ideological and institutional structures that maintain queer oppression. The punch that started Stonewall continued to reverberate among those who saw DeLarverie as a gender-bending performer whose identity choices were not only about theatrical entertainment but also about oppositional consciousness.

QUEER REALITIES

Despite the unique identity bentness and potential resonance of butch queerness, standard drag discourse would not necessarily acknowledge it as a gender-bending performance; if it did, it would likely identify it as male impersonation. In the first framing, queer butch acts are deemed a quotidian iteration of the butch's "true self" and thus a natural rather than performance-based gender expression. This classification leads to uncomfortable generalizations about what is authentic versus performative, and it also discounts the performer's efforts to design and deploy a cultivated masculine stage aesthetic. Moreover, if a butch's life is already deemed a queering of gender expectations from assigned sex, then an intense problem of power dynamics is front and center here: the butch is positioned as not capable of creatively and theatrically bending masculinity because butches are assumed to already be personally living this bentness. Thus, a traditional understanding of gender-bending (fictive gender is presented in contrast to the real identity of the performer) leaves butch women as well as trans and gender-non-conforming people with limited performance options. The result is that if this queer person does participate in gender-bending, they have little discursive agency to define their work as such.

The presumption that butches are not gender-bending if they present a masculine stage persona is sidestepped entirely by simply calling them male impersonators. Such a label identifies the performer as bending masculinity not from their offstage gender identity but from their institutionally assigned sex (their identities as nonmale). This solves one problem but creates a slew of others. For instance, male impersonation has historically been defined as the gender-bending act of a woman impersonating a man or playing at what she is fundamentally not. Thus, this label frames masculinity as the normalized purview of male bodies: to perform masculinity is to perform as a man. Simultaneously, it frames the nonman performer as a woman who must embody some degree of femininity because she is capable only of impersonating (rather than inhabiting) masculinity. Naming these acts male impersonations diminishes the complex queerness of butchness, and it leads to significant misidentification of the performers. It also wholly discounts what the actor wanted to do, what methods they used to do it, and what they hoped to achieve with such a performance.

Because of the pitfalls associated with standard drag discourse, I have found it necessary to frame any identity-focused stage act as a potentially queered iteration of said identity; I suggest that this should be a standard presumption about staged identity acts unless the act directly proves otherwise. In concrete terms, this means that instead of presuming that DeLarverie's stage masculinity was a normative projection of the actor's self or an impersonation of a normative man, I presume that DeLarverie was bending the standard notion of masculinity. And my presumption could have been easily disproven had DeLarverie provided evidence to the contrary. Indeed, I found this exact kind of contrary evidence in the statements, literature, advertisements, and performance methods of variety and vaudeville male impersonators, who were very clear about the relationship between their offstage identities and the men they portrayed onstage. But this chapter asserts the value of initially looking at staged identity acts as potentially bent: it allows us to immediately speculate *whether* the act is a politically potent expression of bent identity, rather than first drawing on limited ideas and words to justify the act's inclusion within such a speculative framework. This mode of investigation makes clear, for example, that both DeLarverie and Bentley were deeply invested in cultivating a stage expression that would result in being publicly read as queer and also that such readings were intended to lead to specific micro- and macroeffects.

These last three chapters have demonstrated how gender-bending acts are more complicated than the terms and logic that constitute drag discourse. Queer butchness was in some ways similar to what Annie Hindle did onstage, yet, because Hindle was middle-class, White, nationally popular, and able to publicly identify within normative sex and gender parameters, her reception and impact were very different. Hindle's identity privileges and targeted advertising campaigns allowed her public gender acts to be presumptively interpreted as playacting rather than queerness or deviance. In the same vein, the particular impact of queer butchness cannot be separated from the unique racial, socioeconomic, and cultural contexts it was constructed and deployed within. Hindle's gender-bending allowed her to get paid for leading the life she wanted (for a time); teatristas' gender-bending made them active members rather than passive objects of el Movimiento; queer butchness, examined within Black performance traditions and a strongly expressed intentionality toward queer alignment, had the effect of forming defiant community bonds. Attention to these nuances does not discount the accomplishments of any bending act but does measurably help illustrate its unique and situated qualities.

NOTES

1. Drorbaugh describes DeLarverie's voice like this in "Sliding Scales," 123.
2. This phrase was used on marquees and newspaper advertisements. The number of "men" fluctuated (as many as thirty-five) and the particular actor commissioned to be "the girl" changed as well (other notables were Mickey Mercer, Corky Davies, Tommy Williams, and Jo Vaughn). However, the tagline of "[x number] men and one girl" (or "... *a* girl") was routinely used starting around 1939 and continuing after DeLarverie left the revue in 1969.
3. Newton, "Dick(less) Tracy and the Homecoming Queen," 162.
4. Bailey, *Butch Queens Up in Pumps*, 130–131.
5. Wilson, *Bulldaggers, Pansies, and Chocolate Babies*, 135.
6. Bailey, *Butch Queens Up in Pumps*, 130–131.
7. It is common to refer to Stonewall as a "riot." However, the term is too often associated with violent or out-of-control actions and used to delegitimize the resistance of minority racial groups. Conversely, terms such as *rebellion*, *revolt*, and *revolution* have been historically used to characterize heroism against oppressive

powers. I frame Stonewall with DeLarverie's own preferred term as a rebellion against homophobic, transphobic, and racist police actions and government policies.

    8. For example, see Maltz, "Real Butch," 280; Drorbaugh, "Sliding Scales," 121. See also Jewel Box Revue program booklets.

    9. De Frece, *Recollections of Vesta Tilley*, 137. Rainey (writer and singer), "Prove It on Me Blues" (1928).

    10. Bailey, *Butch Queens Up in Pumps*, 40.

    11. Maltz, "Real Butch," 274–275.

    12. Halberstam, *Female Masculinity*, 250–255.

    13. Ibid., 246.

    14. Ibid., 245–246.

    15. Maltz, "Real Butch," 275.

    16. Halberstam, *Female Masculinity*, 240.

    17. Maltz, "Real Butch," 275.

    18. Bailey, *Butch Queens Up in Pumps*, 33.

    19. For example, see Newton, "Dick(less) Tracy and the Homecoming Queen," 162; Dauphin, "A Bit of Woman in Every Man," 12; and articles on gay history and culture websites such as afterellen.com (Chu, "An Interview") and pride.com (Ring, "Who the F Is . . .").

    20. For example, see Garber, "Gladys Bentley," 55, 58–59; Wilson, *Bulldaggers, Pansies, and Chocolate Babies*, 174.

    21. Mansbridge, "Making of Oppositional Consciousness," 4–5.

    22. For a longer discussion of what is considered "traditional activism," see Piepzna-Samarasinha, "Time to Hole Up," 170.

    23. Cohen, "Deviance as Resistance," 30.

    24. Ibid., 37.

    25. Bentley, "I Am a Woman Again," 93.

    26. Bailey, *Butch Queens Up in Pumps*, 130–131.

    27. Giddings, *When and Where I Enter*, 86.

    28. Garber, "Gladys Bentley," 58–59. Waters and Baker were not as overt in their sexual interests and connections as Bentley and Rainey, and thus there is less evidence about their relationships.

    29. Halberstam, "Mackdaddy, Superfly, Rapper," 113–114.

    30. Maltz, "Real Butch," 278.

    31. Wilson, *Bulldaggers, Pansies, and Chocolate Babies*, 174.

    32. Bentley, "I Am a Woman Again," 94.

    33. Wilson, *Bulldaggers, Pansies, and Chocolate Babies*, 172.

    34. Young, quoted in Garber, "Gladys Bentley," 58.

    35. Bentley, "I Am a Woman Again," 94.

    36. Ibid., 93.

37. Wilson, *Bulldaggers, Pansies, and Chocolate Babies*, 188.
38. Newton, *Mother Camp*, 5.
39. Dauphin, "A Bit of Woman in Every Man," 3.
40. Jewel Box Revue programs, Queer Music Heritage Archives.
41. Dauphin, "A Bit of Woman in Every Man," 4. See also "Its an Old Mannish Custom," information page toward the front of all Jewel Box Revue programs.
42. Dauphin, "A Bit of Woman in Every Man," 12.
43. *Stormé: The Lady of the Jewel Box*.
44. This information comes primarily from Brown's personal scrapbooks, which contain clippings of newspaper advertisements and other performance memorabilia. These scrapbooks were donated by Brown's estate to Queer Music Heritage, an online archive curated and maintained by music historian JD Doyle.
45. For an example, see the Brown scrapbooks, advertisement for the June 20, 1950, Pittsburgh engagement.
46. Jewel Box Revue programming and advertising materials almost always use the titles "Mr." or "Miss" before performers' names. Titles correspond to the performer's assigned sex rather than stage gender. Thus, Mercer, Williams, DeLarverie, and other MCs are always "Miss" and female impersonators are always "Mr."
47. For example, see Capó, *Welcome to Fairyland*, 274.
48. Newton, "Dick(less) Tracy and the Homecoming Queen," 162; *Stormé: The Lady of the Jewel Box*.
49. According to DeLarverie, DeLarverie's hair was cut short for the Jewel Box job (*Stormé: The Lady of the Jewel Box*). Thus, I date all images with this shorter hairstyle as having been taken during or after 1955. DeLarverie was known for wearing more casual clothing styles after leaving the Jewel Box Revue in 1969. All photos I analyze in this chapter show DeLarverie quite dressed up, so, I surmise, they either are images of DeLarverie in performance clothing or were taken during a time when DeLarverie was representing the Jewel Box.
50. Queer Music Heritage holds twelve complete program booklets and one nightly handbill from the Jewel Box Revue's national touring days (also two booklets from Club Jewel Box). These booklets are not clearly dated, their pages are not numbered, and many programs contain similar content (although all have different covers and thus can be identified as separately released booklets). Doyle speculates that these booklets span the touring era of the 1950s and 1960s. Booklets released before DeLarverie joined the Jewel Box are easy to identify because Mickey Mercer is the featured MC. However, some of DeLarverie's performance pictures and headshots may have remained in booklets after DeLarverie's 1969 departure. For example, one program has images of both DeLarverie and "Miss Joe Vaughn," the person that appears to have replaced DeLarverie as the MC. Because of the overlapping information in these booklets as well as a lack of dates and

page numbers, I refer to the recurring images or other items generally, as program booklet material, and I identify any item specific to one booklet by reference to the booklet's cover.

51. DeLarverie's image was not included in the final magazine spread.
52. Doyle found this handbill sandwiched in the pages of a program booklet. The handbill is currently filed with the program booklet it was found in; the booklet has a black cover and two drawings of Danny and Doc.
53. DeLarverie, quoted in *Stormé: The Lady of the Jewel Box*.
54. Drorbaugh, "Sliding Scales," 123.
55. Jewel Box Revue handbill, Queer Music Heritage Archives. The images of DeLarverie in a Navy uniform are printed in several program booklets.
56. Martin and Kazyak, "Hetero-Romantic Love and Heterosexiness," 323–328.
57. *Stormé: The Lady of the Jewel Box*; Drorbaugh, "Sliding Scales," 129.
58. Drorbaugh, "Sliding Scales," 129.
59. Ibid., 123.
60. Jewel Box Revue program booklets, Queer Music Heritage Archives.
61. Newton, "Dick(less) Tracy and the Homecoming Queen," 162.
62. Ibid.; Drorbaugh, "Sliding Scales," 123.
63. *Stormé: The Lady of the Jewel Box*.
64. Newton, "Dick(less) Tracy and the Homecoming Queen," 162.
65. Maltz, "Real Butch," 281.
66. Bailey, "Gender/Racial Realness," 379.
67. Walker, *Looking Like What You Are*, 7.
68. Newton and Maltz use this language or otherwise insinuate DeLarverie's homosexuality. This type of language also appears in Hinds, "Uncovering the Stonewall Lesbian"; Chu, "An Interview with Lesbian Stonewall Veteran Stormé DeLarverie"; and Yardley, "Storme [sic] DeLarverie." Occasionally, DeLarverie is ostensibly proven to be a lesbian via reference to a long-term live-in relationship with a woman named Diana.
69. It is likely that DeLarverie's gender and sexuality identity narratives were well known by friends and coworkers, but DeLarverie did not identify them in public interviews or statements.
70. *Stormé: The Lady of the Jewel Box*.
71. Yardley, "Storme [sic] DeLarverie."
72. Ibid.
73. Butler, "Performative Acts and Gender Constitution," 527.
74. Bailey, *Butch Queens Up in Pumps*, 58.
75. Halberstam, "Shame and White Gay Masculinity," 223.
76. Ibid.
77. DeLarverie, quoted in *Stormé: The Lady of the Jewel Box*.

78. The details I supply in this narrative are also supported by several mentions in newspapers and gay-community blogs about DeLarverie's life and death.

79. Piepzna-Samarasinha, "Time to Hole Up," 166.

80. Stonewall's popular positioning as the first or most important "trigger" of the US gay civil rights movement is highly contested. Acts of violent and nonviolent resistance occurred before the Stonewall Rebellion, and many were quite significant on both local and national scales. There is a need to scrutinize why this particular rebellion has risen to the top of the gay rights narrative. But regardless of its contested historicization, Stonewall was still an important public manifestation of oppositional consciousness formulated by a persecuted minoritarian community resisting systems of institutionalized discrimination and persecution.

81. Mansbridge, "Making of Oppositional Consciousness," 4–5.

82. Rupp and Taylor, *Drag Queens at the 801 Cabaret*, 219.

83. Sandoval, *Methodology of the Oppressed*, 54

84. Cohen, "Deviance as Resistance," 30–33.

85. Ibid., 30.

86. Ibid., 42.

FIVE

Bent Means "Not Quite Straight"

Kinging as Disidentification

AROUND 11:00 P.M., Mr. Luxe—a masculine figure with light skin who is dressed in a rust-colored zoot suit with a black fedora over short brown hair—walks onstage. After taking a swig from a metal flask, Luxe begins to swagger and dance. He removes his suit jacket. Then the fedora. Suddenly his shirt and tie are gone, revealing the bubblegum-pink bra underneath. Luxe pulls off his brown wig and a ponytail of straight white-blond hair cascades down his back. After unhooking and removing the bra, in tempo with what has become a fast-paced cymbal beat, Luxe swings his breasts (marginally covered with silver-tasseled nipple pasties) in a circular motion. Turning his back to the audience, Luxe pulls down his trousers to reveal satin panties and fishnet stockings. The now nearly naked Luxe is not quite done yet. As the music climaxes, Luxe turns forward and reveals a large dark-colored erect phallus, which shoots a small stream of liquid over the heads of the audience. The crowd around me explodes into whistles and applause. We expected nothing less from the fifteenth annual Drag King Contest.[1]

As I watched Luxe from the left side of the audience pit, I thought about Vesta Tilley. Luxe initially presented as a dandy character in full men's suit and trendy menswear accessories, performing "men's business" such as drinking from a flask. Also, like Tilley, Luxe employed racially and socioeconomically coded feminine "tells" about the embodied "truth" under the act. Tilley's soprano register, subtle suit tailoring, and stage wig were visual nods to her public persona as the genteel Miss Vesta Tilley. Luxe invited a similar reading by wearing false eyelashes, showing the white-blond ponytail, unveiling luxury women's undergarments, and—undoubtedly a step farther than Tilley would take it—revealing breasts. Suzanne Kessler and Wendy McKenna classify certain visible body parts as "cultural genitals," or physical characteristics interpreted as evidence of an individual's assigned sex.[2] Breasts certainly fit this category (usually perceptible via cleavage or curves under clothing), as does body hair such as beards. But despite using a reveal, Luxe was not performing an identification gender-bending act. In fact, the feminine reveals were red herrings: a seeming disclosure of cisgender truths that were quickly revealed to be one more bend. The next reveal was, of course, the semirealistic, erect, and functioning phallus. Drawing once more from their study on public gendering, Kessler and McKenna contend that the visible presence of a penis operates as prime and overriding proof of assigned sex.[3] In this regard, mass publics will often identify a body with both breasts and a phallus as male because penises trump other signifiers. And yet, the phallus reveal did not bring Luxe back into a masculine look, nor did it appear to be him revealing his offstage quotidian identity. In fact, Luxe's final body tableau did not locate him within any hegemonic ideologies of self, nor within a particular minoritarian group. Rather, I argue that drag acts such as these disidentify from both majoritarian and minoritarian identifications by "genderfucking"—that is, exploding what concepts such as gender, sex, and desire can mean. Such an unintelligible identity product was both welcomed and celebrated by the audience that night.

The previous two chapters discussed acts that centralized their bending work in the development of particular queer stage pictures rather than in the contrast between lived and staged gender. Likewise, at the Drag King Contest, I did not need to know Luxe's offstage identity to apprehend how this act was bent. And that is a good thing, because I had no access to knowledge about Luxe's offstage self before or after the show. From my spectator standpoint, it remained completely unclear which parts of Luxe's offstage self were akin to or dissimilar from this act. Yet, it was obvious that Luxe intended to mess with identity categories and their usefulness as classification systems. Thus, he created a character who embraced many pleasurable aspects of gender and sexuality and also shifted the meanings attached to these signs. The contrast between the lightness of Luxe's own body and the dark phallus he employed was, I argue, another type of genderfucking: it suggested the intent to blend racial signifiers and divisions along with gender and sexuality. Later in this chapter, I explore how the bending of racial markers can be a powerful act of disidentification when done by racially oppressed individuals. However, when performed by White or light-skinned subjects such as Luxe, these actions might reinforce racialized stereotypes and power structures under the seemingly progressive umbrella of queering identity. Luxe's act had the intent of bending many things, and the impacts of such bending methods must be carefully parsed.

I have witnessed similar acts performed throughout California at small community-centered drag king shows and queer drag shows featuring drag kings.[4] People who have attended such shows will attest to the diversity of drag practiced there. But because these acts often employ multiple, complex, or nontraditional forms of bending and infrequently include a traditional reveal, they do not always fit well into the standard drag definition. Therefore, most scholarly literature that discusses these acts and shows translates them into a more familiar discursive format for the purpose of description and analysis. To once again reference Halberstam's famous description of the HerShe Bar drag king shows, a drag king is "a female (usually) who dresses up in a recognizably male costume and performs theatrically in that costume."[5] Senelick characterizes the genre of drag kinging as an emergent mimetic alternative to queening and female impersonation, which he defines as the "adult male decked out in seductive feminine frippery."[6] Luxe's act was intended to be unintelligible; thus it is difficult to linguistically illustrate how Luxe's act is drag without ignoring its contradictory gender expressions or naming an offstage sex and gender that was never disclosed. To add one more factor to this, it is notable that such an unintelligible act was met with deafening yells and hollers of pleasure from an audience that came to see a drag king show. I propose that Luxe's reception was positive precisely because it could not easily be understood in conventional identity terms or standard drag definitions, although that makes it harder to discuss.

In earlier versions of my work, I called Luxe a drag king. Luxe's act easily meets the criteria for gender-bending I have outlined in this book, and, moreover, the act was performed at a drag king show. At that point in my writing, I had a strong inclination to refer to all acts occurring at drag king shows or queer drag shows featuring drag kings as drag kinging: it was my way of articulating how the act was an important form of gender-bending within drag king forums. As I demonstrate, there is a vast range of acts and performers that self-identify as drag kinging/drag kings, and this range is not delimited by the standard definitional parameters offered by Halberstam and Senelick. But I never heard Luxe call himself a drag king, and he was a featured performer rather than a competitor at the Drag King Contest that year. Sometimes acts similar to Luxe's are called burlesque or "faux/bio queening," and sometimes these acts go unnamed altogether. So, instead of using drag kinging as my umbrella designation for all acts that occur at these events, I make the case that the omnipresence of diverse bent acts at drag king shows challenges not only common knowledge about drag kinging but also the popular notion of what drag is. To develop this more comprehensive picture, I connect my own ethnography at shows in Los Angeles, Oakland, and San Francisco between 2008 and 2012 to an online video archive of acts performed at these same venues. My ethnographic observations and archival analysis are supported by conversations I had with research partners who attended shows with me as well as statements made by performers in personal essays, interviews, and social media.

So, based on this data, what might one encounter at a small-forum drag king show or queer drag show featuring drag kings taking place in a liberal urban setting? There would undoubtedly be some traditional forms of impersonation: actors clearly identified as women who are mimetically replicating what Senelick calls "coarse, womanizing boors."[7] These hypermasculine acts might be laced with sexist language or behavior, and they might be racist as well; I have seen several White kings enact stereotyped "thug" characters while lip-synching to rap songs by Black artists. In my experience, the more racially homogeneous the space (favoring White or light-skinned audiences), the more emboldened White performers are to replicate pernicious racial stereotypes as a form of play without attending to the cultural messages or consequences of such expressions. So, sexist and racist acts will likely happen. But also, some drag kings will create nuanced versions of masculinity that are not heteronormative or cisgender. An example is Noah Boyz's depiction of youthful homosexual attraction or, as he describes it, "two nerds at summer camp [. . .] two awkward young boys falling in love."[8] Some acts will express identity as shifting, multiple, unstable, androgynous, absent, or as actively confrontational. For instance, a woman performer might visually distort the relationship between femininity and objective sexual desirability. I am describing a crowd favorite that I refer to as "female-femmeing": when a woman- or femme-identified performer enacts stylized, exaggerated, or otherwise queered femininity. Some drag acts will present a queer stage picture as an overt political statement on how bodies are defined and regulated by medicine and law. This is often accomplished by performances I call "body-breaking": acts where performers confront embodied meaning by doing gender or sexuality in ways that conflict with the body parts they are exposing. Some acts I just described will be directly referred to by performers or in show promotions as drag kinging, or generally as drag, and others will not. However, I found it most useful during my ethnographic work to presume that unless the performer said otherwise, all acts at these shows were some form of drag, and thus that all were using specific bent methods to achieve particular reception goals.

These acts model a performance process I call disidentification or, in its more aggressive iteration, genderfucking. Muñoz characterizes disidentification as a form of identity negotiation that acts "within and outside the dominant public sphere simultaneously."[9] A disidentification drag process enables the actor to embrace cultural identities in ways that are different from how those identities are conceived by the hegemony to operate. Disidentification actions incorporate some aspects of a hegemonic identity and simultaneously dismiss or reorder its "pathetic or abject" positioning of the subject.[10] By working inside identities to refigure their parameters and thus their personal and cultural implications, Muñoz argues that individuals are actually claiming power over the oppressed identities assigned to them. In short, disidentification gender-bending presents known identities in deliberately queered ways for the express purpose of triggering a conscious rethinking of how those dominant identifications can operate on the body of the performer, in the microspace of performance, and in larger ideological contexts. In drag spaces, this process is sometimes referred to as genderfucking, and I use this term to explore disidentification acts with an overtly confrontational style. Rather than simply expanding or tweaking identifications, genderfucking twists identity relationships to the point of breakage by deploying them in multiple, contradictory, and unintelligible ways.

To illustrate the innovation and uniqueness of disidentification bending, I must first take up two components of drag discourse that this book has not yet fully tackled. The first concerns the ideological implications of the reveal. Not all the acts I have discussed in this book employ a reveal, however, acts that do generally use it to show the performer's quotidian reality or personal truth—or at least qualities performers intend their audiences to see as such. Reveals are frequently facilitated by a visual or verbal disclosure of some capacity of the physical body such as the voice, chest, or haircut. When gender-bending is contextualized traditionally, as a performance that conceals and contrasts with the performer's real self, exposure of the actor's body can be assumed to represent the disclosure of this reality and is thus a sign the performance is over. This is certainly the format of some gender-bending acts, but it is a mistake to presume that every body exposure represents this.

A compelling example comes from Halberstam's aforementioned taxonomy of 1990s drag king styles. Halberstam describes a "femme pretender" drag king as a performer who presents onstage in a masculine way but "blows her cover by exposing her breasts or ripping off her suit in a parody of a classic striptease."[11] Although Halberstam uses positive terms to discuss Dred and Bridge Markham—artists who perform in drag king venues and use strip transformation in queer and interesting ways—Halberstam suggests that the display of certain body parts (breasts) dissolves the gender-bending portion of these drag acts. Similarly, in a conversation with Halberstam for *The Drag King Book*, drag king Mo B. Dick asserts that "it takes great concentration to stay in character and keep it convincing [...] it's too easy to strip and be a girl, for God's sake, you're a girl every day."[12] In this characterization, stripping ends the drag element of the act because it visually reestablishes the performer's ostensibly real status as "the girl." However, in my ethnographic research, I found it common that drag performers would expose skin and body parts as a method of confronting the essentialism assigned to sexed bodies rather than as a method of stopping their acts. Some strip acts were just sexualized skin shows, and some were traditional reveals. But body exposure during a drag act can also be a disidentificatory method that calls into question larger cultural beliefs, such as that having breasts means you are "the girl" and not the boy or the nonbinary person.

So, the visual display of body parts is not necessarily defining the end of the act, nor is it necessarily a revelation of the performer's quotidian or lived identity. Relatedly, the second component of drag discourse I question concerns those performers who *do* incorporate a reveal to show audiences their quotidian or lived identity. When an offstage self is intentionally disclosed at the end of a gender-bending act, that information can and should be used by audiences to understand who the performer really is in relation to their acts. However, such a reveal is also traditionally employed by audiences to rank the performer's particular talent. That is to say, audiences assume a gender-bending performer is skilled not because they produce a queer stage picture but because they are performing something that exists in fundamental contrast with what they are. As I have demonstrated throughout this book, a performer's quotidian self does not need to exist in stark, dichotomous contrast to whatever they produce onstage; in fact, many performers' lived realities inform their stage methods and many stage acts influence performers' personal identities. Yet, the logic of a traditional reveal invites audiences to use the real self as the means of articulating the skill it must have taken to create what was just performed. In other words, if the self is revealed, the revealed identity becomes a fulcrum of contrast to the performance, and that formula is then used to gauge the bent accomplishment.

Take, for instance, Esther Newton's progressive account of Joan Van Ness, the first woman to be crowned the "homecoming" drag queen of Cherry Grove, New York. Van Ness almost lost the competition because of a presumption that drag queens were men and that, if women dressed in a feminine manner, they were "dressing grandly or in costume rather than [. . .] in drag."[13] According to Newton, Van Ness was ultimately awarded the drag queen crown because she was a well-known butch lesbian who worked as a volunteer firefighter and did not wear dresses and makeup. So, although Van Ness was a woman, her daily lived masculinity and expressed discomfort with feminine aesthetics formed a recognizable contrast to her drag queen persona. Newton calls this "compound drag" because it stretches beyond drag's traditional sex and gender difference to include contrasting "representations of conventional masculinity by a 'nellie' gay man [. . .] or of femininity or nelliness by a 'butch' lesbian."[14] In this case, a woman's theatrical presentation of femininity is identified as successful drag through the revelation that her lived reality is markedly masculine. I have personally witnessed this type of compound drag. At a holiday charity show at the White Horse Inn in Oakland, California, a performer in a corset, blond wig, heels, diamond jewelry, and elbow-length gloves lip-synched to Madonna's "Material Girl." This performer later emerged during the curtain call in very butch street clothes. Because of this revelation, I understood that the bending component of the act was located in the divergence between lived masculinity and feminine character. Thus, I do not discount the power or significance of drag acts that intentionally reveal how the quotidian self identifiably contrasts with the stage representation. While Newton's articulation of compound drag does expand the scope of traditional gender-bending, my point is that it does not displace how drag success is measured by putting reality in culturally meaningful opposition to what is performed.

A caveat here: in my experience, audience members speculate about the body and identity of drag performers for a variety of reasons, including curiosity and desire. I distinctly remember leaving a drag show late one evening and engaging in hushed speculation with my research partner about whether an extremely masculine performer, aptly named Lucky Johnson, was "really" a butch woman, a transman, a man assigned female at birth, or a man assigned male at birth. We both knew these identifications would yield us little useful or important information . . . but we wanted to know anyway. Gender taxonomy is so central to contemporary Western culture that even the famous gender theorist Judith Lorber caught herself trying to pin down the "real" gender identity of a toddler.[15] And I have done some educated speculating in this book about the bodies and identities of certain historical performers.[16] However, I argue that interest or speculation about a performer's body or identity is not the same as using that information as a fulcrum to determine the accomplishment of the act. My friend and I were interested in Johnson's offstage identity, but our speculations did not lead us to validate or debunk the act. Johnson's act was drag because Johnson identified as a drag king and performed a clearly discernible bent character. Johnson absolutely could have declared a lived identity to define the relationship to the stage character, but this particular methodology was not employed. So, while the body or lived reality of the performer can constitute a point of queerness or a method of bending, it should not unequivocally be used by audiences to rank the quality of the bend. Unmooring the reveal from these ideological components opens a critical space for acknowledging the nuance and complexity of disidentification drag. To reiterate, some gender-bending performers employ standard identification or counteridentification reveals, and these methods do create "bentness" by disclosing a lived self in contrast to the performance. But I argue that disidentification methods employ bodies and revelations in nonstandard ways specifically because they are less focused on revealing hegemonic contrast than on reworking the meanings and implications of overarching cultural identification systems.

So, here are my goals with this final chapter. First, I document a range of practices that occur in small-forum drag king and queer drag spaces. Minimal literature on drag kings and shows exists, and what does exist primarily produces a singular vision of kinging aesthetics within a very clear hierarchy of queening, kinging, and all other acts. My second goal is to contextualize the range of important and moving drag acts I have witnessed—acts I argue are forms of disidentification—as occurring primarily in spaces that allow for such practices. The term *genderfucking* is connected to progressive, queer communities for a reason: as my account of the Los Angeles–based event series Bent demonstrates, a genderfucking space linguistically marks its performance lineups and policies to indicate that all identity iterations will be treated as valid and legitimate. This vision of "inclusivity" can allow or even encourage the production of sexist or racist drag under the umbrella of a shared queer community and project. In this regard, attention to who attends these forums and how the spaces outline their policies and expectations for performer conduct is also important. But a disidentification-based genderfucking process most often thrives in spaces that are dedicated to growing the number of identifications that exist, encouraging those identifications to complicate and overflow group affiliations, and spreading such iterations beyond the limitations of the stage.

DRAGGING KINGS

I start with how certain theatrical acts become identified as drag kinging. Such an entry point is not intended to assign drag kinging primacy in my discussion of disidentification; actually, it is not a given that kings will employ this particular drag process. But among all types of drag acts, kinging is second in the cultural imagination only to queening. That is to say, not everyone knows what drag kinging is, but certainly many more people are aware of this practice than other acts I discuss in this book. Moreover, the linguistically parallel relation between queening and kinging is used by mass publics to formulate knowledge about kinging—what this act might possibly be, even if they have not seen or considered it before. However, there is a significant gap between (1) the standard image of drag kinging in literary references and drag queen comparisons and (2) the varied shape and scope of kinging as discussed by its performers and practiced at drag king events.[17] I suggest that while there is an identification-based version of kinging, the overarching shape of this practice is rooted in specific queer intents and methods. To better illustrate the range of disidentification drag, then, I first work to challenge popular perceptions of the standard drag king act as well as demonstrate the real priorities and values of the people who claim this practice.

The earliest scholarly mention I have found that might be alluding to contemporary drag kinging is from Esther Newton's *Mother Camp* (1972). This text has one footnote describing the relatively scarce practice of "women who perform as men: male impersonators ('drag butches'). They are a recognized part of the profession, but there are very few of them."[18] Newton uses "male impersonator" and "drag butch" simultaneously, which she then treats as analogous to the drag queens ("female impersonators") in her book. Let us, once again, play the name game. I have outlined both why and how male impersonation must be specifically contextualized, and these parameters do not reflect the lived masculinity and same-sex sexual implications of a term like *drag butch*. I have also explained why DeLarverie, who possibly could be described as a drag butch, was not a male impersonator. In the previous chapter, I also referenced Newton's account of surprise when discovering DeLarverie was a gender-bending performer. Therefore, it is unlikely that "drag butch" refers to the queer butch aesthetic or resonance of performers like DeLarverie. Factoring in the time period and location of Newton's data collection (gay clubs in the late 1960s), it is more likely that she is describing an earlier iteration or an early form of what would come to be termed *drag kinging*.

So, "drag king" is relatively new, at least to our popular lexicon (I have not seen it referenced prior to the late 1980s). However, some have attempted to code drag kinging as a contemporary iteration of older forms of bending including male impersonation, cross casting, and drag queening. Some scholars and practitioners describe 1990s drag kinging acts by making connections to the work of White male impersonators in late nineteenth-century US variety and vaudeville and British music hall and variety acts. In this framework, these practices share key qualities such as being song-and-dance acts done in a gender persona fundamentally different from the gender identity of the performer. In the documentary *A Drag King Extravaganza*, a performer calls Annie Hindle and Vesta Tilley the mothers of modern drag kinging. Halberstam also refers to these particular male impersonators but articulates their influence not on kinging techniques but rather on the scope of quotidian masculine presentations favored by audience members at kinging shows.[19]

Contemporary drag kinging has also been descriptively bound to the early work of performance artists Lois Weaver and Peggy Shaw. Weaver and Shaw formed the theater troupe Split Britches with Deb Margolin in 1980, and their plays infused topics of economics, nationalism, race, and domesticity with feminist and lesbian concerns. In *The Art of Drag Kinging*, Dante DiFranco surmises that the butch looks and twisted representations of heteronormative coupling that so heavily characterized Split Britches productions directly informed contemporary kinging practices.[20] It is of note that Shaw and Weaver rarely performed as men or as nonwomen characters. For example, in *Belle Reprieve*, Split Britches' revision of *A Streetcar Named Desire*, Stanley (played by Shaw) is identified in the cast list as "a butch lesbian" rather than a man character or even a drag king/male impersonator.[21] Nevertheless, some scholars classify these acts as early forms of drag kinging because a known woman was doing a readably masculine stage persona.

Yet another popular articulation of drag kinging is built through reference to Diane Torr's late 1980s and 1990s performance art shows and Drag King/Man for a Day workshops. In *Sex, Drag, and Male Roles*, Torr and Stephen

Bottoms explain that "while Diane was not the only figure responsible for the emergence of drag king culture in the 1990s, she was undoubtedly one of the most influential."[22] However, Halberstam proposes that while "news articles attribute the origins of New York drag [king] culture to Diane Torr (as does Torr herself)," her workshops did not reflect the intent or impact of drag kinging.[23] Torr began her workshops in 1989 for women-assigned participants to learn how to "wear" and thus acquire men's power and privilege. Torr promoted a form of mimetic impersonation she felt would create "realistically plausible male characters who could pass on the street rather than simply remaining within the confines of club performance."[24] Torr believed that confining these gender practices to the "safe" atmosphere of a drag show would reduce their personal impact on the performer, so she had her students do men characters in dangerous men-dominated or women-restricted public areas. Because of the workshop's removal from a theatrical venue, emphasis on public passing, and lack of opportunities both for queer and nonconforming practitioners and for exploring queer and nonconforming identities, Halberstam concludes that it "has little to do with drag kings or kinging."[25]

According to Torr, the workshop has operated differently since the early 2000s. The current format emphasizes a process of playing with identity and is not restricted to woman-assigned participants. Torr describes a workshop in Glasgow, Scotland, where a heterosexual ciswoman named Paula and her trans- and queer-identified sibling Joey created masculine characters because "having grown up as sisters, the idea of exploring their mutual relationship as 'brothers' had a particular appeal."[26] Paula created a character that was sexually aggressive toward women, yet rather than reading her as a butch woman with sexual desire for women, other workshop attendees treated Paula like a heterosexual man. Joey also created a masculine character, but one that more closely resembled the nonhegemonic masculinity of Joey's everyday self. Even though both siblings created masculine personae and Joey's more closely reflected his quotidian masculinity, Joey was still interpreted by other attendees as the queerer of the siblings: an effeminate or "gay" man in relation to Paula's heteronormative man.[27] Rather than congratulating Paula on her passability and working with Joey to be more hegemonic, as might have happened in earlier workshops, Torr instead relished the complexities of these identities and encouraged exploring and picking apart dominant identities to create complex identity iterations. This workshop format was not the precursor to drag kinging, as it began in 2000, but it actually does reflect many of the intents, methods, and outcomes of the contemporary drag kinging I explore in this chapter.

The final method used to contextualize drag kinging is one of simple relational equivalence: drag kinging is the woman version of the historical practice of drag queening. Senelick explains that several 1980s and 1990s drag queens achieved mass public acceptance by "Disney[fying]" or toning down their lascivious stage content, and thus drag kinging is the shadow that filled this entertainment gap.[28] Relatedly, mass public knowledge about drag kinging is often inferred via reference to popular commercialized drag queening practices or famous drag queens. DiFranco asserts that "if you walked down the street and asked say 50 people in the general public, 'what they thought about drag kings,' maybe (if you were lucky) three of those people would even know what a drag king was. Furthermore, probably all three of those people's knowledge would be based on the assumption that a drag king must be the opposite of a drag queen."[29] In a similar exercise, the filmmakers of *A Drag King Extravaganza* asked random people in a park to describe what a drag king is. One individual says a drag king is the opposite of a drag queen. Another answers, "someone who dresses in women's clothing and goes on parade." When the interviewers reply, "that's a drag queen," the interviewee reanswers with "a woman who dresses in men's clothing and goes on parade."

This book does not directly focus on drag queening, but it is important to note that the scope and methodology of this practice can be more complex than these statements imply. Nevertheless, the most common and popular characterizations of drag queening are frequently used to situate kinging. Such equivalence is problematic in many regards. For instance, calling kinging a copycat practice implies that it lacks what Newton terms queer *culture production*.[30] In other words, it is not an original queer product but an imitation of the historical cultural labor of gay men. Another concern is how this equivalence is built not via similarity of intent or method but through reference to assigned sex and its divergence from gender performance. Schacht and Underwood call drag queens "individuals who publicly perform being women in front of an audience that knows they are 'men,' regardless of how compellingly female—'real'—they might otherwise appear."[31] Senelick describes drag kings in similar terms: "'men's men': coarse, womanizing boors clad in velvet lounge jackets or baggy soccer shirts and shorts" that claim to be "pimps" or voice "grossly retrograde sentiments."[32] Senelick then argues that the more stereotypically heteromasculine the drag king appears, the more lesbian audiences will be sexually drawn to the essential womanhood they know lies just underneath the act. And perhaps such a reading happens in some clubs and is cultivated by some performers, but this is far from a complete picture of kinging practices, performers, or show audiences.

The contextual picture of drag kinging as developed from references to historical queening is a limited one. However, a careful and critical comparison between the two can illustrate important commonalities in bending intent, method, and impact. In fact, Rupp, Taylor, and Shapiro propose that this side by side comparison could be one "key to understanding the boundary" of drag.[33] Kinging and queening are usually separated because of assumptions regarding performers' assigned sex, as well as limited ideas that queens perform hegemonic femininity and kings do hegemonic masculinity. In Rupp, Taylor, and Shapiro's estimation, kings and queens may differ in "contexts and styles" but can still engage similar strategies and tactics of critiquing the fixity of gender and sexuality.[34] They argue that the significant equivalence between queening and kinging is that these cultural entertainments use bending techniques methodologically to invest in and work toward political projects such as "resistance to the gender structure and heteronormativity."[35]

In sum, the most common way of defining drag kinging is to root it in the work of other historical practices, a contextualization that deprives it of originality and uniqueness. However, the drag kinging I have witnessed does share a few qualities with these referenced drag practices. For example, like US male impersonation, drag kinging often highlights the performability of gender as well as its cultural connection to assigned sex and sexuality. Like Split Britches' productions, drag kinging is often a visible act of nonnormativity played to audiences that are interested in recognizing such queerness. Like Torr's later drag king workshops, kinging personae do not have to fit into hegemonic identity boxes but rather can reflect identity experimentation. And like some drag queening, kinging can be built and deployed as a political action of cultural and institutional pushback. Thus, I suggest that contemporary drag kinging is best defined via its relationship not to other forms of drag but to practices of identity visibility, identity queerness, the deconstruction of dominant identities, or the political deployment of identities. I realize this does little to nail down the concrete elements of a kinging practice. But, as a performer in *A Drag King Extravaganza* surmises, "The beauty of being a drag king is that the stage is wide open."

What kinging ends up being really comes down to the intentions of each of its performers. So, who performs drag kinging? The answer offered by Halberstam is that drag kings are female people (usually).[36] However, DiFranco lists a range of people who call themselves drag kings: "Boychicks, Gender Outlaws, Transmen, Tomboys, Gender Benders, Passing Women, Dykes, Butches, Heterosexuals, Bisexuals, Gays, Lesbians, Men, Women, or anyone else who has a desire to 'put on the trousers.'"[37] Similarly, Shapiro describes the drag king troupe the Disposable Boy Toys as assigned women, lesbians, and dykes as well as individuals in transition and transpeople.[38] DiFranco's and Shapiro's lists do not encompass all bodies and identities, but they do highlight a range of individuals who might identify as drag kings. For this very reason, DiFranco concludes that "being a drag king only takes saying that you are one" and performer Del LaGrace Volcano surmises that drag kinging can done by "anyone (regardless of gender)" as long as their focus is on creating a conscious gender performance[39] (see fig. 5.1).

Thus, I suggest a more apt way to define kinging is via performers' expressed intentionality. Indra Windh explains that kinging is "at its best" when it is a "mocking crotch-kick to a gender system that tyrannizes and reduces us all."[40] To extend from this, no drag king I have talked with or read about repudiates the queerness of their stage expressions. So, while Vesta Tilley would rather have died than said her performance was intended to read as queer, I argue that kinging is fundamentally marked by performers' intents to express identity queerness or highlight oppressive identity norms. Drag kinging is not required to break down hegemonic identity parameters, but an overwhelming number of kings feel this is the appropriate vehicle for doing so. For example, performer and drag scene aficionado Kentucky Fried Woman surmises that the common thread among acts at drag king and queer drag venues is the "intentional gendered performance" of evoking different versions of selfhood and confronting "normal."[41] Scholar-performer Kathleen LeBesco similarly characterizes kinging as the creation of a "corporality that mark[s] an individual [as] somehow different from culturally determined norms."[42] I likewise assert that drag kinging is accurately contextualized as an intentional production of altered identity norms. And such a process should be recognized as a form of disidentification.

What is the value of a disidentification act that does not directly lead to commercial gain (like identification does) or minoritarian community gain (like counteridentification)? Extending Rupp, Taylor, and Shapiro's articulation of the key thread between kinging and queening, I propose that disidentification drag is a political act and thus its goals move beyond commercial or minoritarian community gains. A performer interviewed for *A*

Fig. 5.1. Richelle South, a member of The Beauty Kings, often performs femme characters but poses here as a masculine king. *Photo courtesy of Vanessa Adams.*

Drag King Extravaganza states, "When you take that act [drag kinging] and make it deliberate and do it in a public arena, that to me is a political act." Rupp and Taylor similarly argue that cultural entertainments that employ identity strategically can advance the politically potent agenda of promoting "resistance to domination."[43] And Rupp, Taylor, and Shapiro propose that performance-based actions or stories that "challenge binary gender and sexual identities" are working toward such political goals.[44] Thus, disidentification is an intentional queering for the sake of instigating microcommunity gains or larger cultural worldmaking effects.

The political efficacy of the open-ended performance practice I have defined as kinging can be subjective. However, Rupp and Taylor suggest starting with "intentionality, because doing so reveals what both the performers and audience interpret as political about the performance."[45] Such intent can be gleaned from the written or spoken statements of performers, troupes, and events. For instance, a troupe called the Miracle Whips describes their acts as taking on "gender and social issues" by modeling "progressive femininity," creating "radical erotic possibilities," and disrupting "conventional notions of sexiness."[46] This statement—posted to their Facebook page—speaks to both their performance methods and their intended goals of growing queer femininities. Similarly, members of the drag king troupe The Beauty Kings characterize their "broad range of gender-based performances" as intended to help audiences "think about and play with gender outside the binary system of male/female."[47] They also articulate their overarching performance goal of increasing "awareness and visibility of a wide spectrum of gender-bending, twisting, turning, playing, fucking, ambiguous, queer, straight."[48] Below, I describe several acts that evidence how these troupes put their articulated intents and methods into practice. For now, it suffices to say that both The Beauty Kings and the Miracle Whips clearly express the intent to model queer identity toward the politically oriented goal of expanding or building identity possibilities. Not every troupe or performer puts their mission statement on social media. Sometimes, like with Bent's master of ceremonies Landon Cider, verbal declarations of intent happen in real time at the show. In the absence of direct written or verbal statements, though, I also mark intentionality as displayed in clear and overt performance methods. Luxe did not state his intention to queer the relationships among body, gender, and desire. However, his visual engagement of feminine signifiers, an erect phallus, and an active sexual act was plainly readable.

DISIDENTIFICATION PROCESSES

In the next two sections, I explore some of the practices—including those I refer to as female-femmeing and body-breaking—that are omnipresent at drag king or queer drag events. My use of labels for particular practices is not intended to build substantive divides among kinging, queening, and other bent acts. Just the opposite: I use these terms to linguistically illustrate particular disidentificatory and genderfucking processes that are shared among various types of acts. Moreover, acts such as Luxe's fit my description of both female-femmeing and body-breaking and might very well also be identified as drag kinging. In short, labels are not indicative of delineated and rigid performance genres but rather are a discursive method I use to discuss the range of aesthetics and actions that can constitute a politically rich disidentification drag process.

At drag king shows and queer drag shows featuring drag kings, it is common for performers to do masculine-to-feminine, feminine, high femme, burlesque, or strip numbers, and many of these performers publicly identify as women or femmes. During the drag king show at the previously mentioned White Horse Inn, I watched a highly feminine-presenting performer with Betty Page bangs and bows tattooed on the backs of her thighs do a strip routine. Richelle South, whose drag name is Papa Cherry, is a member of The Beauty Kings and predominantly (but not always) performs feminine characters.[49] The Miracle Whips perform their "queer femme" numbers alongside The Beauty Kings at Bent performance events in Los Angeles.[50] Sometimes these femme acts are referred to via the biological and essentialist label "faux queening" or "bio-queening," and sometimes they go unnoted in programming materials or are advertised as the titillating skin show background to the drag show. In an effort to acknowledge the bentness of these acts—an omission that has been a point of contention among practitioners such as Kentucky Fried Woman—I refer to any theatrical act that happens in these spaces, is done by a woman-identified or visually femme performer, and consciously constructs and expresses queer, queered, or new iterations of femininity by my drag term *female-femmeing*.[51] Based on my observations at many drag shows, I argue that female-femmeing often engages with a disidentification drag process. However, these acts are rarely considered drag and rarely treated as equals to kinging or queening practices. Thus, a critical consideration of these extremely popular acts must first acknowledge that femininity can be queerly expressed by a woman or a femme person and that this practice is as bent as any kinging or other disidentification drag act.

Female-femmeing bends identity in (at least) three ways. First, acts may present femininity in a manner different from the performer's declared personal gender identity. Second, acts may twist or reimagine relational ideologies among femininity, beauty, body, and sexuality. Third, performers may express femininity as a multiple and shifting identification. Yet, in spite of these very clear gender bends, female-femmeing has not been fully embraced as drag because the gender presented onstage does not dichotomously oppose the lived sex or gender of the performer. In both stage and quotidian contexts, an expression of femininity by a woman is not generally framed as a bending of gender. In fact, the prevailing cultural ideology posits that femininity layered over a woman's body is a nontransgressive, hegemonic, and cisgender doing of identity. However, Laura Harris and Liz Crocker suggest that women can do femininity in conscious ways if they choose and that such an actively cultivated and "sustained gender identity"—what they refer to as "femme"—does not have to represent a normal and natural expression or acquiesce to hegemonic standards of femininity.[52] Some women embody race, body size, or ability identities that preclude their femininity from easily blending with hegemonic standards. Moreover, Harris and Crocker illustrate how women might not be considered "properly or conventionally feminine" if their femininity is not connected to heterosexuality or if they do not reproduce the femininity they were socialized into as children.[53]

To be clear, not all staged feminine expressions by women are disidentification bending practices. However, I draw on and extend Harris and Crocker's concept of "femme" to characterize those staged feminine expressions that are consciously chosen, actively sustained, and intended to disrupt hegemonic femininity or present an alternative version. Disidentification is actually very useful here for apprehending how a feminine expression by a woman or femme performer can be a transgressive or disruptive action. According to Muñoz, disidentification allows individuals to use their race, gender, or sexuality strategically to define their own cultural power and refigure the most oppressive attributes assigned to them.[54] Femme performers queer oppressive cultural attributes of femininity, including sexual passivity, assumed heteronormativity, and hegemonic beauty standards. Unlike the counteridentification process DeLarverie used to declare membership in a particular queer community, disidentification works toward "recycling and rethinking" the parameters that define and order both majoritarian and minoritarian groups.[55] And unlike some White drag kings who reproduce racism by performing stereotyped masculinities of Color, almost all female-femmeing acts I have seen target the cultural standards to which the performers' own bodies are held. Thus, women or femmes who theatrically perform femininity employ disidentification to manipulate, expand, or refashion rather than fully reject or embrace representations assigned to or thrust upon them in daily contexts.

At the fifteenth annual Drag King Contest, a troupe called the Diamond Daggers performed a dance act in vintage swimsuits, heels, red lipstick, and pin-curled hair. The Daggers' choreography and aesthetic evoked an iconic "pinup girl" look, and the troupe even included a strip component. For me, this strongly echoed the historical performance tradition of US burlesque, a form of entertainment centered on the sexualized, objectifying display of unclothed women's bodies. On a surface level, the Daggers' act could likewise be read as sexual "eye candy" entertainment or a "skin show." In their study of children's films, Martin and Kazyak demonstrate how femininity, represented via a cartoon woman's beauty and exposed body, is significant "in the construction of heteronormative sexuality."[56] A woman character's femininity is always portrayed in tandem with her sexiness, and her sexiness is established when men characters desire her. If a woman character is not feminine because, for example, she is fat, ugly, or old, then she is not sexually desirable; on the other hand, if a woman character is feminine, her femininity marks her as beautiful and also available for men's desire. Martin and Kazyak term this relationship among a woman's beauty, her femininity, her sexiness, and men's desire for her as *heterosexiness*.[57] The Daggers' act could have solidified the performers within this heterosexiness matrix except for the fact that they had nonhegemonic bodies: some were thin with small breasts; some were pear shaped and curvy; some did not shave their underarms or legs; some had large tattoos; one Dagger had visible facial hair. While not having hegemonically feminine body shapes and grooming practices, all the Daggers projected the image of sexy and desirable women. By staging their diverse bodies in sexually provocative ways, the Daggers confronted the connection between sexiness and hegemonic beauty and body standards. These presentation methods stretched and tweaked the definition of sexy and sexually desirable to include many different types of women.

This disidentification process acknowledges and also queers the hegemonic cultural ideology that women become interpellated as adult women by being sexually objectified. Eli Clare argues that disabled women are often treated like children or asexual beings, and therefore becoming objects of sexual desire can be critically important for their cultural value and self-worth.[58] In a related vein, Kentucky Fried Woman argues that thinness is a key component of adult feminine sexiness for both heterosexual and homosexual communities. According to her, this is why "so many of the representations of queer desires can easily be found in the pages of any heterosexual magazine."[59] Even if Martin and Kazyak's heterosexiness were translated to "homosexiness"—such that feminine women were sexy objects for women to desire and sexually consume—the sexy corollary of femininity remains linked to hegemonic body size and ability standards. The Daggers' act is sexy in ways that bend the exclusivity of feminine presentation by refiguring which bodies can (or should) automatically attract desiring gazes. Likewise, Kentucky Fried Woman performs in corsets, miniskirts, fishnet stockings, heels, wigs, and makeup and explains that this stage presentation is inspired by the general perception that fat bodies are not feminine. Her "fat femme" strip act is subversive—and, I argue, a salient form of gender-bending—specifically because she presents her unclothed body as feminine and thus aesthetically pleasing and sexually titillating.[60] Both the Daggers and Kentucky Fried Woman bend feminine gender when they render fat, hairy, or differently shaped bodies as beautifully feminine and therefore sexually desirable.

Other female-femmeing acts reproduce hegemonic standards of body and beauty but then bend their relationship to feminine ideologies such as sexual roles. At a Bent event called *Holidays Are a Drag*, I watched the Miracle Whips perform a number in tight blue wrap dresses, fishnet stockings, heels, red lipstick, and erect strap-on dildos. They began by introducing themselves as flight attendants aboard F.U.C.K. Airlines (an acronym for "Femmes Use Cock, [OK!?]"). Talking to the audience as if we were airline passengers, the Whips delivered preflight announcements such as "other carriers assume that, if femme, no strapping. We're here to kick that notion in its sorry little ass." The Whips then performed a routine to Ricky Martin's "She Bangs" with choreography that simulated both penetrator and penetrated (what Rupp calls "enveloper") sex positions.[61] The routine ended with this postflight message: "We recognize it's your choice whether to strap or not to strap." By enacting a penetrator sexual role without ever compromising or altering their hyperfeminine presentations, the Whips both confronted and reimagined the relationship between femininity and "natural" sexual receptivity. The key bending quality in the Whips' performance was not a developed contrast between sex and gender but rather the pairing of recognizable hegemonic femininity with a culturally nonfeminine sexual position.

By never compromising their feminine aesthetics even while wearing and using phalli, they tweaked rather than acquiesced to or completely rejected a binary understanding of gender and its relation to sexuality. I argue that the stage picture these acts produced encouraged a queer reading of embodiment: penetrator sex acts can be feminine acts, and the feminine people who enact them will continue to be read as feminine. As the Whips put it, "The sting means it's working!"[62] In this case, what "stings" is the way femininity is being bent away from limited sexual scripts; this may leave a lingering mark on spectators who have been automatically organizing certain bodies—even queer bodies—into certain sexual roles.

Like the Daggers and Kentucky Fried Woman, the Whips often end their acts by stripping to nipple pasties and panties. Martin and Kazyak's concept of heterosexiness also illuminates how a feminine woman's unclothed body is always framed as serious (never a joke) because it triggers heterosexual objectification via men gazing at it. This form of sexual objectification can occur in nonheterosexual contexts if individuals who desire women have the opportunity to gaze at women's naked bodies. Homosexual gazing is certainly a possibility at drag shows in local gay bars and other spaces populated by queer people. As evidenced by the Daggers, Kentucky Fried Woman, and other acts that feature fat, differently shaped, or hairy bodies, eliciting this desiring sexual gaze is a major goal of some performers. Even if the performers intend to cultivate this gaze, such acts nevertheless exemplify Martin and Kazyak's point that unclothed women's bodies are automatically foregrounded as sexually consumable products. Yet, in her study of contemporary "neo-burlesque," Lynn Sally argues that a consciously constructed and carefully performed striptease can work to "dismantle (or, at least, to question)" singular meanings ascribed to women's unclothed bodies.[63] Thus, female-femmeing that includes a strip component may inspire an array of objectifying desires or it may inspire alternate forms of desire.

I witnessed an example of this at Bent's *Drag in the Name of Love* show, where the Whips performed a cooking segment called "Whip It" wearing aprons, nipple pasties, panties with a keyhole cutout in the back, and little else. The number ended with them drizzling honey down their exposed skin. The audience went wild with shouts and applause, a reaction I interpreted as sexual pleasure derived from gazing at seminude, honey-coated, femme bodies. Reinforcing my interpretation, drag king Landon Cider—the show's MC—went onstage and proclaimed that the Whips made him "want honey." It was not surprising that Cider's masculine persona (he was a James

Dean–esque character that night) enjoyed gazing at and fantasizing about eating honey off the Whips' feminine bodies. But then Cider immediately also proclaimed that the performance made him want to wear "nipple tassels and [have] baby butt crack" (in reference to the keyhole cutout panties). Certainly, his desire was objectifying—he desired sexual access to the Whips' bodies. But his desire was also inclusive and personally embodied—he found it exciting to think of himself in the feminine clothing that had elicited such sexual desire. A desire to wear nipple pasties and panties, perhaps a desire to be seen as sexy in those items, did not mesh with Cider's masculine persona. So, the Whips' act triggered two distinct forms of desire, which then inspired Cider's queer sexual reaction. Reinforcing my interpretation of this moment, Bent founder and organizer Richelle South explains that although some Bent spectators might gaze at feminine artists and "desire that body to sleep with," others might "desire that body for [themselves]."[64] In these terms, female-femmeing presents sexiness in bent ways that not only extend femininity across bodies and expressions but also complicate desire paradigms.

Rather than wholly identifying within or wholly counteridentifying against hegemonic parameters of femininity, female-femmeing engages with a disidentification process to present powerful queer iterations of feminine beauty, sexiness, and sexuality. In this regard, performers who consciously intend to enact public "resistance to domination" will often use this form of drag to do so.[65] The acts I saw did not queer all problematic aspects of femininity. For example, few acts highlighted or expanded how femininity is entrenched with socioeconomic, racial, colorist, or ability standards. However, I argue that this mode of performance is an apt method of taking up those relationships if performers so choose. Thus, female-femmeing is both an ideologically positioned political identity practice and a materially effective one.

GENDERFUCK IT

Body-breaking drag acts have a similar set of intentions and goals as female-femmeing, though they might look quite different. Body-breaking twists the assumptive meanings attached to primary or secondary sex characteristics through this formula: performers present uncovered body parts—generally parts used to assign sex—and then perform gender, race, and sexuality in ways that conflict with a hegemonic reading of the disclosed sex. These acts are disidentificatory in that they engage with how publics use visible physical markers to categorize bodies but frame alternate or expanded models as better methods of interpreting embodiment. Reading the body, or making assumptions about an individual's personhood based on their visible parts, is a standard mode of taxonomy and cultural interaction, and such readings aid publics as they select pronouns or pursue sexual encounters. Obviously, reading can also compartmentalize an individual within limited notions of race, ability, and gender as well as reify essentialist notions and cultural hierarchies connected to sex assignment. For example, a study conducted by Kessler and McKenna demonstrated how people most often assign gender to bodies according to the presence or absence of a visible penis (rather than the presence or absence of other visible genitalia).[66] But, because penises are not regularly visually available in public contexts, Raine Dozier argues that secondary characteristics such as beards and breast shape take over this gendering job.[67] Certain readable body parts evince medically designated sex, which then becomes a vehicle for understanding not only a person's gender expression but also their sexuality, behavior, identity, and overall subjectivity. This is an incredibly problematic cultural method for assigning meaning to people, but the framework provides a promising basis for body-breaking drag.

Robyn Wiegman's discussion of racial designation in US history is useful in exploring both the cultural habit of visually reading bodies to assign them personhood and the ways bodies can manipulate such readings. Wiegman argues that race constitutes a "real" embodied difference only if it can be visually categorized as such. Black individuals in US history who were able to visually pass as White individuals were legally and culturally considered White as long as they continued to pass. This institutional racial status might have been divorced from what the individual personally regarded as their "true" and "embodied" racial identity. Nevertheless, their racial classification had strong implications for their life outcomes. Wiegman uses the term *economies of visibility* to identify the process of building racialized social meaning though the visual perception of body difference.[68] The meanings of embodied qualities are products of cultural perception, even while their embodied see-ability is framed as ontological proof of meaning. In this regard, if a person can change the cultural perception and classification of their body, their body will not change but they nevertheless will be able to alter how so-called embodied truths can result in specific life outcomes for them.

To return once more to Mr. Luxe: his act started out as a masculine dandy character, then transitioned into a sexy feminine character, then finished by presenting divergent gender and perhaps racial signifiers on a single body to express his sexual prowess and objectified desirability. We could certainly analyze this act as one of female-femmeing, but I also want to note how Luxe employed both primary and secondary sex characteristics as a way of messing with popular perceptions of what certain body parts imply about gender and sexuality. Disidentification is generally a subtler process of shifting and stretching identities. Body-breaking, on the other hand, employs visually jarring and confrontational tableaux that bend an embodied identity to the point of breaking it. Accordingly, I suggest, many body-breaking acts reflect the quality and spirit of what is referred to in these spaces as genderfucking. Luxe's performance fucked with the meanings of a sexy feminine body and an active, masculine phallus by placing them in seeming harmony. And the act also seemed designed to fuck with the singularity of race designation by pairing a dark phallus with a light-skinned body. If this were the case, Luxe's choice ultimately reinforced the pernicious racial stereotype that Black men have large penises because they are aggressively hypersexual. Below I discuss two acts that successfully genderfuck racial-gendered power relationships. However, genderfucking is not a flawless vehicle for breaking down any and all identity hierarchies and thus cannot be treated as a catchall queering methodology. Drag performers must always attend to the intersectional cultural privileges and positions their bodies and identities can access outside these theatrical spaces.

Disidentification and genderfucking are two sides of the same methodological coin: both queer identities and both present new identities as a type of positive identity expansiveness that can spread queer space or thought. But, because genderfucking is a startling, sexy, and taboo word, it shows up more at drag shows. For example, Bent events have been promoted as "a night of drag, burlesque and genderfucking."[69] When used in this way, genderfucking discursively marks the atmosphere of a space as welcoming and supportive of various queer identity iterations. Genderfucking is also used to describe certain forms of embodied action that target hegemonic thinking. For example, the online, user-generated Urban Dictionary offers the definition for *genderfuck* as "deliberately sending mixed messages about one's sex [. . .] based upon the belief/idea that either gender does not exist (but only in the context of culture) or that there are multiple genders (beyond male and female)."[70] Evident in this definition is how strongly gender and assigned sex are ideologically connected and also how genderfucking works to confuse this relationship. In one of the few scholarly articles to reference the word, June L. Reich defines genderfucking as a deconstruction of the "psychoanalytic concept of difference without subscribing to any heterosexist or anatomical truths about the relations of sex to gender."[71] Thus, genderfucking is an action that confronts notions of embodied truth or reality by presenting gender in unintelligible ways. I add two components to this definition. First, genderfucking acts are capable of targeting-for-the-sake-of-deconstructing not only the relationship between embodied sex and gender *but also* other essentialized identifications such as sexual orientation and racial-gendered power dynamics. Second, genderfucking presents queer identity iterations that do not just break ontological assumptions but also add to the scope of identification possibilities.

Many of these components were evident in Dillon St. Dong's runner-up performance at the fifteenth annual Drag King Contest. Dong presented as a highly styled yet very masculine Black man by pairing a black dress shirt and vest with gray slacks, a paisley tie, and diamond stud earrings (his look was completed by a black goatee and groomed flathawk). R. W. Connell asserts that this type of Westernized business attire has become a transnational symbol of not only wealth and power but also hegemonic masculinity.[72] In addition to his clothing and grooming, Dong possessed another important symbol of masculinity: an extremely long, tube-shaped light-pink balloon (the type used for making balloon animals) protruding from the zipper of his pants. Dong presented an interesting tableau as a sleek, "business masculine" Black man with a comically long, erect, pink phallus. In creating a taxonomy of masculinity, Connell ranks White, heteronormative masculinity as the most honored or desired, and other types of subordinated masculinity—feminine, homosexual, or of Color—as having less cultural cachet and thus less steady access to power.[73] And Dong's nodding smile and confident body language seemed to acknowledge the use-value attached not just to his masculine presentation but specifically to his extremely long light-pink phallus.

As Dong's drag act played out onstage, all did not go smoothly. The balloon-phallus repeatedly took control of his body, pulling him across the stage and hitting him. Dong yanked the phallus from his pants and attempted to wield it like a sword, but the phallus-sword continued to attack him, eventually stabbing him in the ribs. The phallus-sword also simulated sexual violence by thrusting itself into Dong's mouth and "ejaculating" into his eye. Although this bit elicited uproarious laughter from the audience, the pantomime strongly recalled US histories of race-based sexual violence and domination of Black individuals by White men. At the act's climax, Dong grabbed the phallus-sword and reshaped it into a balloon puppy, which he playfully floated into the audience. As I stood in the audience pit watching, the implications of this final action reverberated strongly with me: after failing to fully acquire the violent power of the White phallus, Dong had no option but to deconstruct and refigure it. Once this was done, the object no longer had the means or opportunity to hurt him and in fact elicited positivity (in the form of a collective "awww" from the audience). In a provocative denouement, Dong clutched at his wounds and limped offstage, exhibiting the lasting bodily damage from his racial-gendered power struggle.

Even within the diverse entertainment lineup of the Drag King Contest, Dong's act stood out to me as particularly politically rich. Dong made no verbal or written statement about his act that I could find, but his careful selection of objects clearly illustrated racial-gendered cultural power and its attendant embodied violence and also suggested how this oppressive structure might be successfully reordered. I occasionally show a video of this act in my Women's and Gender Studies courses. Students quickly identify how Dong's performance is a commentary on masculine power structures, yet they are often divided on whether Dong intended to illustrate a racially designated form of masculine power with the light-pink balloon. Some feel that the balloon color is unintentional or arbitrary and thus unimportant, and others believe that a Black performer at a drag show in San Francisco would be conscious of the associations a light-pink phallus would elicit. For me, the proof of the act's racial meanings lies in the students' initial acknowledgment that it was about masculine power structures, because any doing or interpretation of gender is inextricably connected to race. Crenshaw's articulation of intersectionality directly contradicts notions that any singular identity can account for the whole of a person's life experiences, and Connell's theory of masculinity explicates how heteropatriarchy replicates racial stratification.[74] Thus, the effect of Dong's masculine balloon-phallus-sword cannot be divorced from racial meaning. If his penis-signifier visually represented masculinity as cultural domination, then it also demonstrated how masculinity was privileged or subordinated by the power holder's race, sexuality, gendered behavior, and socioeconomic status.

Dong did not verbally identify himself or name his act before, during, or after the show. But Dong was clearly identified as a drag king performer in the event's advertising, and he also registered as a participant in the Drag King Contest rather than just a performer in the show. The identification of Dong's act as drag kinging classifies it, on the most basic level, as an act of gender-bending. But I furthermore argue that the centrally bent quality of the act was its illumination of how power flows through sex- and race-marked body parts. He deliberately queered these categories of meaning by physically manipulating and refiguring them as well as shifting the audience's reaction to them. To return to Lorde's famous metaphor of the master's tools, which can never dismantle the master's house, Dong could not properly use his "master's tool," so he had to break it down and create something else. Dong's representation of the power certain body parts wield and his active, embodied refiguration of it was a disidentification drag practice. Moreover, his overt presentation of the violent White phallus and his epic physical struggle to produce something new exemplified the parameters of genderfucking.

Other body-breaking acts target desire rather than racial paradigms to show how embodied classifications are limiting or irrelevant modes of understanding. An example is by Mickey Finn and another performer I call "Lola" at the fourteenth annual Drag King Contest.[75] At the top of the act, Finn was wearing plaid bell-bottoms, a brown suit jacket, white oxfords, a loose black tie, and a brown fedora over short curly hair. Behind him stood Lola in a short black dress, thigh-high stockings, white platform boots, and dangly earrings. Although Finn was in menswear and Lola wore women's clothing, neither had the body shape or size stereotypically connected to their gendered presentations. Finn was short and relatively thin, at least compared to Lola, who stood a head taller and had broad shoulders and impressively muscled legs. As "Lola" by the Kinks began to play, the two performed a courtship story in which Lola took the more dominant pursuer role: she chased Finn around the stage, yanked off his tie, lifted him off his feet while dancing, and sat him on her lap. The performers' behaviors clashed with the traditional racialized gender mores they would ordinarily be expected to comply with (both are light skinned and appear White). In fact, the tableau they created was of two individuals presenting in traditionally gendered ways but behaving in the opposing gendered roles. Or as the song goes, Lola "looks like a woman and acts like a man" and Finn looked like a man but took on the passive romantic position middle-class White women are expected to occupy.[76]

Back to the scene, at this point, I suggest, Finn and Lola were intentionally encouraging the audience to read feminine-presenting Lola as a man and masculine-presenting Finn as a woman. This conclusion would not be a stretch for any person familiar with gender-bending because the traditional definition nudges audiences to apprehend this disjunction as at the root of all drag acts. And several of Finn and Lola's stage actions seemed to evidence the validity of this reading. For instance, Finn removed Lola's dress to reveal a broad and muscular body scantily covered by a bra and pink panties. However, when Lola removed Finn's shirt, the audience did not see breasts as they might have expected but rather a flat chest covered in thick brown hair. Lola then knelt in front of Finn to pantomime oral sex, and her physical position indicated that she was performing sex on a penis. Decoding these new signs via cultural gender rules would lead audiences to see Finn's chest hair and implied penis as unequivocal evidence he was a man. Thus, rather than a courtship ritual between a cross-dressed woman (Finn) and a cross-dressed man (Lola), the audience could infer they were watching a same-sex romance between a cross-dressed yet physically masculine man (Lola) and an effeminate but still male-assigned man (Finn).

The confusion escalated when Finn took off Lola's bra: her flat, muscular chest remained marginally covered by nipple pasties. Female-assigned performers must often use nipple coverings to avoid breaking antinudity regulations or laws. While male-assigned people or men who have completed top surgery are legally allowed to be topless in public settings, many US counties and cities—including, at the time of this performance, areas of California—have "obscenity" laws prohibiting similar public exposure of "female" nipples.[77] Therefore, Lola's nipple pasties seemed to indicate that her body had secondary sex characteristics that are legally and medically defined as female. So, whereas Finn and Lola could have been a binary but gender-bending couple or a same-sex couple with differing gender presentations, they now presented as a binary and cisgender heterosexual couple (Lola was the she and Finn was the he). Reflecting Dozier's conclusions about individuals in gender transition, their "behavior ha[d] not really changed, but people's assignation of meaning to that behavior" shifted based on public inferences of their bodies.[78] It was at this point that I realized (with some frustration) what a fool's errand I was on, trying to pin down the performer or the character or the relationship according to the body parts I was identifying.

The act ended as Lola shimmied her shoulders, grabbed the front of Finn's belt, and led him willingly offstage. In one respect, the audience was left without resolute answers or even stable building blocks about which identity elements constituted the real characters, the real performers, and the real relationship. Traditional drag logic would lead us to assume the stage picture could be accurately classified in opposition to the actor's reality. Thus, if we had concrete information that Finn was a woman performer, we could assume Finn's character was a man, and vice versa for Lola. The next logical step would be to classify the stage romance as heterosexual because of the gender contrast we nailed down through our sex-identity knowledge. However, this conclusion relies on some large assumptions about the performers and I actually do not know how these actors personally identified. Furthermore, even if Finn was competing in the Drag King Contest, I have already described how the title of drag king does not mean the performer is a woman. And, anyway, Finn and Lola were clearly deploying gender, body characteristics, and sexual overtures in ways incongruous with the ideological concept that "sex, gender, and sexual orientation align in highly correlated, relatively fixed, binary categories."[79] In short, their bodies and expressions were presented as too slippery to be fixed in any type of discrete box. Thus, I argue, Finn and Lola's act was intended to confront the method of publicly sexing bodies and then using this knowledge to categorize relationships and desires.

Finn and Lola might not have presented readable gender and sexual orientation identities, but the audience did have a very clear way of understanding them: they were completely comprehensible in terms of their mutual interest and connection with one another. Their increasingly queer presentations and behaviors did not disrupt their romantic and sexual interest for one another at any point. On the contrary, their exploration of these different levels of expression and connection propelled them into multiple romantic tableaux. Genderfucking is a method of not only aggressively deconstructing identity but also developing new forms of identification and presenting them as valid even though (or especially if) they are culturally unintelligible. In light of the thunderous applause this act received and its second-place finish in the contest, I suggest Finn and Lola's act effectively presented a bent picture of romance, broke the authority of sexed bodies and hegemonic gender roles in defining this, and created a coupling that was enthusiastically accepted as both queer and legitimate.

The final example I analyze here is the one I use every semester in my Introduction to Queer Studies class to illustrate the concept of genderfucking. It is Delicio Del Toro's winning act from the fourteenth annual Drag King Contest. Dressed in a silky red and yellow robe, black wrestling singlet, and short golden cape, with a gold and purple mask zipped over his head, Del Toro presented himself as a luchador (a lucha libre wrestler). As Pitbull's Spanish-language-infused song "I Know You Want Me" began to play, Del Toro wrestled with a doll resembling a *miniestrella* (short luchador). As exemplified in the description of masculine calavera figures in chapter 3, machismo connotes a form of masculine sexual prowess, pride, and power that is also specifically racialized (Latino or Chicano). Del Toro was performing as a Mexican wrestler, and, after winning his violent match against the miniestrella, he stripped off his mask to reveal brown skin, short curly hair, and a thick black mustache. Paired with his stout build, dark armpit hair, and bulging crotch, these features suggested the embodiment of this type of racialized machismo masculinity.

Next, Ricky Martin's "The Cup of Life" began to play, and Del Toro aggressively pulled down the top of his wrestling singlet, revealing very large breasts marginally covered by red-tasseled, silver nipple pasties. In the absence of a phallus, breasts make the short list of secondary sex characteristics most often employed to gender bodies. Ordinarily, Del Toro's reveal of breasts (further coded as women's breasts by the pasties) would serve as clear visual evidence that Del Toro was actually a woman under the macho wrestler act. As previously discussed, reveals have traditionally marked the ending of the drag performance by establishing the reality of the performer's body in contrast to the performance. So, in theory, the exposure of Del Toro's breasts should not only have indicated his offstage identity but also dissolved his machismo performance. Yet, Del Toro's body exposure did not trigger a change in his masculine physicality. In fact, he seemed to become more masculine, aggressively replicating the victory actions of men soccer stars who strip off their jerseys after a goal. Del Toro's continued (and convincing) embodiment of machismo shattered the assumed relationships between breasts and femininity, breasts and women's identities, and breasts and reduced masculinity.

But Del Toro's act was not simply a tribute to machismo, nor was it a one-note demonstration of how people with breasts can inhabit masculinity; Del Toro's act was also a critical disidentification with how racialized gender codes were culturally imposed on his brown body and simultaneously denied to his breasted body. Two parts of his act most clearly demonstrated this. First, Del Toro arranged to be showered with tortillas—an often pejoratively employed marker of Mexican culture—during a particularly aggressive moment in his topless victory dance. This moment mirrored the showering of Spanish bullfighters with roses but twisted this metaphor to build an uncomfortably racist tableau. Second, at the climax of his act, Del Toro exposed what had been bulging in his crotch area: a thick, tinfoil-wrapped burrito. Tearing back the top of the wrapping, Del Toro took a large bite and, in a symbolic act of ejaculation, sprayed the rest of the burrito's contents onto the (cheering) crowd. This action confronted the embodied parameters of machismo by reimagining how it might function on a body with breasts and a temporary-yet-functional phallus. Both parts of the act employed stereotypical and racist imagery to ridicule the seriousness of machismo. But Del Toro also successfully performed this masculine virility with exposed breasts and a burrito phallus and then was publicly "praised" for it with a tortilla shower. Thus, his act not only broke the assumed connection between body and gender expression but also genderfucked the solemn authority this racialized masculinity holds.

At first blush, a pink balloon, nipple pasties, or a burrito in the pants might not seem like very political objects. They certainly made the scenes silly and fun, weird and provocative, and greatly entertaining. But such qualities do not reduce their potential for political resonance or efficacy. In fact, each of these acts very carefully broke down limiting ideological relationships among gender, body, and sexuality and also reordered or reimagined what embodied selfhood could be. Furthermore, while many White performers I witnessed stayed away from actively queering racial identities, the performers of Color I analyzed here actively used this forum to disidentify from and fuck with constructs imposed on the racially marked body. And the drag acts that most explicitly utilized genderfucking techniques to problematize identity categories and express new ones were the ones that placed highest in the Drag King Contest.

QUEER COMMUNITY SPACE

Most of the acts I have discussed do not fit comfortably into canonical drag king parameters, and many are not even explicitly identified by performers or show literature as gender-bending. But all clearly demonstrate identity-queering intentions and employ bending methods, and all work toward the goal of producing micro- or macroforms of identity disjunction. A final critical step, then, is to explore where and how this type of wide-ranging disidentification drag can be most effective. Any performer may engage in a deviant identity practice or a defiant identity behavior, but such queer expressions can become acts of political resistance only when they engage with and influence others.[80] If one purpose of a disidentification act is to break down existing identities and build up new ones, its corollary second purpose is to alter audiences' thought processes or behaviors about what is a valid, important, and spreadable expression of selfhood. In this regard, the potential efficacy of this drag process—its impact factor—is tightly connected to the parameters of its performance space.

Throughout this book, I have demonstrated how a performer's intents and methods necessarily operate in conjunction with the atmosphere of a particular performance space and the majority audience such a space attracts. Here is an example that highlights the critical connection between disidentification drag and the place where it is enacted. While there are aesthetic similarities between historical US burlesque and female-femmeing, a big difference is that historical burlesque was performed predominantly in less reputable commercial theaters known for offering heterosexual erotica shows. In this regard, even if a performer were interested in incrementally expanding desire paradigms or shifting the parameters of feminine sexuality, it is unlikely her performance would have been accepted or interpreted as such by the majority of the clientele. Relatedly, Shapiro describes how members of the Disposable Boy Toys were uncomfortable doing their body-focused rendition of "Hey Big Spender" on a local university campus. While the act itself was intended to be both queer and transgressively femme, the troupe was concerned that the audience for this campus show would interpret their sexuality through a traditionally heteronormative lens.[81] In other words, the Disposable Boy Toys did not believe the audience most likely to attend this space would apprehend the act as a disidentification and thus be prompted to rethink and accept new forms of identity.

A critical feature of effective disidentification drag must then be a receptive audience or, more broadly, the development of a queer community space that audiences respect. While having a homogeneously like-minded queer audience might help drag artists accomplish their disidentification goals, this is likely an impossible audience to cultivate for any given theatrical performance. Rupp and Taylor note that the Key West–based 801 Cabaret attracts locals, tourists, queer people, and people who identify in heteronormative ways. But, despite the heterogeneity of audiences' beliefs, the 801's drag queens feel they are able to effectively expand concepts of gender, race, and sexuality as well as increase spectators' capacities for accepting differences.[82] The key is that, while the 801 Cabaret attracts all kinds, each audience member "buys in" when they make the choice to attend a drag queen show above a gay bar in queer-friendly Key West. In other words, everyone who steps into the space is very likely aware of what they are getting into (at least that they will need to be open to queer things) and what is generally expected in terms of nondiscriminatory behavior and reactions. The efficacy of these performances can then be measured in individual spectator's responses or in how each audience member says their attitudes and actions have changed as a result of their experience. While Rupp and Taylor collected this kind of detailed focus group data, they propose that efficacy can also be measured in terms of a sustained atmosphere, specifically the cultivation of a "sense of we-ness" among audience and performers.[83]

Relatedly, I argue that the efficacy of disidentification drag can be gauged by the most pervasively followed codes of conduct and iterated expressions of sentiment at community-based drag king events and queer drag events featuring drag kings. Disidentification acts present queer relational identities that model a queerer world or at least envision a queer space that celebrates such expressions. Actors certainly cannot fully control each spectator's interpretation of their acts, but I have witnessed ways performers and producers actively support this queer worldmaking goal in their environments. Take, for example, the Los Angeles–based event series Bent, which is held several times a year at small local venues such as Mr. T's Highland Park Bowl and Nightclub (see fig. 5.2). Bent shows are collections of solo and group acts, lip-synching, dancing, comedy, skits, and specialty skill acts. A show called *Drag in the Name of Love* began with a performance of "The Wanderer" by the drag king MC Landon Cider. The Beauty Kings then put on a choreographed musical number, the Miracle Whips led a sing-along about STI transmission among lesbians called "Showdown against Shame," a masculine belly dancer executed a sword dance, and several performers competed in a "baby drag king" contest. At their *Holidays Are a Drag* show some months later, performers presented a series of holiday-themed skits, Lucky Johnson did a masculine striptease, and Marlon Brandingo first performed in a tuxedo and then later did a femme strip as SheShe Chambray. Bent shows heavily incorporate audience participation and end with a dance party hosted by local DJs such as DJ Dru Wave.

Many of these acts engage in body-breaking or female-femmeing, and many also clearly reflect capacities of disidentification and genderfucking. Such lineups are carefully prepared by Bent organizer, Richelle South. South told me that any act is welcome to perform at Bent as long as it commits to Bent's overarching themes of inclusivity and queer community celebration.[84] Bent also advertises itself as a "genderfucking mind-altering experience" and "a night of drag, burlesque and genderfucking."[85] Its use of the term "genderfucking" linguistically marks the tone producers and organizers expect their shows to reflect. As South told me, Bent is intended to be an event where everyone feels comfortable doing identity in "whichever way" they desire.[86] In particular, South believes this atmosphere will encourage participants and spectators to be more open to seeing all expressions that occur at Bent as

Fig. 5.2. Right to left: Richelle South (Papa Cherry) and drag king Landon Cider preparing for a performance. *Photo courtesy of Vanessa Adams.*

"slightly bent" or "not quite straight."[87] In fact, South told me a prime reason for creating the Bent series in the first place was to build an inclusive space free from judgments about who did and did not belong in a queer community.[88] In other words, rather than suggesting that only some expressions in the Bent space are queer—or that some are more queer than others—Bent encourages spectators to assume all identity iterations are equal and similar in their queerness.

In addition to diverse lineups and welcoming promotional word choices, Landon Cider conveys Bent's inclusive ideology as the show's MC. During the *Holidays Are a Drag* show, Cider asked, "Do we have any lesbians or gay men in the audience?" immediately followed by "Do we have any queers in the audience?" When cheers were uproarious for the two categories in the first question, Cider verbally instructed audience members to also cheer for the second question and therefore identify themselves together in the third choice. Cider's sentiment here was clear: he felt that all people should behave in this space as if related and connected. This exemplifies an active way that producers both expressed Bent's overarching ideology and enforced it via group participation.

The appeal for audiences to apprehend all Bent acts and attendees as similar in their queerness reflects the politically salient method of creating group solidarity by emphasizing a shared identity of difference. However, as Cohen illustrates in her discussion of "mall invasion" actions, such as kiss-ins, this queerness rhetoric occludes intersectional issues that maintain stratification systems in minoritarian groups.[89] So, under the ideological umbrella of a unified queer community, some White drag actors feel empowered to appropriate and reproduce non-White racial signifiers in their performances. Halberstam mentions White drag kings who did "masculinities of Color" because racialized masculinities were more culturally visible and thus more theatrically accomplishable than the hegemonic invisibility of White heteromasculinity.[90] Given the genderfucking intents of disidentification drag, it makes sense that some performers will take up the relationships among race, gender, and sexuality in their deconstruction and fashioning of new identities. However, White drag performers can trivialize racial inequalities and reproduce racist structures if queer inclusivity is presumed to dissolve all other power structures or provide a space for groups in racial power to play with racial tropes without consequence. Thus, in designing an inclusive queer drag space—one that both unites and is attentive to power and difference—producers must be clear about their guidelines for genderfucking to ensure that it is actively antiracist.

There is one more important way that Bent maintains its specific atmosphere. South calls Bent a "community stage show" because it does not insist on building a figurative "fourth wall" to divide stage practices from audience participation. I witnessed many acts in which performers came off the stage to interact with the crowd, sing to individual audience members, hand out favors, or perform a call-and-response with them. One of the most visible aspects of this interactional structure is Cider's regular "get to know your neighbor" segment. Around the halfway point of Bent shows, the house lights go up and Cider asks everyone to introduce themselves to one another, shake hands, and talk about their foremost "passion." Cider explains to the audience that describing a passion is more meaningful than identifiers such as employment or sexual orientation. At the *Holidays Are a Drag* show, I shook hands with an individual who discussed their love of riding motorcycles, and I, like an academic nerd, described my passion for learning. South told me that Cider chooses to do this activity at almost every Bent show and that these segments are important because they create a context for attendees to verbally interact and physically touch. The integration of interludes such as these into Bent events are clear forms of coalition building: they foster familiarity among individuals who might then feel more compelled to accept, defend, and celebrate each other. Actually, South told me that it is often hard to get Bent shows back on track after this segment because audience members will not stop sharing with each another.[91]

At Bent, a variety of queer performances, and their unequivocal acceptance as such, point spectators away from assuming they can definitively mark what is and is not queer. While audience members are free to infer what they will about a given act, making narrow conclusions about it will conflict with the overarching sentiment designed by and continually telegraphed at Bent. Bailey similarly documents the types of labor that ballroom organizers and participants do in order to ensure balls are inclusive community atmospheres, or spaces where individuals can self-fashion and express a range of gender and sexual identities without fearing the same degree of censure or violence they face in phobic public spheres.[92] Balls and Bent events are ostensibly framed as theatrical shows featuring, among other things, a variety of gender-bending acts and interesting queer possibilities. Yet, the formation and maintenance of queer physical and ideological space around these shows is intrinsic to the efficacy of these acts' intents and methods, especially if they employ a disidentification process. This framework encourages spectators and performers alike to accept all expressions as queer and to celebrate the potentiality of such expressions.

QUEER WORDS, QUEER WORLDS

The Drag King Book, published in 1999, cautions spectators to "assign no biological sexes [. . .] in fact, realness or authenticity is not the best measure of Drag King status, and we can only measure realness in terms of each king's investment and each audience's response."[93] Although it is unclear which author (or if a performer) expressed this sentiment, the statement offers a clear and valid critique of the canonical drag discourse model that echoes my own. In each chapter of this book, I have illustrated how rote biological categorization and hegemonic concepts of authenticity are poor tools for apprehending drag and can in fact act as red herrings for our explanations and analyses. If we do not question the canonical premise that theatrical gender-bending is a projection of gender that contrasts to the reality of the performer's assigned sex, then the majority of acts described in these pages cannot be known as drag. In fact, some acts I have discussed in this chapter alone—female-femmeing, for example—would be categorized as the opposite of drag.

It is true that defining a particular performance as drag or not drag does little to alter its physical parameters and perhaps little to influence the transmission of meaning between one performer and one spectator. Many performances have a visceral impact that will not change simply or easily just by changing what we choose to call them. But discourses are not just definitional terms; they are also forms of knowledge that can be archived, disseminated, and used as authoritative measures of meaning. Moreover, if the queer world that an act creates is spreadable to macrorealms only via spectators' communications about it, then indeed drag discourse has the power to stymie the performance's full potentiality. The disidentification and genderfucking acts described in this chapter were designed to expand the scope of queer possibility. And I suggest that a simple way to nudge both microperformance spaces and larger mass publics into acknowledging and spreading this type of queerness is simply to call these acts drag. The fact that there are acts in contemporary drag king and queer drag forums that have never been documented or discussed in drag scholarship is strong evidence for why we need to start referring to them as drag. But instead of simply squishing these acts into the canonical parameters of drag discourse (as the director did when contextualizing the *I Dream of Jeannie* act described in chapter 1), I see more value in discursively refiguring drag to capture the intents, methods, and impacts of a broad range of queer identity acts. From this discursive position, it is much easier to investigate how a given embodied expression could substantively contribute to a queerer world.

Let me take one step back: not all acts in contemporary drag king forums—not even all those that call themselves drag kinging—are intended to be political attempts at queer worldmaking. In fact, Halberstam writes that "many [drag king] performers are not necessarily that interested in the theoretical import of their acts or even in identifying a larger context" for their performances.[94] When I asked about the political significance of Bent events, South replied: "At the end of the day [it's] just entertainment."[95] Sometimes a drag show or a drag act is just intended as a bit of fun. Accordingly, performers engage with whatever methods and ideologies best enable them to achieve this desired product. And yet, I return to the concept of space, or where drag kings and queer drag performers most frequently locate their work. The acts I describe are produced for small-scale events and queer clubs in progressive cities. Neither these spaces nor these acts are profitable large-scale commercial enterprises that must create products to appease certain mass markets. Yet, even when the primary reason for this type of drag is "only" fun, the fun is almost always rooted in breaking apart those solemn identity rules that order majoritarian and even minoritarian communities. In this regard, acts are modeling "a disempowered politics or positionality that has been rendered unthinkable by the dominant culture."[96] Acts that take place in these forums and exhibit disidentification and gender-fucking drag processes should be assessed for their political efficacy, specifically in their ability to bring forth a queerer world space. These types of gender-bending acts are certainly fun, but they also queer identity in a way that, to borrow Cohen's terminology, demonstrates the "radical potential of queer politics."[97]

NOTES

1. The Drag King Contest is held annually in San Francisco, California. It includes featured and competing acts, group song-and-dance numbers, specialty talents, strip artists, transformation performers, go-go dancers, celebrity guest judges, and often the political drag queen troupe the Sisters of Perpetual Indulgence makes an appearance.

2. Kessler and McKenna, *Gender*, 150.

3. Ibid., 151.

4. Some events clearly label themselves and their acts with the term *drag king* (e.g., the annual Drag King Contest). However, most events featuring drag kings include a variety of acts. Moreover, many shows featuring drag kings do not bill themselves strictly as drag king shows (e.g., the Bent series). In this chapter, I make an effort to refer to both drag king shows and queer drag shows that feature drag kings, although this distinction is largely linguistic rather than to highlight an important difference in performance makeup.

5. Halberstam, *Female Masculinity*, 232.

6. Senelick, *Changing Room*, 492, 295.

7. Ibid., 492.

8. Shapiro, "Disposable Boy Toys," 4. Noah Boyz is the drag king persona of Shapiro, a former member of the Disposable Boy Toys.

9. Muñoz, *Disidentifications*, 5.

10. Ibid., 3.

11. Halberstam, *Female Masculinity*, 246–255, 249.

12. Quoted in Volcano and Halberstam, *Drag King Book*, 111.

13. Newton, "Dick(less) Tracy and the Homecoming Queen," 172.

14. Ibid., 175.

15. Lorber, *Paradoxes of Gender*, 13.

16. I say "educated speculating" because my claims about performers' assigned sex, gender identity, and sexuality are largely inferred from performers' own word choices and public promotion.

17. Only a handful of studies on drag kinging exist, and most of these are dated. Some major differences between well-known scholarly accounts of kinging and my own ethnographic observations are undoubtedly due to the development of new theatrical conventions and changes in cultural, social, and political sentiments toward gender and sexuality. This chapter represents an updated source on drag kinging and other drag practices that occur in drag kinging spaces. But I also acknowledge that this work is located in its own specific time and place context (2008–2012) and should be met with future critiques and updates.

18. Newton, *Mother Camp*, 5.

19. Halberstam, *Female Masculinity*, 233.

20. DiFranco, *Art of Drag Kinging*, 34.

21. Bourne et al., "Belle Reprieve," 150. Case ("Toward a Butch/Femme Aesthetic") and Davy ("Fe/Male Impersonation") argue that when Shaw or Weaver performed masculinity, it was intended to represent a readable aspect of butch/femme lesbian identity and was not traditional drag.

22. Torr and Bottoms, *Sex, Drag, and Male Roles*, 34.

23. Halberstam, *Female Masculinity*, 250, 250–253.

24. Torr and Bottoms, *Sex, Drag, and Male Roles*, 28.

25. Halberstam, *Female Masculinity*, 252.

26. Torr and Bottoms, *Sex, Drag, and Male Roles*, 198.

27. Ibid., 199.

28. Senelick, *Changing Room*, 492.

29. DiFranco, *Art of Drag Kinging*, 286.

30. Newton, "Dick(less) Tracy and the Homecoming Queen," 165.

31. Schacht and Underwood, "Absolutely Flawless," 4.

32. Senelick, *Changing Room*, 492.

33. Rupp, Taylor, and Shapiro, "Drag Queens and Drag Kings," 278.

34. Ibid., 276.

35. Ibid., 277.

36. Halberstam, *Female Masculinity*, 232.

37. DiFranco, *Art of Drag Kinging*, 9.

38. Shapiro, "Disposable Boy Toys," 5.

39. DiFranco, *Art of Drag Kinging*, 12. While anyone can do kinging, in Volcano's estimation the gender created onstage by a drag king will be masculine (Volcano and Halberstam, *Drag King Book*, 16).

40. Windh and Volcano, "Gender Fusion," 133.

41. *A Drag King Extravaganza*.

42. LeBesco, "Introduction," 2.

43. Rupp and Taylor, *Drag Queens at the 801 Cabaret*, 218.
44. Rupp, Taylor, and Shapiro, "Drag Queens and Drag Kings," 278.
45. Rupp and Taylor, *Drag Queens at the 801 Cabaret*, 218.
46. Miracle Whips, Facebook.com. Accessed September 9, 2015. (Note that the page is currently deactivated.)
47. The Beauty Kings, Facebook.com. Accessed September 9, 2015.
48. Ibid.
49. Richelle South is a founder/organizer of Bent and was a member of The Beauty Kings during my ethnographic work. I am much indebted to South for actively participating in and supporting this project.
50. Miracle Whips, Facebook.com. Accessed September 9, 2015.
51. For example, see Kentucky Fried Woman's discussion of the marginalization and disavowal of "faux queens" at events like the International Drag King (Community) Extravaganza during the late 1990s and early 2000s, "Fat... Fierce... Kentucky Fried," in *Femmes of Power* (175–179) and *A Drag King Extravaganza*.
52. Harris and Crocker, "Introduction to Sustaining Femme Gender," 1.
53. Ibid., 3.
54. Muñoz, *Disidentifications*, 4.
55. Ibid., 31.
56. Martin and Kazyak, "Hetero-Romantic Love and Heterosexiness," 330.
57. Ibid., 328.
58. Clare, *Exile and Pride*, 111–114.
59. Quoted in Shapiro, "Disposable Boy Toys," 175.
60. Kentucky Fried Woman, "Fat... Fierce... Kentucky Fried," 175–179; Shapiro, "Disposable Boy Toys," 175–200.
61. Rupp, in conversations with the author.
62. Miracle Whips, Facebook.com. Accessed September 9, 2015.
63. Sally, "It Is the Ugly That Is So Beautiful," 7.
64. South, interview with the author, December 18, 2011.
65. Rupp and Taylor, *Drag Queens at the 801 Cabaret*, 218.
66. Kessler and McKenna, *Gender*, 151.
67. Dozier, "Beards, Breasts, and Bodies," 304–305.
68. Wiegman, *American Anatomies*, 4.
69. Bent, Facebook.com. Accessed December 5, 2011.
70. Although Urban Dictionary is not a scholarly source, it is peer reviewed: definitions are voted on by users. This is the top entry on the site because it has received 542 positive and 197 negative votes as of July 23, 2019.
71. Reich, "Genderfuck," 255.
72. Connell, "Masculinities and Globalization," 16.
73. Connell, *Masculinities*, 76–77.
74. See Crenshaw, "Mapping the Margins" and Connell, *Masculinities*.

75. I call Finn's partner Lola because the entertainer was unnamed but the couple performed to the song "Lola" by the Kinks and partially acted out narratives from the song.

76. The Kinks, "Lola," written by Ray Davis (1970).

77. As a public entertainment location, the DNA Lounge may have been subject to a California Penal Code regarding "indecent exposure." Although legal debates over the classification of breasts or nipples as "genitals" are ongoing, many female-assigned performers cover nipples to avoid potential charges.

78. Dozier, "Beards, Breasts, and Bodies," 308.

79. Ibid., 297.

80. Cohen, "Deviance as Resistance," 40.

81. Shapiro, "Disposable Boy Toys," 110, 197.

82. Rupp and Taylor, *Drag Queens at the 801 Cabaret*, 219.

83. Ibid.

84. South, interview with the author, December 18, 2011.

85. Bent, Facebook.com. Accessed December 5, 2011. Bent's public Facebook profile now reads: "A variety show dedicated to bending the gender binary" (July 2019). The language I cite was on Bent's Facebook page for many years and still remains in some online materials that advertise and promote its events.

86. South, interview with the author, December 18, 2011. South personally prefers the term *gender-bending* to *genderfucking* and feels that they have similar meanings. *Genderfucking* was more heavily used in Bent advertising at the time of my ethnographic work, and South told me it was because the term was more attention grabbing.

87. Ibid.

88. Ibid. When asked about the participation of individuals who identify as heterosexual, South stated that they are welcome. Although the inclusion of heteronormative people might conflict with Bent's "not quite straight" ideology, I find South's statement to further reflect the mission and tone of inclusivity cultivated at Bent events.

89. Cohen, "Punks, Bulldaggers, and Welfare Queens," 449.

90. Halberstam, *Female Masculinity*, 234–235.

91. South, interview with the author, December 18, 2011.

92. Bailey, *Butch Queens Up in Pumps*, 33–37.

93. Volcano and Halberstam, *Drag King Book*, 36.

94. Halberstam, *Female Masculinity*, 242.

95. South, interview with the author, December 18, 2011.

96. Muñoz, *Disidentifications*, 31.

97. Cohen, "Punks, Bulldaggers, and Welfare Queens," 458.

Conclusion

Bending Rhetoric

IN ATTEMPTING TO trace the discourse of drag, I have explored many examples of gender-bending performance. I was fortunate enough to witness some of the acts I discuss, and I also have a strong personal background in theater performance and production. But many acts described in these pages are accessible only via curated archives and other published accounts. I—like other scholars—necessarily draw from these materials to describe historical drag acts and their impact. My experience with these textual sources has been that they most often centralize or emphasize drag's significance in visible contrast between whatever is being performed onstage and whatever might constitute offstage authenticity. So, when performance scholars such as I draw on these materials, we must always remember to resist seeing their mediated framing as objective truth or even baseline reality. My task in this book has been to prove the necessity of this active engagement, and I have attempted to do so by demonstrating the limitations of drag discourse when compared with the complexities of bending practices. Similarly, Taylor cautions against using "authenticity" to measure theatrical performance. Instead, she guides us to focus on a performance's "efficaciousness," or how successful a given theatrical act is at transmitting its intended message.[1]

I have scrutinized the bending work of male impersonators who staked their livelihoods on the successful transmission of cisgender identities while singing, "If you'd like to love a soldier, you can all love me."[2] I have documented the form of bending that teatristas used to give themselves a revisionary "freedom" over the implications of their embodied racial-gendered subject positions.[3] I have outlined how the bending work DeLarverie did with the Jewel Box Revue transmitted a queer counteridentification that was both dangerous and also a politically salient call to "rebellion."[4] And I have documented how acts at drag king and queer drag shows are "not quite straight" when they disidentify from cultural identity formations and model new forms of identity.[5] These are innovative and complex bending acts that cannot be fully captured by myopically focusing on the comparison of "authentic" sex to performed gender. I have shown how shifting the focus to specific intents—money, activism, affiliation, genderfucking—and readable performance methods reveals a more comprehensive picture of drag. Yet, even when united under my revised gender-bending umbrella, these performances do not build toward any singular objective narrative or authentic definition. Just the opposite: they offer a fragmented mosaic of gender-bending, a series of partial drag perspectives that enrich our overall understanding of what the genre could be as well as what an efficacious drag practice could accomplish.

I conclude this project as all good scholars feel compelled to do, by dwelling on its limitations. Specifically, I use these final pages to discuss three important issues that have continually bracketed this project: (1) the issue of taxonomy, (2) the issue of queer spread, and (3) the issue of stage practice. In chapter 1, I addressed these as delimiting components of my project. Here, I consider them in the context of the careful negotiations scholars must attend to when translating performance into prose and prose into applicable theory. First is the issue of taxonomy projects. I built a redefinition for drag, and thus I reshaped the parameters of the existing drag taxonomy. Taxonomies are tricky things: they not only classify organisms and objects but also position themselves as the objective authority in forming such boundaries. In my Feminist Theories course, I spend a week and a half going over feminist concerns regarding taxonomy and typology projects. This discussion is critically important because the West has a fraught history with taxonomy projects, both building these divisions in culturally biased (and individually harmful) ways and also cementing them into the cultural imagination as objective and essential truths. Foucault famously describes the Victorian process of naming, grouping, cataloging, explaining, and ranking nonmarried (and therefore deviant) sexual practices. The institutionalization of this taxonomy served to actualize sexual "heterogeneities," which was the opposite of the expressed intention of "banish[ing]" bad sex from popular knowledge and practice. But Foucault articulates another key outcome of the taxonomy of sexual acts: it also served as a taxonomy of individuals and identities, an ideological "implantation" that enabled even more punitive forms of cultural oppression and stratification.[6]

By reworking the existing definition of drag, I might be forming boundaries akin to those that have stalled scholars' abilities to convey the complex queerness of drag. I likewise understand that by placing a range of queer practices into my revised drag taxonomy, I might be removing them from an important peripheral realm; one might argue that it is the very quality of being undefined, unnamed, and unintelligible that makes queer performance queer. I do not wish to limit or foreclose queer performance by smooshing it into a new drag discourse or taxonomy. But neither do I desire to continue limiting and foreclosing these acts by using the terms and logic presently available. To be honest, I did not originally set out to write a theoretical intervention in drag language or to refashion the taxonomy of drag. As a graduate student in theater studies, I was interested in the directorial motivations, actor methods, and audience reactions connected with contemporary cross casting. But at a certain point in my studies it became nearly impossible to communicate my thoughts about gender-bending without employing assumptive, essentialist, and nonintersectional language about the performer and the product. Perhaps this would have troubled me less had I not been a teaching assistant in the Department of Feminist Studies at the time, where I was constantly reiterating to students the importance of language and logic choices that frame identities as cultural constructs rather than givens. So, I set out to build myself a little linguistic tool to help me avoid problematic words and ideas when explaining my work on gender-bending. Since I built it, I have used this tool almost every day of my life.

Lorde writes about the use-value and complicity of tools that help some social actors navigate the master's house but do not dismantle its divisive structures.[7] My redefinition is a tool, and my drag taxonomy is a renovation. By functioning within the framework of the house, the produced materials may still "sustain and reinforce social-political power structures."[8] But there is also value in undoing some of the reductions and exclusions that the existing structures of the house have maintained. I have attempted to do this by tracing the feminist path Code outlines for her own taxonomy project, the *Encyclopedia of Feminist Theories*: first, to form "working definition[s]" that do not "claim once-and-for-all accuracy" and, second, to design a taxonomy that future scholars can add to, reframe, and reshape as suits the changing need of the field.[9]

The second issue is regarding the scope of queer spread, which became the unintended through line of my graduate course on the politics of gender-bending. My savvy students enjoyed parsing the queer worldmaking potential in a range of bent public identity practices. However, drawing on the definition of queer as askew from or out of sync with the hegemony, they constantly queried the point at which queer spread spreads too far into the public domain to remain queer. Berlant and Warner characterize queer worlds as unbounded by community or group affiliation; they are defined instead by the inclusion of unlimited people and "more spaces than can be mapped beyond a few reference points."[10] I have likewise characterized the queerness of drag as being able to include but not be tethered to a particular minoritarian identity or queer counterpublic. As I argued in the previous chapter, the purpose of radically queer drag is to enact influential queer ideas about identity that "unsettle the garbled but powerful norms" of both majoritarian and minoritarian systems.[11] But at what point is this queer work accomplished, and does its completion unmoor queer acts from their queerness?

In addition to considering the end goal of queer accomplishment, as I have done in this book, we must also consider the end point of effective queer spread. That is to say, we must interrogate when and how a queer act loses its ability to produce a culturally queer (thus effectively queer) impact. Drag practices are rooted in the presentation of queer identity relationships, and I have shown how that queerness can materialize as various forms of disjunction from either majoritarian or minoritarian ideologies. In removing sex-gender contrast as the "fixed referent" for drag, I have also illustrated drag's various potentialities for producing this queer cultural effect.[12] And yet, these various potentialities must always be located in opposition to centralized cultural standards because the division between compliance and queerness is culturally contingent. In this regard, a queer act (or the production of a queer effect) is not guaranteed to maintain its queerness forever but only for as long as it holds an outsider or marginal position. If a radically queer gender-bending act is successful in achieving its intended goal of spreading queerness, its accomplishment may render it no longer effectively queer.

This loss of a position at the margins because of effective centralization is aptly characterized in Duggan's articulation of homonormativity.[13] In cultures that value heteronormativity and presume compulsory heterosexuality, people with same-sex desires will be marked by medical, government, law, and other institutions as different and deviant, and therefore marginal. But Duggan demonstrates how a homosexual identity can be integrated into this majoritarian system if the subject's lifestyle otherwise reflects what the hegemony values. So homonormative people are more welcomed into the Western cultural center when they have privileged identities such as Whiteness and cisness and when they participate in consumer culture, nationalism, and domesticity. In contrast, Muñoz notes, queerness is always "not quite here."[14] Queer people and queer acts can be integrated into the center, but queerness cannot. Thus, the process of spreading queer ideas or actions is also the process of unqueering them.

My graduate students and I agreed that an effective, radically queer practice would, at some point, spread to the point of dilution. An important aspect to consider, though, is whether that queer iteration becomes diluted by norms or whether norms become fundamentally altered by queerness. The fact that there is an end point to queer effectiveness does not invalidate the queering process itself. In a not-too-distant point in US history, the type of drag queening on *RuPaul's Drag Race* was far too queer for mainstream television broadcasting. Like many acts discussed in this book, drag queening was seen as an action of outright defying rather than subtly reifying gender divisions. Queening was also known as the cultural product of homosexual men—a decidedly queered social group. Whereas cross casting and female impersonation made the rounds in respectable theaters and early cinema, drag queening was generally relegated to nightclubs, bars, queer events, and house parties. Even the most basic form of queening could be an act of defiance, of genderfucking, or of actively bolstering a queer space that allowed such queer expressions to happen. In the preface to this book, I discussed Mary Cheney's reaction to *RuPaul's Drag Race*, specifically her suspicion that drag queening mocked women. It is of note that Cheney was not scandalized by the notion of drag queens in general nor by how performers might contextualize queening as a public extension of their homosexual identities. In fact, her nonchalance is a sign that, at some point between that not-too-distant history and now, there was a significant shift in the positions of gay men and drag queening within the cultural imagination. This shift is, in part, connected to the worldmaking efforts of drag queens in nightclubs, bars, queer events, and house parties and, in part, to queens like RuPaul who spread this work into larger and more mainstream public domains. The fact that drag queening is no longer guaranteed to manifest queerness is proof of its potential efficaciousness. As with taxonomy projects, the queer part of a queer act must always constitute a working definition and methodological process rather than a fixed object, ideology, or outcome.

My final issue is regarding my dogged primary engagement with theatrical stage practice; reflecting on this aspect of my study also allows me to discuss the potential applicability of drag discourse analysis to other forms of public performance. As my background in theater studies suggests, I have always been keen to explore practices that occur in that magical, cordoned space devoted to fictive play. As noted in chapter 1, individuals do many mundane or fantastic forms of gender expression, play, and performance in their daily lives. These gender doings and gender bendings make for many types of rich discussion and analysis. In fact, my sibling field of performance studies often frames such non-formally staged public acts of expressive communication as key cultural performances. But as I mentioned in that first chapter, there is a specific quality of the formalized theater space that fascinates me, and this quality is intrinsic to the way gender-bending performance has been framed. Everyday doings of gender and even strategic public gender expressions are contextualized as realities or as fictive expressions that are nevertheless part of the real world and carry real and lasting consequences. Theater performers certainly deploy acting methods that draw on their realities and express messages that can have lasting and spreadable consequences. Despite this, the theater is contextualized as a space apart, where realities do not constitute a critical factor in what is done and what is done does not have critical consequences in reality. Theater is instead framed as a space that facilitates the transmission of a particular narrative message or a particular sensory or emotional experience. Thus, performance-based elements (a man playing a woman character) that deviate from offstage norms or realities are presumed to be done for the sake of effect or practical necessity (the show must go on!). And audiences are asked to willingly suspend their disbelief in order to experience the fullness of this.

That magical, cordoned aspect of the theater—and its prioritization of narrative over authenticity or reality—is the reason that I, as a high schooler, was able to play Shakespearean characters even though I had braces on my teeth; why I played characters decades older than me; why I played parts written for men actors. At my all-girls high school, plays were primarily cast with the available pool of actors, which was teen girls. Audiences were aware of our embodied divergences from our characters, but they willingly suspended this realization to follow the meaning and message of the show. In college, I wanted to audition for the role of Roy Cohn in *Angels in America* because I thought I would be good at it. Roy is a man, the character is traditionally played by a man actor, the director for this particular production had no vision for cross-casting the role, and there were ample men to play the part. Thus, despite the audience's *capacity* to willingly suspend their disbelief regarding the gender divergence between me and the character, I did not even read for the role.[15] I was cast in the show, though, as the Angel, a mystical and divine character that floats down from a shattered obelisk and talks to people in their dreams. This casting experience taught me that while theater is a space for fantasy and telling stories about the fantastical, there are indeed some key lines of reality and permissibility that permeate even this space. When it comes to bending or breaking gender rules onstage, there must be a clearly articulated impetus and a clearly communicated message about its intended meaning. Certainly, theater spaces and performances can be as open and progressive as we choose to make them. But the space itself is not automatically free from the ideologies that shape everyday life or the regulations that force gender compliance. The mythos that theater is free from the punitive consequences that beset offstage gender bending is ultimately just that—a mythos.

With that said, my focus on the intents, methods, and impacts of theatrically staged bending necessarily leads me to speculate about the use of such analysis when evaluating other public forms of gender performance. I have begun to catalog how drag discourse is used in entertainment news, television shows, and social media to characterize public figures that do gender in nonnormative ways. Drag terms are not just reserved for what happens on *RuPaul's Drag Race*; they are also used to explain why "Casey Legler, the first female to be signed as a male model" is commercially successful (she has a "knack for gender-bending").[16] Zoe Chace, a reporter for National Public Radio's music site *The Record*, declares that "there are some pop stars right now who look a lot like drag queens—Lady Gaga, Nicki Minaj, Beyoncé, Katy Perry, even Ke$ha."[17] Since these celebrities have publicly identified as ciswomen, I am not assuming that Chace means these performers look like they are "individuals who publicly perform being women in front of an audience that knows they are 'men' regardless of how compellingly female—'real'—they might appear otherwise."[18] However, Chace is drawing on an assumption embedded in traditional drag discourse that heightened or queer public exhibitions of gender are not real and, in fact, contrast with reality. Thus, drag is mobilized to explain why the femininity expressed by these ciswomen does not look normal or natural, as Chace implicitly assumes it should on normal or natural ciswomen. This drag tag ultimately implies that the gender done by Gaga or Beyoncé or Legler is not an authentic expression of their selfhood but rather a fictive performance with a clearly articulated impetus and a clearly communicated message about its intended meaning.

It disturbs and fascinates me that entertainment media are so casual about using drag discourse to explain these types of gender expression. While I have centered my study on theater practice, it is clear that the scope of drag discourse extends far beyond the formalized stage. In theory, referring to various public gender expressions as drag could unmoor them from sex essentialism and trigger a discussion about the performativity of gender within various cultural contexts. So perhaps this is a useful linguistic tool for starting conversations about the performability of identity, the constructedness of cisgender realities, and the many ways people do gender. But rather than simply accepting drag metaphors as good tools for unpacking offstage gender doings, we must first consider what is built into such discourses. My focus in this book has been to illuminate a major problem with how gender-bending intents and methods have been translated and disseminated as discursive knowledge products and to propose new models for doing this work. This same focus can help illuminate the cultural impacts of applying terms such as *gender-benders* and *drag queens* to women menswear models and fabulously femme pop stars. And while I must leave this work for another project, academics do write second books.

NOTES

1. Taylor, *Archive and the Repertoire*, 13.
2. De Frece, *Recollections of Vesta Tilley*, 137.
3. Diane Rodriguez, quoted in Broyles-González, "Living Legacy of Chicana Performers," 50.
4. This phrasing is in reference to DeLarverie's preferred term for Stonewall.
5. South, interview with the author, December 18, 2011.
6. Foucault, *The History of Sexuality*, 36–37.
7. Lorde, *Sister Outsider*, 112.
8. Code, "Introduction," xvi.
9. Ibid., xvii.
10. Berlant and Warner, "Sex in Public," 558.
11. Ibid., 548.
12. Eng, Halberstam, and Muñoz, "What's Queer about Queer Theory Now?" 1–2.
13. Duggan, "New Homonormativity," 179.

14. Muñoz, *Cruising Utopia*, 21.

15. The role was earned by Eric Parks, who is now a successful professional stage and screen actor, so it was probably the right casting choice.

16. Peppers, "It's Easier to Model as a Man Than a Woman," 2013.

17. Chace, "Pop Personae," 2010.

18. Schacht and Underwood, "Absolutely Flawless," 4.

BIBLIOGRAPHY

Althusser, Louis. *Lenin and Philosophy and Other Essays*. Translated by Ben Brewster. New York: Monthly Review, 1971.

Anzaldúa, Gloria. *Borderlands/La Frontera: The New Mestiza*. San Francisco: Spinsters/Aunt Lute Books, 1987.

Aston, Elaine. "Male Impersonation in the Music Hall: The Case of Vesta Tilley." *New Theatre Quarterly* 4, no. 15 (1988): 247–257.

Bailey, Marlon M. *Butch Queens Up in Pumps: Gender, Performance, and Ballroom Culture in Detroit*. Ann Arbor: University of Michigan Press, 2013.

———. "Gender/Racial Realness: Theorizing the Gender System in Ballroom Culture." *Feminist Studies* 37, no. 2 (2011): 365–386.

Barad, Karen. "Posthumanist Performativity: Toward an Understanding of How Matter Comes to Matter." *Signs* 28, no. 3 (2003): 801–831.

Beauty Kings, The. Facebook. Accessed September 9, 2015. https://www.facebook.com/pages/The-BeautyKings/114499308583403?sk=info.

Bent. Facebook. December 5, 2011. Accessed July 23, 2019. https://www.facebook.com/pages/Bent/165426663939?sk=info.

Bentley, Gladys. "I Am a Woman Again." *Ebony Magazine*, August 1952.

Berlant, Lauren, and Michael Warner. "Sex in Public." *Critical Inquiry* 24, no. 2 (1998): 547–566.

Bornstein, Kate. *Gender Outlaw: On Men, Women, and the Rest of Us*. New York: Vintage Books, 1994.

Bourne, Bette, Paul Shaw, Peggy Shaw, and Louis Weaver. "Belle Reprieve." In *Split Britches: Lesbian Practice/Feminist Performance*, edited by Sue-Ellen Case, 149–184. London: Routledge, 1996.

Brockett, Oscar G., and Franklin J. Hildy. *History of the Theatre*. 10th ed. Boston: Pearson, 2008.

Broyles-González, Yolanda. "Foreword." In *Teatro Chicana: A Collective Memoir and Selected Plays*, edited by Laura E. Garcia, Sandra M. Gutierrez, and Felicitas Nunez, x–xviii. Austin: University of Texas Press, 2008.

———. "The Living Legacy of Chicana Performers: Preserving History through Oral Testimony." *Frontiers* 11, no. 1 (1990): 48–52.

———. "The Powers of Women's Words: Oral Tradition and Performance Art." In *A Companion to Latina/o Studies*, edited by Juan Flores and Renato Rosaldo, 116–125. Malden, MA: Blackwell, 2007.

———. *El Teatro Campesino: Theater in the Chicano Movement*. Austin: University of Texas Press, 1994.

Butler, Judith. *Bodies That Matter: On the Discursive Limits of "Sex."* New York: Routledge, 1993.

———. *Excitable Speech: A Politics of the Performative*. New York: Routledge, 1997.

———. *Gender Trouble: Feminism and the Subversion of Identity*. 1990. 10th anniversary ed. Reprint, New York: Routledge, 1999.

———. "Performative Acts and Gender Constitution: An Essay in Phenomenology and Feminist Theory." *Theatre Journal* 40, no. 4 (1988): 519–531.

Capó, Julio, Jr. *Welcome to Fairyland: Queer Miami before 1940*. Chapel Hill: University of North Carolina Press, 2017.

Cárdenas de Dwyer, Carlota. "The Development of Chicano Drama and Luis Valdez's Actos." In *Modern Chicano Writers: A Collection of Critical Essays*, edited by Joseph Sommers and Tomás Ybarra-Frausto, 160–168. Englewood Cliffs, NJ: Prentice-Hall, 1979.

Case, Sue-Ellen. "Classic Drag: The Greek Creation of Female Parts." *Theatre Journal* 37, no. 3 (1985): 317–327.

———. "Toward a Butch/Femme Aesthetic." In *Camp: Queer Aesthetics and the Performing Subject*, edited by Fabio Cleto, 185–199. Ann Arbor: University of Michigan Press, 1999.

Chace, Zoe. "Pop Personae: Why Do Some Women Perform in Character?" *NPR Music*, August 12, 2010. Accessed July 24, 2019. http://www.npr.org/blogs/therecord/2010/08/11/129134759/pop-personae-why-do-some-women-perform-in-character.

Chu, Grace. "An Interview with Lesbian Stonewall Veteran Stormé DeLarverie." *After Ellen*, July 26, 2010. Accessed July 19, 2019. http://www.afterellen.com/people/77167-an-interview-with-lesbian-stonewall-veteran-storm-delarverie.

Clare, Eli. *Exile and Pride: Disability, Queerness, and Liberation*. Durham, NC: Duke University Press, 1999.

Code, Lorraine. "Introduction." In *Encyclopedia of Feminist Theories*, edited by Lorraine Code, xv–xxvi. London: Routledge, 2000.

Cohen, Cathy J. "Deviance as Resistance: A New Research Agenda for the Study of Black Politics." *Du Bois Review* 1, no. 1 (2004): 27–45.

———. "Punks, Bulldaggers, and Welfare Queens: The Radical Potential of Queer Politics?" *GLQ: A Journal of Lesbian and Gay Studies* 3, no. 4 (1997): 437–465.

Coleridge, Samuel Taylor. *Biographia Literaria: or Biographical Sketches of My Literary Life and Opinions*, vol 1. New York: Holt and Williams, 1872.

Connell, R. W. *Masculinities*. Berkeley: University of California Press, 2005.

———. "Masculinities and Globalization." *Men and Masculinities* 1, no. 1 (1998): 3–23.

Crenshaw, Kimberlé. "Mapping the Margins: Intersectionality, Identity Politics, and Violence against Women of Color." *Stanford Law Review* 43, no. 6 (1991): 1241–1299.

Dauphin, Mara. "'A Bit of Woman in Every Man': Creating Queer Community in Female Impersonation." *Valley Humanities Review* (Spring 2012): 1–16.

Davy, Kate. "Fe/Male Impersonation: The Discourse of Camp." In *The Politics and Poetics of Camp*, edited by Moe Meyer, 130–148. London: Routledge, 1994.

De Frece, Lady. *Recollections of Vesta Tilley*. 3rd impression. London: Hutchinson, 1934.

Diamond, Elin. *Unmaking Mimesis*. London: Routledge, 1997.

DiFranco, Dante (Julie "Jitterbug" Pearce). *The Art of Drag Kinging: Drag'ging Out Your Inner King*. Louisville, KY: Wasteland, 2004.

Dolan, Jill. "Gender Impersonation Onstage: Destroying or Maintaining the Mirror of Gender Roles?" *Women and Performance: A Journal of Feminist Theory* 2, no. 2 (1985): 5–11.

Dozier, Raine. "Beards, Breasts, and Bodies: Doing Sex in a Gendered World." *Gender and Society* 19, no. 3 (2005): 297–315.

Drag in the Name of Love. Bent. Mr. T's Highland Park Bowl and Club, Los Angeles, April 4, 2011.

Drag King Contest, 15th annual. Dragstrip. The DNA Lounge, San Francisco, August 17, 2010.

"Drag King Contest: 2007–2015." Youtube. Accessed September 15, 2015. https://www.youtube.com/dragkingsf.

A Drag King Extravaganza. Directed by Clare Smyth and Meaghan Derynck. Frameline Productions. 2008. DVD.

Drorbaugh, Elizabeth. "Sliding Scales: Notes on Stormé DeLarverie and the Jewel Box Revue, the Cross-Dressed Woman on the Contemporary Stage, and the Invert." In *Crossing the Stage: Controversies in Cross-Dressing*, edited by Leslie Ferris, 120–143. London: Routledge, 1993.

Duggan, Lisa. "The New Homonormativity: The Sexual Politics of Neoliberalism." In *Materializing Democracy: Towards a Revitalized Cultural*

Politics, edited by Russ Castronovo and Dana D. Nelson, 175–194. Durham, NC: Duke University Press, 2002.

———. *Sapphic Slashers: Sex, Violence, and American Modernity*. Durham, NC: Duke University Press, 2000.

Eng, David L., J. Halberstam, and José Esteban Muñoz. "What's Queer about Queer Studies Now?" *Social Text* 23, nos. 3–4 (2005): 1–17.

Enke, A. Finn. "The Education of Little Cis: Cisgender and the Discipline of Opposing Bodies." In *Transfeminist Perspectives: In and Beyond Transgender and Gender Studies*, edited by A. Finn Enke, 60–77. Philadelphia: Temple University Press, 2012.

Fausto-Sterling, Anne. "The Five Sexes: Why Male and Female Are Not Enough." *The Sciences* 33, no. 3 (1993): 20–24.

Foucault, Michel. *The History of Sexuality*, vol 1. Translated by Robert Hurley. New York: Pantheon Books, 1978.

Garber, Eric. "Gladys Bentley: The Bulldagger Who Sang the Blues." *OUT/Look: National Lesbian and Gay Quarterly* 1, no. 1 (Spring 1988): 52–61.

"Genderfuck." Urban Dictionary. Accessed July 23, 2019. https://www.urbandictionary.com/define.php?term=genderfuck.

Giddings, Paula. *When and Where I Enter: The Impact of Black Women on Race and Sex in America*. New York: W. Morrow, 1984.

Greenwald, Michael L., Rodger Schultz, and Roberto D. Pomo. *The Longman Anthology of Drama and Theater*. Compact ed. New York: Longman, 2002.

Halberstam, J. *Female Masculinity*. Durham, NC: Duke University Press, 1998.

———. "Mackdaddy, Superfly, Rapper: Gender, Race, and Masculinity in the Drag King Scene." *Social Text* 15, nos. 3–4 (1997): 104–131.

———. "Shame and White Gay Masculinity." *Social Text* 23, nos. 3–4 (2005): 219–233.

Haraway, Donna. "Situated Knowledges: The Science Question in Feminism and the Privilege of Partial Perspectives." *Feminist Studies* 14, no. 3 (1988): 575–599.

Harris, Laura, and Liz Crocker. "An Introduction to Sustaining Femme Gender." In *Femme: Feminists, Lesbians, and Bad Girls*, edited by Laura Harris and Elizabeth Crocker, 1–12. New York: Routledge, 1997.

Harth, Dorothy, and Lewis M. Baldwin. *Voices of Aztlán: Chicano Literature of Today*. New York: Mentor Books, 1974.

Heller, Meredith. "Drag Queen Asks: Is Drag Degrading to Women?" Interview, *AirTalk*. NPR. Los Angeles: KPCC, February 18, 2015.

———. "Female-Femmeing: A Gender-*Bent* Performance Practice." *QED: A Journal of GLBTQ Worldmaking* 2, no. 3 (2015): 1–23.

———. "Gender-Bending in El Teatro Campesino (1968–1980): A *Mestiza* Epistemology of Performance." *Gender and History* 24, no. 3 (2012): 766–781.

———. "Is She He? Drag Discourse and Drag Logic in Online Media Reports of Gender Variance." *Feminist Media Studies* 16, no. 3 (2016): 445–459.
———. "RuPaul Realness: The Neoliberal Resignifcation of Ballroom Discourse." *Social Semiotics* (2018): 1–15, doi: 10.1080/10350330.2018.1547490.
Hernández, Ellie D. *Postnationalism in Chicana/o Literature and Culture.* Austin: University of Texas Press, 2009.
Hinds, Patrick. "Uncovering the Stonewall Lesbian." *Curve* 18, no. 1 (2008): 64.
Holiday Charity Show. The East Bay King's Club. White Horse Inn, Oakland, CA, December 2008.
Holidays Are a Drag. Bent. Mr. T's Highland Park Bowl and Club, Los Angeles, December 17, 2011.
hooks, bell. *Black Looks: Race and Representation.* Boston: South End, 1992.
Horowitz, Katie R. "The Trouble with 'Queerness': Drag and the Making of Two Cultures." *Signs* 38, no. 2 (2013): 303–326.
Huerta, Jorge. *Chicano Theater: Themes and Forms.* Ypsilanti: Bilingual Review, 1982.
Kaiser, Charles. *The Gay Metropolis: 1940–1996.* Boston: Houghton Mifflin, 1997.
Karkazis, Katrina. *Fixing Sex: Intersex, Medical Authority, and Lived Experience.* Durham, NC: Duke University Press, 2008.
Kentucky Fried Woman. "Fat . . . Fierce . . . Kentucky Fried." In *Femmes of Power: Exploding Queer Femininities,* edited by Del LaGrace Volcano and Ulrika Dahl, 175–179. London: Serpent Tail, 2008.
Kessler, Suzanne J., and Wendy McKenna. *Gender: An Ethnomethodological Approach.* New York: Wiley-Interscience, 1978.
Krafft-Ebing, R. V. *Psychopathia Sexualis, with Especial Reference to the Antipathic Sexual Instinct: A Medico-Forensic Study.* Rev. ed. Translated by F. J. Rebman. London: Medical Books, 1928.
Largillière, Nicolas de. "Portrait of a Boy in Fancy Dress," oil on canvas, ca. 1710–14 (Getty Center, Los Angeles).
LeBesco, Kathleen, with Donna Jean Troka and Jean Bobby Noble. "Introduction." In *The Drag King Anthology,* edited by Donna Jean Troka, Kathleen LeBosco, and Jean Bobby Noble, 1–14. New York: Harrington Park, 2002.
Lloyd, Moya. *Beyond Identity Politics: Feminism, Power, and Politics.* London: Sage, 2005.
Lorber, Judith. *Paradoxes of Gender.* New Haven, CT: Yale University Press, 1994.
Lorde, Audre. *Sister Outsider: Essays and Speeches.* Berkeley: Pressing, 1984.
Maitland, Sara. *Vesta Tilley.* London: Virago, 1986.
Maltz, Robin. "Real Butch: The Performance/Performativity of Male Impersonation, Drag Kings, Passing as Male, and Stone Butch Realness." *Journal of Gender Studies* 7, no. 3 (1998): 273–286.

Mansbridge, Jane. "The Making of Oppositional Consciousness." In *Oppositional Consciousness: The Subjective Roots of Social Protest*, edited by Jane Mansbridge and Aldon Morris, 1–19. Chicago: University of Chicago Press, 2001.

Marrero, Maria Teresa. "Out of the Fringe? Out of the Closet." *Drama Review* 44, no. 3 (2000): 131–153.

Martin, Karin A., and Emily Kazyak. "Hetero-Romantic Love and Heterosexiness in Children's G-Rated Films." *Gender and Society* 23, no. 3 (2009): 315–336.

Meyer, Moe. "Unveiling the Word: Science and Narrative in Transsexual Striptease." In *Gender in Performance: The Presentation of Difference in the Performing Arts*, edited by Laurence Senelick, 68–85. Hanover, NH: University Press of New England, 1992.

Miracle Whips. Facebook. Accessed September 9, 2015. http://www.facebook.com/themiraclewhips?fref=ts.

Miz Cracker. "Drag Isn't Like Blackface. But That Doesn't Mean It's Always Kind to Women." *Slate*, February 17, 2015. Accessed July 23, 2019. http://www.slate.com/blogs/outward/2015/02/17/is_mary_cheney_right_about_drag_being_like_blackface.html.

Mohanty, Chandra. "Under Western Eyes: Feminist Scholarship and Colonial Discourses." *Boundary 2* 12, no. 13 (1984): 333–358.

Moore, Fiona. "One of the Gals Who's One of the Guys: Men, Masculinity and Drag Performance in North America." In *Changing Sex and Bending Gender*, edited by Allison Shaw and Shirley Ardener, 103–118. New York: Berghahn Books, 2004.

Moraga, Cherríe L., and Gloria Anzaldúa. *This Bridge Called My Back: Writings by Radical Women of Color*. 3rd ed. Berkeley: Third Woman, 2002.

Morinaga, Maki. "The Gender of Onnagata as the Imitating Imitated: Its Historicity, Performativity, and Involvement in the Circulation of Femininity." *Positions* 10, no. 2 (2002): 245–284.

Muñoz, José Esteban. *Cruising Utopia: The Then and There of Queer Futurity*. New York: New York University Press, 2009.

———. *Disidentifications: Queers of Color and the Performance of Politics*. Minneapolis: University of Minnesota Press, 1999.

Newton, Esther. "Dick(less) Tracy and the Homecoming Queen: Lesbian Power and Representation in Gay-Male Cherry Grove." In *Inventing Lesbian Cultures in America*, edited by Ellen Lewin, 161–193. Boston: Beacon, 1996.

———. *Mother Camp: Female Impersonators in America*. Chicago: University of Chicago Press, 1972.

Odell, George. *Annals of the New York Stage*. Vols. 8–10, 12, 14. New York: Columbia University Press, 1936–1945.

Peppers, Margot. "'It's Easier to Model as a Man Than a Woman': Casey Legler, the First Female to Be Signed as Male Model, on Her Knack for

Gender-Bending." *Daily Mail*, April 15, 2013. Accessed July 24, 2019. http://www.dailymail.co.uk/femail/article-2309598/Its-easier-model-man-woman-Casey-Legler-female-signed-male-model-knack-gender-bending.html.

Pérez, Emma. *The Decolonial Imaginary: Writing Chicanas into History*. Bloomington: Indiana University Press, 1999.

Piepzna-Samarasinha, Leah Lakshmi. "A Time to Hole Up and a Time to Kick Ass: Reimagining Activism as a Million Different Ways to Fight." In *We Don't Need Another Wave: Dispatches from the Next Generation of Feminists*, edited by Melody Berger, 166–179. Berkeley: Seal, 2006.

Reich, June L. "Genderfuck: The Law of the Dildo." In *Camp: Queer Aesthetics and the Performing Subject*, edited by Fabio Cleto, 254–265. Ann Arbor: University of Michigan Press, 1999.

Ring, Trudy. "Who the F Is . . . Blues Singer Gladys Bentley?" *Pride*, January 8, 2014. Accessed July 19, 2019. http://www.pride.com/who-f/2014/01/08/who-f-...-blues-singer-gladys-bentley.

Robertson, Jennifer. *Takarazuka: Sexual Politics and Popular Culture in Modern Japan*. Berkeley: University of California Press, 1998.

Robertson, Pamela. "What Makes the Feminist Camp?" In *Camp: Queer Aesthetics and the Performing Subject*, edited by Fabio Cleto, 266–282. Ann Arbor: University of Michigan Press, 1999.

Rodger, Gillian M. *Champagne Charlie and Pretty Jemima: Variety Theater in the Nineteenth Century*. Urbana: University of Illinois Press, 2010.

———. "'He Isn't a Marrying Man': Gender and Sexuality in the Repertoire of Male Impersonators, 1870–1930." In *Queer Episodes in Music and Modern Identity*, edited by Sophie Fuller and Lloyd Whitesell, 105–133. Urbana: University of Illinois Press, 2002.

———. "Male Impersonation on the North American Variety and Vaudeville Stage, 1868–1930." PhD diss., University of Pittsburgh, 1998.

Rose, Margaret. "Traditional and Nontraditional Patterns of Female Activism in the United Farm Workers of America, 1962 to 1980." *Frontiers* 11, no. 1 (1990): 26–32.

Royle, Edwin Milton. "The Vaudeville Theatre." *Scribner's Magazine* 26, no. 4 (October 1899): 485–495.

Rupp, Leila J., and Verta Taylor. *Drag Queens at the 801 Cabaret*. Chicago: University of Chicago Press, 2003.

Rupp, Leila J., Verta Taylor, and Eve Ilana Shapiro. "Drag Queens and Drag Kings: The Difference Gender Makes." *Sexualities* 13, no. 3 (2010): 275–294.

Sally, Lynn. "'It Is the Ugly That Is So Beautiful': Performing the Monster/Beauty Continuum in American Neo-Burlesque." *Journal of American Drama and Theatre* 21, no. 3 (2009): 5–23.

Sandoval, Chela. *Methodology of the Oppressed*. Minneapolis: University of Minnesota Press, 2000.

Schacht, Steven P., and Lisa Underwood. "The Absolutely Flawless but Flawlessly Customary World of Drag Queens and Female Impersonators." In *The Drag Queen Anthology*, edited by Steven P. Schacht and Lisa Underwood, 1–18. New York: Harrington Park, 2004.

Schilt, Kristen, and Laurel Westbrook. "Doing Gender, Doing Heteronormativity: 'Gender Normals,' Transgender People, and the Social Maintenance of Heterosexuality." *Gender and Society* 23, no. 4 (2009): 440–464.

Scudera, Domenick. "Dear Mary Cheney: Here Are Reasons Why Drag Is Socially Acceptable and Blackface Is Not." *Huffington Post*, February 1, 2015. Accessed July 24, 2019. http://www.huffingtonpost.com/domenick-scudera/dear-mary-cheney-here-are_b_6589910.html.

Senelick, Laurence. *The Changing Room: Sex, Drag, and Theatre*. London: Routledge, 2000.

Shapiro, Eve Ilana. "The Disposable Boy Toys: Identity Transformation in a Drag King Community." PhD diss., University of California, Santa Barbara, 2005.

———. "Drag Kinging and the Transformation of Gender Identities." *Gender and Society* 21, no. 2 (2007): 250–271.

Slide, Anthony. *The Encyclopedia of Vaudeville*. Westport, CT: Greenwood, 1994.

Smith-Rosenberg, Carroll. "Discourses of Sexuality and Subjectivity: The New Woman, 1870–1936." In *Hidden from History: Reclaiming the Gay and Lesbian Past*, edited by Martin Duberman, Martha Vicinus, and George Chauncey Jr., 264–280. New York: New American Library, 1989.

———. *Disorderly Conduct: Visions of Gender in America*. New York: Alfred A Knopf, 1985.

South, Richelle. Interview with the author, December 18, 2011.

Spade, Dean. "Resisting Medicine, Re/modeling Gender." *Berkeley Women's Law Journal* 18, no. 1 (2003): 15–37.

Stormé: The Lady of the Jewel Box. Directed by Michelle Parkerson, documentary. Women Make Movies, 1987.

Tasker, Yvonne, and Diane Negra. "Introduction: Feminist Politics and Postfeminist Culture." In *Interrogating Postfeminism: Gender and the Politics of Popular Culture*, edited by Yvonne Tasker and Diane Negra, 1–26. Durham, NC: Duke University Press, 2007.

Taylor, Diana. *The Archive and the Repertoire*. Durham, NC: Duke University Press, 2003.

El Teatro Campesino. *El Teatro Campesino: The Evolution of America's First Chicano Theatre Company 1965–1985*. San Juan Bautista, CA: El Teatro Campesino, 1985.

Tian, Min. "Male Dan: The Paradox of Sex, Acting, and Perception of Female Impersonation in Traditional Chinese Theatre." *Asian Theatre Journal* 17, no. 1 (2000): 78–97.

Tilley, Vesta. "The Mannish Woman." *Pittsburg Gazette Home Journal*, April 3, 1904: 5.
Titterton, W. R. *From Theatre to Music Hall*. London: Stephen Swift, 1912.
Torr, Diane, and Stephen Bottoms. *Sex, Drag, and Male Roles: Investigating Gender as Performance*. Ann Arbor: University of Michigan Press, 2010.
Tracer, Dan. "RuPaul's Perfect Response to Mary Cheney Proves That Drag Can Be a Class Act," *Queerty*, February 2, 2015. Accessed July 24, 2019. http://www.queerty.com/rupauls-perfect-response-to-mary-cheney-proves-that-drag-can-be-a-class-act-20150202.
Troka, Donna Jean, Kathleen LeBesco, and Jean Bobby Noble. *The Drag King Anthology*. New York: Harrington Park, 2002.
Valdez, Luis, and El Teatro Campesino. *Actos*. San Juan Bautista: Cucaracha, 1971.
Valentine, David. "'I Went to Bed with My Own Kind Once': The Erasure of Desire in the Name of Identity." *Language and Communication* 23, no. 2 (2003): 123–138.
Vicinus, Martha. "Turn-of-the-Century Male Impersonation: Rewriting the Romance Plot." In *Sexualities in Victorian Britain*, edited by Andrew H. Miller and James Eli Adams, 187–213. Bloomington: Indiana University Press, 1996.
Volcano, Del LaGrace, and J. Halberstam. *The Drag King Book*. London: Serpent's Tail, 1999.
Walker, Lisa. *Looking Like What You Are: Sexual Style, Race, and Lesbian Visibility*. New York: New York University Press, 2001.
Wandor, Michelene. "Cross-Dressing, Sexual Representation and the Sexual Division of Labour in Theatre." In *The Routledge Reader in Gender and Performance*, edited by Lizabeth Goodman with Jane de Gay, 170–175. London: Routledge, 1998.
Webb, Jenn. *Understanding Representation*. Los Angeles: Sage, 2009.
Welter, Barbara. "The Cult of True Womanhood: 1820–1860." *American Quarterly* 18, no. 2 (1966): 151–174.
West, Candace, and Don H. Zimmerman. "Doing Gender." *Gender and Society* 1, no. 2 (1987): 125–151.
Wiegman, Robyn. *American Anatomies: Theorizing Race and Gender*. Durham, NC: Duke University Press, 1995.
Wilson, James F. *Bulldaggers, Pansies, and Chocolate Babies: Performance, Race, and Sexuality in the Harlem Renaissance*. Ann Arbor: University of Michigan Press, 2010.
Windh, Indra, and Del LaGrace Volcano. "Gender Fusion." In *Queer Theory*, edited by Iain Morland and Annabelle Willox, 130–141. Houndmills: Palgrave Macmillan, 2005.
Yarbro-Bejarano, Yvonne. "Chicanas' Experience in Collective Theatre: Ideology and Form." *Women and Performance: A Journal of Feminist Theory* 2, no. 2 (1985): 45–58.

———. "The Female Subject in Chicano Theatre: Sexuality, 'Race,' and Class." *Theatre Journal* 38, no. 4 (1986): 389–407.

———. "Gloria Anzaldúa's *Borderlands/La Frontera*: Cultural Studies, 'Difference,' and the Non-Unitary Subject." *Cultural Critique* 28 (1994): 5–27.

Yardley, William. "Storme [sic] DeLarverie, Early Leader in the Gay Rights Movement, Dies at 93." *New York Times*, May 29, 2014.

Zellers, Parker R. "The Cradle of Variety: The Concert Saloon." *Educational Theatre Journal* 20, no. 4 (1968): 578–585.

ARCHIVAL NEWSPAPERS

National Police Gazette, 1880–1886

"Annie's Indignant Hands," January 3, 1880: 10
"Stage Whispers," July 3, 1886: 2.
"Stage Whispers," August 21, 1886: 2.

New York Clipper, 1868–1886

"Amusements," August 1, 1868: 186.
"Amusements," September 5, 1868: 175.
"Amusements," October 17, 1868: 224.
"Amusements," October 24, 1868: 281.
"Amusements," August 26, 1876: 175.
"Amusements," September 16, 1876: 199.
"City Summary," August 6, 1870: 142.
"City Summary," May 30, 1874: 70.
"Music Halls," September 26, 1868: 198.
"Music Halls," December 19, 1868: 295.
"An Unexpected Marriage—One Woman Marries Another—Is She He?" June 12, 1886: 198.
"Variety Halls," December 16, 1876: 303.

New York Times, 1917

"Ella Wesner Lies in Man's Garb," November 14, 1917: 15.

Sun [New York], 1891

"Stranger Than Fiction," December 27, 1891: 13.

QUEER MUSIC HERITAGE ARCHIVES

Danny Brown Scrapbooks. 1935–1944. Accessed September 5, 2016. http://queermusicheritage.com/jbr.html.

Jewel Box Revue program booklets (11). Approximately 1950s–1970s.

"The New Jewel Box Revue" [pink and white diamond cover]. Accessed September 8, 2016. http://queermusicheritage.com/fem-jewl10.html.

"The New Jewel Box Revue" [black, white, and gold diamond cover]. Accessed September 8, 2016. http://queermusicheritage.com/fem-jewl7.html.

"The New Jewel Box Revue" [blue and white diamond cover]. Accessed September 8, 2016. http://queermusicheritage.com/fem-jewl13.html.

"The New Jewel Box Revue" [gray and white cover with drawings of Danny and Doc]. Archivist date estimates 1950s. Accessed September 8, 2016. http://queermusicheritage.com/fem-jewl3.html.

"The New Jewel Box Revue" [black and gold cover with drawing of woman]. Accessed September 8, 2016. http://queermusicheritage.com/fem-jewl8.html.

"The New Jewel Box Revue" [black cover with drawings of Danny and Doc]. Archivist date estimates 1950s. Accessed September 8, 2016. http://queermusicheritage.com/fem-jewl15.html.

"The New Jewel Box Revue" [blue and pink cover with drawings of Danny and Doc]. Accessed September 8, 2016. http://queermusicheritage.com/fem-jewl.html.

"25th Anniversary" [gray cover with white wreath]. Hand dated 1968. Accessed September 8, 2016. http://queermusicheritage.com/fem-jewl14.html.

"28th Edition" [black cover with photograph of cast]. Accessed September 8, 2016. http://queermusicheritage.com/fem-jewl5.html.

"30th Edition" [red cover]. Accessed September 8, 2016. http://queermusicheritage.com/fem-jewl12.html.

"30th Edition" [cream cover with photographs of Danny and Doc]. "Sold in 1967." Accessed September 8, 2016. http://queermusicheritage.com/fem-jewl6.html.

"30th Edition" [pink and white zigzag pattern]. Accessed September 8, 2016. http://queermusicheritage.com/fem-jewl2.html.

Jewel Box Revue nightly handbill (1). Archivist date estimates 1950s. Found in program with black cover and drawings of Danny and Doc. Accessed September 8, 2016. http://queermusicheritage.com/fem-jewl15.html.

CALIFORNIA ETHNIC AND MULTICULTURAL ARCHIVES (CEMA)

American Perspectives: Another View [video], Show no. 110. CEMA 5, series 5. Accessed March 19, 2018. http://stream.library.ucsb.edu/visual/1000/1169/cusb-v1169b.mov.

Broyles-González, Yolanda. Manuscript draft of chapter 3, *El Teatro Campesino: Four Cardinal Points*, October 8, 1990, CEMA 97, Box 1.

"Casting Sheet." *La pastorela*, Winter 1980, CEMA 5, Series 1, Box 22, Folder 5.

Catch 2: "Los Vendidos." Interview with Phil Esparza, Diane Rodriguez, and Jose Delgado [video], Denver: KWGN, Ch. 2. 1976, CEMA 5, series 5. Accessed January 2, 2018. http://stream.library.ucsb.edu/visual/1000/1150/cusb-v1150b.mov.

Chumacero, Olivia. Interview by Cecelia Trujillo [audio cassette], San Juan Bautista, 1972, Album 3, Cat.02 007, CEMA 5, series 9.

———. [photograph]. *El fin del mundo* (Europe), 1980, CEMA 5, Series 6, Box 8, Folder 3, photograph #7.

Company (calaveras). [photograph]. *El fin del mundo*, 1977, CEMA 5, Series 6, Box 7, Folder 4, photograph #17.

El fin del mundo, first/revised draft [script]. San Juan Bautista: El Teatro Campesino, 1980, 150 pp., CEMA 5, Series 1, Box 18, Folder 2.

El fin del mundo [flyer]. Phoenix Arts Coming Together and Glendale Community College Associated Students, 1978, CEMA 5, Series 14, Box 9, Folder 17.

La carpa de los rasquachis [script]. San Juan Bautista: El Teatro Campesino, 1973, 70 pp., CEMA 5, Series 1, Box 13, Folder 5.

La pastorela, original ed. [script]. San Juan Bautista: El Teatro Campesino; 1976, 29 pp., CEMA 5, Series 1, Box 22, Folder 2.

Las cuatro apariciones de la Virgen de Guadalupe [program]. San Juan Bautista, Fiestas Navideñas, 1979, CEMA 5, Series 14, Box 10, Folder 23.

Las cuatro apariciones de la Virgen de Guadalupe and *La pastorela* [program]. San Juan Bautista, Fiestas Navideñas, 1978, CEMA 5, Series 14, Box 10, Folder 5.

Las cuatro apariciones de la Virgen de Guadalupe, *La pastorela*, and *Posadas* [program]. San Juan Bautista, Fiestas Navideñas, 1977, CEMA 5, Series 14, Box 9, Folder 3.

Nine AM Morning Show: "Part II." Interview with Luis Valdez, Olivia Chumacero, and Phil Esparza [video], Monterey, KMST, Ch. 46. 1980, CEMA 5, series 5. Accessed January 2, 2018. http://stream.library.ucsb.edu/visual/1000/1160/cusb-v1160b.mov.

Rodriguez, Diane. Interview by Paulina Sahugan [audio cassette], San Juan Bautista, 1983, Album 3, Cat.02 013 CEMA 5, Series 9.

———. [photograph]. *La pastorela*; 1978. CEMA5, Series 6, Box 39, Folder 1, photograph #10.

Valdez, Socorro. [photograph]. *La carpa de los rasquachis*; 1976. CEMA 5, Series 6, Box 12, Folder 3, photograph #3.

———. [photograph]. *La carpa de los rasquachis*; 1976. CEMA 5, Series 6, Box 12, Folder 3, photograph #5.

———. [photograph]. *La carpa de los rasquachis*; 1976. CEMA 5, Series 6, Box 12, Folder 3, photograph #10.

———. [photograph]. *La carpa de los rasquachis;* 1976. CEMA 5, Series 6, Box 12, Folder 3, photograph #15.

———. [photograph]. *La carpa de los rasquachis,* 1976, CEMA 5, Series 6, Box 12, Folder 4, photograph #18.

———. [photograph]. *El fin del mundo* (Europe), 1980, CEMA 5, Series 6, Box 8, Folder 5, photograph #59.

———. [photograph]. *El fin del mundo* (Europe), 1980, CEMA 5, Series 6, Box 8, Folder 6, photograph #70A.

———. [photograph]. *El fin del mundo* (Europe), 1980, CEMA 5, Series 6, Box 9, Folder 1, photograph #75.

———. [photograph]. *El fin del mundo* (Europe), 1980, CEMA 5, Series 6, Box 9, Folder 1, photograph #76.

INDEX

Page numbers in *italics* indicate figures.

activist practices, 78, 85, 142–43
Agate, James, 64
AirTalk (Southern California Public Radio show), xi–xii
Althusser, Louis, 12–13, 145
androcentrism, 29, 39n89
Angels in America, 198–99
Annals of the New York Stage (Odell), 66
Anti-Concert Saloon Bill, 46
Anzaldúa, Gloria, 35, 79, 82, 107
Arbus, Diane, 131, *132*
archive, 2–3, 6, 11, 24–26, 188, 193; of drag king shows, 155; Jewel Box Revue materials, 131; for male impersonation, 34, 42–44, 73n20, 75n58; for queer butch acts, 127–28, 131, 149–50n50, 149n44; spreadability and, 28; El Teatro Campesino, 34–35, 78–79, 83, 88–92, 95–96, 98, 103, 105–6, 110n5, 112n5; two-pillar model, 19–21, 25–26. *See also* taxonomies
The Art of Drag Kinging (DiFranco), 161

assigned sex, 4, 14, 25–26, 36n8, 187; "cultural genitals," 153; disidentification and, 153, 157–59, 162–65, 169–70, 175; elevated above gender, 16–17; intersex people and, 13, 16–18, 37n45, 58; Jewel Box Revue titles based on, 130, 149n46; male impersonators and, 44, 58, 61; queer butchness and, 123, 135, 145–46, 149n46; teatristas and mythical sexless characters, 98, 108
Aston, Elaine, 41–42, 44
audience, 11; active decoding by, 41–42, 45; awareness of performer's offstage identity, 3–4, 19–20, 24–25, 43–44, 52–56, 157; cross casting and, 20–21, 23, 26–27; cross identification and, 54–55; disidentification and, 152, 154, 178–79; heterosexual, 40, 55–56, 192n88; mixed-race, 116, 131; participation, 186–87; revisionary separation of lived identity from stage product, 82, 95, 97–98; sexless characters, multiple interpretation

audience (*cont.*)
  choices, 95; sexual desires of, 23, 55–56; speculation about body and identity, reasons for, 158–59, 187–88, 190n16; willing suspension of disbelief, 19, 22–23, 199. *See also* intention of performer
"authenticity," 12, 18, 187, 193–94, 198–200; counteridentification and, 120, 135–37, 145; identification and, 53–54, 63

Babushka (dog character), 100–1
Bailey, Marlon, 16, 21, 22, 37n40, 116, 119–21, 123, 139, 142, 187
Baker, Josephine, 118, 123, 124, 148n28
Ball, Harry, 66
ballroom culture, 16, 21, 120–21, 123, 139, 187; "realness," 136, 142–43
Barad, Karen, 8, 18
Barbara Eden / *I Dream of Jeannie* act, 25–26, 188
The Beauty Kings troupe, 166, 167, 168, 191n49
Beijing Opera, 21
Belle Reprieve (Split Britches), 161
Benner, Doc, 130
Bent (Los Angeles-based event series), 159, 167, 168, 188, 192n85; as "community stage show," 186; Drag in the Name of Love show, 172; "get to know your neighbor" segment, 186–87; *Holidays Are a Drag* show, 171, 186
Bentley, Gladys, 117, 118, 120, 121, 123–25, 138, 148n28; *Ebony Magazine* testimonial, 126–27
bentness, 33, 159, 168; bending taxonomies, 17; definition, 7; of male impersonation, 71; of mythical sexless character roles, 78, 82, 98; of queer butch acts, 120, 145. *See also* gender-bending
Berlant, Lauren, 5, 34, 196
Bernhardt, Sarah, 29
Betty (character, *Cloud 9*), 26, 29–30
binary sexed body, 4–5, 9; as baseline for reality of self, 14–16; disidentification and, 171–72; intersex and, 13, 16–18, 37n45, 58
blackface minstrelsy, xi
Black performers (1910–1969), 10, 73n6, 115–51; in Black community spaces, 125–26, 128; "Black vaudeville," 123, 125; commercial success of, 126; earlier LGBT methods, 116; masculine acts by women, 118–19; queer cultural space and, 123–30. *See also* racial markers
Black women, as not true women, 123–25
"blue" content, 40, 46, 49, 124
Bodies That Matter (Butler), 28
body: concrete individual, 12–13; cultural assumptions about, 4, 17; of drag king, disidentification and, 165; embodied truth, challenges to, 174–76; gestus (readable feeling or attitude), 26, 29–30; intersex, 13, 16–18, 37n45, 58; stability of cisgender assumed, 4, 14, 17–18, 27, 30, 41, 53, 164, 180, 196; visible markers of sex, 80, 94, 153, 157, 173–74, 179. *See also* racial markers
body-breaking, 155, 168, 173–82; racial markers and, 174–75
Bonehill, Bessie, 66
Bornstein, Kate, 13–14
Bottoms, Stephen, 9–10, 161–62
"boy body," 2, 25, 35n2
Boyz, Noah, 155, 189n8. *See also* Shapiro, Eve Ilana

bracketing, geographic, 4, 5
breasts, visible, 153, 157, 179, 181
British music hall and variety acts, 161
Brockett, Oscar, 20
Brown, Danny, 130, 149n44
Broyles-González, Yolanda, 84–91, 101, 104–5, 110n5, 112n51, 112n53, 113n72
burlesque, British, 28–29
burlesque, US, 169, 172
business attire, Westernized, 176
Buswell, Stephanie, 80, 92
butch, as term, 119. *See also* queer butchness/queer butch acts
Butler, Judith, 6, 8, 27–28, 139

Calavera (character), 99–102, 107, 108–9
calaveras (skeletons) roles, 35, 80, 93, 93–97, 110n13, 180–81; baseline neutrality of, 94; La Flaca, *103*, 103–4; Huesos (Bones) character, 96–100, 101, 104; multiple gender choices for, 94–95; sex signifiers layered onto, 94, 96–97. *See also* mythical sexless characters
California Ethnic and Multicultural Archives (CEMA), 88–89, 110n5
Canon: in analytic practice, 26–30; building, 19–26
carpa (variety show) format, 77
La carpa de los rasquachis (El Teatro Campesino), 79, 80
Carter, Lynn, 133, *134*
Case, Sue-Ellen, 20–21
Catch 2 (talk show), 94
celebrity interviews, 68
Chace, Zoe, 199–200
character delineation, 40, 46, 48
character studies, 41, 63
Chata (calavera character), 94
Chavez, Helen, 85

Cheney, Mary, xi–xii, 1, 31, 197
Cherry Grove homecoming drag queen competition, 37n32, 158
Chicanas, 34–35, 78–82, 85, 91, 95, 109n2; mestiza consciousness and, 35, 79, 82, 99, 101, 105–9; multiple identities, 79, 82. *See also* teatristas
Chicanismo, 77, 84, 102, 109n3
children's cartoon films, 170
China: Beijing Opera, 21
Chitlin' Circuit, 47, 116. *See also* Theater Owner's Booking Association (TOBA)
Christmas pantomime shows, 29, 47, 63
Chumacero, Olivia, 84, 87, 92, 102–5, *103*, 106
Churchill, Caryl, 26
Cider, Landon (master of ceremonies), 167, 172–73, *185*; "get to know your neighbor" segment, 186–87
cisgender identity, 36n8; not intended by DeLarverie, 132, 136–37, 141–42; queer butchness as divergent from, 119–20; stability of cisgender assumed, 4, 14, 17–18, 27, 30, 41, 53, 164, 180, 196
ciswomen performers, drag discourse and, 199–200
civil rights movements, 143
Clam House (Harlem), 124, 125
Clare, Eli, 170–71
clarity of method, 33, 41–42
Clipper (publication), 42, 48, 54, 58, 60
Cloud 9 (Churchill), 26, 29–30
Club Jewel Box (Miami and Tampa), 130
Code, Lorraine, 36n20, 39n98, 195
Cohen, Cathy J., 5, 32, 121–22, 144, 186, 189
collective primary identification, 85
colonization, 37n48

commercial goals, 128–29, 188–89; identification and, 29, 34, 45, 118, 147, 165
communication, gender as tool for, 16
compound drag, 158
concert saloons, 46–48
concrete individual, 12–13, 145
Connell, R. W., 176, 177
context: for drag kinging, 160–67; minoritarian, identification and, 127, 138, 139; nonthreatening spaces, 2, 3, 12, 139, 159, 175; precarity, 139–40; El Teatro Campesino and, 84–89
contradiction, 41, 120
conversion therapy, 126–27
Corridos (El Teatro Campesino), 85
counteridentification, 25, 34–35, 127, 165, 169, 194; "authenticity" and, 120, 135–37, 145; impacts of, 137–45; minoritarian group identity and, 5, 32, 35, 117–18, 121, 143–44, 165; oppositional consciousness and, 35, 121, 143–44; process, 130–37; queer cultural space and people of Color, 123–30; readable queerness, 117–20, 124; resistance and, 121–22, 142–43; reveals as, 135–37, 139, 142, 144, 159. *See also* queer butchness/queer butch acts
Crenshaw, Kimberlé, 45, 177
Crocker, Liz, 169
cross casting, 129, 161, 195; audience and, 20–21, 23, 26–27; in *Cloud 9*, 26, 29–30; dictated, 23–24, 30, 83; historical, 20–21, 23, 24–25; Peter Pan, 29; scripted, 23–24, 26, 30
cross identification, 34, 40, 61, 81, 117; agency of performer and, 56–57; audience exposure to information, 54–55; cultural norms replicated by, 43–45, 53–54, 59–60; process, 50–60
Cruz, Angela, 80, 92

"cultural genitals," 153
culture production, queer, 163
Cushman, Charlotte, 29

Dauphin, Mara, 129
decolonial imaginary, 102
defiance, 5, 11, 12, 121–22, 144–45. *See also* resistance
definitional guidelines, 7
De Frece, Walter, 69, 76n87
Delano, California, 77
DeLarverie, Stormé (drag performer), 35, 115–17, 127, 169, 194; characterized as male impersonator, 117–18, 160–61; cisgender presentation not intended by, 132, 136–37, 141–42; counteridentification process, 130–37; formal attire vs. lived identity, 120, 149n49; as guardian of lesbians, 138–39; intentions of, 132, 136; Jewel Box Revue roles, 130–34; master of ceremonies (MC) role, 130, 131, 133; in Navy dress uniform, 132, 133; oppressed identity categories, 139–40; photographs of, 131–32, 134; police identification of as queer, 117, 122, 140–41; reveals, 135–37, 139, 142, 144; sexual and gender identity not declared by, 122–23, 150n68, 150n69; as singer, 128, 135; Stonewall Rebellion and, 117, 122, 140–45
Delgado, Joe, 84
Del Toro, Delicio (drag performer), 180–81
Dennis, Blackie, 127, 128
desire, 23; cross identification and, 55–56; disidentification and, 172–73
deviance, social, as resistance, 121, 144
Diablo (character), 99
diablos (devils) roles, 35, 80, 92, 99
Diamond, Elin, 26, 27, 29–30
Diamond Daggers troupe, 169

DiFranco, Dante, 161, 163, 165
discourse, 3; importance of to gender, 12–18; language and, 3, 6, 8; limited choices, 5; mass public uses of, 8–9; materialization of, 8; participatory, 12; sign-chains, 8–9; as what can be said, 18. *See also* drag discourse
"disguise and reveal" folktales and stories, 25
disidentification, 25, 34, 35, 135, 194; audience and, 152, 154, 178–79; binary sexed body and, 171–72; definitions, 156; desire and, 172–73; essentialism, confronting, 157; female-femmeing, 168–73; genderfucking and, 153, 156, 159–60, 173–82, 192n86; intention and, 183; as political act, 182–83, 188–89; processes, 168–73; queer community space, 182–87; queer worldmaking and, 187–89; readability and, 173–74; as resistance, 167; reveals and, 159, 178–81; unintelligibility intended, 153–54
Disposable Boy Toys troupe, 9, 22–23, 165, 183
DNA Lounge, 192n77
Dolan, Jill, 26–27
St. Dong, Dillon (drag performer), 176–77
Dozier, Raine, 18, 174, 179
drag, 1; as act of political resistance, 5; archive vs. repertoire, 2–3; cisgender identity assumed, 4, 12; differences and similarities, 31; popular conceptions of, 1–3; as progressive deconstruction of identity, 9; revised taxonomy, 32–33, 194–95; safer spaces created by, 2–3
drag butch, as term, 128, 160–61
drag discourse, 3, 7–10, 187–88; as analytic, 7; cisgender

identity assumed, 3–4, 17–18, 25–27; essentialist, 9–10; injurious rhetorical acts, 8, 31; kinging in hierarchy of, 159, 160; as limiting, 3, 5–7, 26, 42–43, 117, 138, 145, 193; male impersonation, mischaracterization of, 41–43, 117–18, 145–46, 160–61; queer butchness not recognized, 145–46; redefining, 30–34; as reductive, 6; reveals, ideological implications of, 156, 180; sign chains, 8–9; status quo reified by, 7, 21, 31
The Drag King Anthology (Troka, LeBesco, and Noble), 9
The Drag King Book (Volcano and Halberstam), 157, 187
Drag King Contests, 29, 152–53, 170, 189n1; Delicio Del Toro, 180–81; Dillon St. Dong, 176–88; "Lola" act, 178–80
A Drag King Extravaganza (documentary), 161, 163, 164, 165, 167
drag kinging/drag kings, xii, 10, 35, 72, 152–92; analogies to queening, 160–61, 163; body-breaking, 155, 168, 173–82; compound drag, 158; context, 160–67; definitions, 4, 9, 154, 164–65; female-femmeing, 101, 155, 168–73; "femme pretender," 157; hypermasculinity, 155; identification-based version, 159, 160; intention and, 163, 165, 167, 183; negative stereotypes portrayed, 163–64; parameters of, 154–56; as political action, 5, 164–66, 182–83, 188–89; racial markers, White drag king appropriations of, 155, 169, 174–75; reveals, 152–54; stripteases, 152–54, 157, 171–72; styles, 120; troupes, 9, 22–23, 161, 164–68, 171–72, 183, 191n49

Drag King/Man for a Day Workshops, 161–63
The Drag Queen Anthology (Schacht and Underwood), 3–4
drag queening: Cherry Grove homecoming competition, 37n32, 158; conversations about, xi–xii, 31, 197; definitions, 3–4; drag kinging as alternative to, 154; essentialist discourse, 9–10; men's socially superior gender position illuminated, 27; popular conceptions of, 1–2; stable cisgender identity assumed, 3–4, 14, 17–18, 25–7
Drag Queens at the 801 Cabaret (Rupp and Taylor), 5, 9, 31
Dred (drag performer), 157
Drorbaugh, Elizabeth, 133, 135
Duggan, Lisa, 32, 43, 196–97

Ebony Magazine, 126–27
economies of visibility, 174
Edward (character, *Cloud 9*), 29–30
efficacy of gender-bending, 25, 27–30
801 Cabaret, 5
El Día de los Muertos (The Day of the Dead) celebrations, 93
El fin del mundo (El Teatro Campesino), 80, 87, 90, 91, 94, 96–98, 99; La Flaca character, 102–5, *103*
Encyclopedia of Feminist Theories (Code), 195
England, Elizabethan, 21, 23
Enke, A. Finn, 36n8
entertainment, nineteenth century, 45–46
Esparza, Phil, 84, 94
essentialism, 4, 10, 11, 18, 41, 157
ethical considerations, 18

farm workers, 77
faux/bio queening, 154–55, 168, 191n51
female-femmeing, 101, 155, 168–73; categorization of, 188
female impersonation, 4, 55, 130, 133, 134, 142; in minstrelsy and circus genres, 47
female masculinity, 120
Female Masculinity (Halberstam), 9
Female Mimics magazine, 131, 132
femininity: in children's films, 170; of ciswomen pop stars, 199–200; high camp, 29; offstage, of male impersonators, 41, 56, 63, 64, 66; racial-sexual position of social respectability, 34, 41–42, 44–45, 47, 62, 64, 71, 118; as visibly done, 29. *See also* female-femmeing
feminist scholarship, 8; on Teatro Campesino, 86–89; theater history critiques, 20–21
femme identity, 169
Finn, Mickey (drag performer), 178–80
La Flaca (character), *103*, 103–5
Foucault, Michel, 5, 194–95
From Theatre to Music Hall (Titterton), 61–62, 63
"The Full Circle" (Arbus), 131, 132

The Gay Metropolis (Kaiser), 141
gay shame/gay pride model, 139
gay versus straight framework, 32
gender: as accomplishment, 16, 25, 37n43; binary cultural assumptions, 3–5, 17; biological, 13–14; doing, 14–16, 155; importance of discourse to, 12–18; as interactional, 16; materialization of, 3–4, 8, 12; medicalized, 5, 13, 49–50, 61, 174; playscript for, 13; self-determination of, 22–23, 120–21; unified body-gender, 120

gender-bending, theatrical:
appearance assumed to be in
contrast with performer's reality,
3–4, 19–20, 22, 43–44; audience
participation, 186; as conceptual
discourse, 1; definitions, 4–5;
efficacy of, 25, 27–30; as fictive play,
19–20, 22; historicization of, 19–21;
mythical sexless characters and,
78–81; as performance of identity
incongruity, 24; queering of, 26–30;
redefinition, 7, 33; reinforcement
of cultural norms, 20–21; reveals,
25–26, 135–37, 142, 144; as source of
individual or group strength, 5; as
stage performance, 1; as support for
status quo, 7, 21, 31, 33; teatristas and,
77–114; two-pillar model, 19–22,
25–26. *See also* audience; drag;
drag kinging/drag kings; female-
femmeing; male impersonation;
male impersonators; mythical
sexless characters; queer butchness/
queer butch acts
genderfucking, 153, 156, 159–60,
173–82, 192n86; definitions,
175–76
genderlessness, 99–102. *See also*
mythical sexless characters
gender performance/lived identity,
21–23, 27–28, 37n48, 198–200;
disidentification and, 157; queer
butchness acts and, 118, 120, 126,
149n49; resistance and lived
social deviance, 121–22, 144–45;
revisionary separation of from stage
product, 82, 95, 97–98
Gender Trouble (Butler), 27–28
geographic and temporal locations, 11;
nonthreatening spaces or contexts,
12, 139, 159, 175

gestus (readable feeling or attitude),
26, 29–30, 33, 100
González, Andres V., 88
Great Depression, 127
great-man conceptual framing, 84
Greek theater, 20–21
Greenwich Village, 125
Gutierrez, Andres, 84

Halberstam, J., 29, 120, 161–62, 188;
definition of drag kings, 4, 9, 154,
164–65; on gay shame/gay pride
model, 139
Haraway, Donna, 8
Harlem Renaissance performers
(1910–1930s), 35, 123–26
Harris, Laura, 169
hegemonic masculinity, 39n90, 120,
125, 140, 164, 176
Hernández, Ellie D., 85
HerShe Bar drag king shows, 154
heteronormativity, 133; in children's
films, 170; drag kinging and,
155, 161–64, 169–70, 176, 183;
homonormativity and, 32, 196–97; of
male impersonators, 45, 123; queer
butch rejection of, 137, 142–43
hetero-romance, 133
heterosexiness, 170–71, 172
heterosexual desire, space created for,
55–56
Hildy, Franklin J., 20
Hindle, Annie (male impersonator),
34, 40, 44, 47, 51, 71, 75n60, 97,
137, 147; active cultivation of cross
identification, 54–55; bookings/
ratings, 48; drag kinging linked
with, 161; marriage to Charles
Vivian, 52, 58–59, 75n59; offstage
masculine appearance, 52–53, 56;
same-sex relationships, 57–58, 75n58;

Hindle (*cont.*)
  sex identity questioned, 58–59;
  variety process, 50–60
Hinds, Patrick, 141
historicization of gender-bending,
  19–21
The History of Sexuality (Foucault), 5
History of the Theatre (Brockett and
  Hildy), 20
Holidays Are a Drag event, 171
homonormativity, 32, 196–97
homosexiness, 171
hooks, bell, xii (note 3)
Horowitz, Katie R., 10
Huerta, Dolores, 85–86, 111n26
Huerta, Jorge, 85
Huesos (Bones) character, 96–100,
  101, 104
hypermasculinity, 155

"I Am a Woman Again" (Bentley), 127
identification, 81, 117; collective
  primary, 85; commercial goals
  and, 29, 34, 45, 118, 147, 165;
  male impersonation and, 41, 45,
  54–55, 62, 64, 68, 193; minoritarian
  context and, 127, 138, 139; Muñoz's
  definition, 43; process, 60–70;
  queered, 156; tactical, 82. *See
  also* counteridentification; cross
  identification; disidentification;
  revisionary identification
identity, 3; cultural construction
  of, 4, 7; drag as progressive
  deconstruction of, 9; essentialist
  views, 4, 10, 11, 18, 41, 157; offstage,
  as unimportant in teatrista roles,
  80, 82, 92, 100–1; offstage, audience
  awareness of, 24–25, 43–44, 54–56,
  157; offstage, drag kinging and,
  127, 130, 135, 146, 153–54, 157, 159,
  181; offstage, queer butchness and,
  116–18, 127, 130, 135, 138–45; offstage,
  theater spaces and, 198–200; offstage
  femininity of male impersonators,
  41, 56, 63, 64, 66; performance
  as incubator for, 22–23; readable
  disjointedness, 33; reimagined by
  drag performances, 5; sex as "master
  status," 18
identity incubator, 22–23
identity pride, 139
I Dream of Jeannie act, 25–26, 188
indigenismo (indigenous legacies),
  77, 81, 109n3
injurious rhetorical acts, 8, 31
intention of performer, 7, 11, 24,
  188–89, 199; as central to gender-
  bending, 33; of drag kings, 163, 165,
  167, 183; of male impersonators,
  42, 56, 60, 71, 118; queer butchness
  and, 118, 128–29, 135–39, 142, 146;
  teatristas, 79, 89–95, 104–5. *See also*
  audience; reveals
interests, gender-based, 16–17
intersectionality, 45, 137–38, 177;
  White privilege and, 175, 186
intersex people, 13, 16–18, 37n45, 58
"inversion," 50, 61, 68–69, 74n3, 124
"Is Drag Degrading to Women?" radio
  show, xi–xii, 31, 197

Japan: Kabuki theatre (ca. 1600–1629
  CE), 21, 28; Takarazuka Revue, 23
Jewel Box Revue, 35, 115, 117, 123,
  128–30, 194; audience base, 130–31;
  as "family entertainment," 129, 131,
  136; framing of show, 133–35; MC
  role, 130, 131; program booklets, 131,
  135, 149–50n50; reveals, 135–37; titles
  based on assigned sex, 130, 149n46.
  See also queer butchness

Johnson, Lucky (drag king), 158–59
Johnson, Marsha P., 141
Jourdan, Alicia, 52

Kabuki theatre, 21, 28
Kaiser, Charles, 141
Karkazis, Katrina, 13, 18, 37n45
Kazyak, Emily, 133, 170, 171, 172
Kentucky Fried Woman (drag performer), 165, 168, 171, 191n51
Kessler, Suzanne J., 153, 174
knowledge production, 2–3, 8, 26
"Know You Want Me" (song, Pitbull), 180–81
Krafft-Ebing, Richard von, 50, 69, 74n3

La carpa de los rasquachis (El Teatro Campesino), 93, 99–100, 105, 107
Lady Gaga, 1, 199, 200
language, 3, 6, 8. *See also* discourse
La pastorela (El Teatro Campesino), 87, 91–92; Luzbel character, 92, 93; Satanás role, 92, 99
La Raza, 85
Largillière, Nicolas de, 14–16, *15*
Las cuatro apariciones de la Virgen de Guadalupe (El Teatro Campesino), 87
Las dos caras del patroncito (El Teatro Campesino), 91
La Virgen de Tepeyac (El Teatro Campesino), 91
LeBesco, Kathleen, 165
Legler, Casey (model), 199, 200
lesbian, as term, 121, 122, 138
lesbian bars, 138–39
"Lingard style," 55
"little theoretical theatre," 12–13, 145
Lloyd, Moya, 82
"Lola" (drag performer), 178–80, 192n75

"Lola" (song, Kinks), 178, 192n75
The Longman Anthology of Drama and Theater, 20
Lorber, Judith, 16, 159
Lorde, Audre, 32, 195
luchadores (lucha libre wrestlers), 180–81
Luxe, Mr. (drag king), 152–55, 167, 168, 174–75

machismo, 93, 96–97, 180–82
macro-oppositional politics, 138
Maitland, Sara, 66, 67
male impersonation, 1, 6–7, 10, 34, 40–76, 95, 193; in academic literature, 43; archive, 34, 42–44, 73n20, 75n58; celebrity interviews, 68; character delineation, 40, 46, 48; commercial goals, 29, 34, 45, 118, 128, 147, 165; conforming subject produced by, 43–45, 57–58, 60, 71–72, 128–29; created to avoid sexual harassment and objectification, 46, 47–48, 56; cross identification in, 34, 40, 43–45, 53–54, 59–60, 61; dandy/swell characters, 40, 48, 62, 119; drag kinging compared to, 152–53, 161; "feminine" attributes not concealed, 40–41, 42, 44; gender-bending aftereffects, 71–72; gendered titles used in publicity, 44, 54, 63–65; heterosexual audience, 40, 55–56, 192n88; identification and, 41, 45, 54–55, 62, 64, 68, 193; masculinity as owned by men, 121; mischaracterization of, 41–43, 117–18, 145–46, 160–61; performance reviews and op-ed pieces, 34, 42, 55, 64; personal flexibility and, 34, 53; publicity, 42, 50–53, *51*, 60–61, 63, 66; racial-sexual position of social

male impersonation (*cont.*)
respectability, 34, 41–42, 44–45, 47, 62, 64, 71, 118; reification of gender norms, 43, 57–58, 71–72; Victorian gender and sexual mores, 26, 41, 44, 48, 49–50, 61, 62, 70; as White-centric practice, 41, 44–45, 47, 71, 123. *See also* male impersonators; variety shows (1860–1880s); vaudeville (1880s–1920s)

male impersonators: agency of, 41–42, 56; assigned sex and, 44, 58, 61; audience for, 41–44; dedicated professionalism, 45, 52–55; DeLarverie characterized as, 117–18, 160–61; heteronormativity of, 45, 123; intentions of, 42, 56, 60, 71, 118; men's clothing in everyday life of, 53; not legally sanctioned, 43, 57; offstage appearance, 52–56, 63–64, 66; as "one of the guys," 47–48; same-sex relationships, 43, 57. *See also* Hindle, Annie; male impersonation; Tilley, Vesta; Wesner, Ella

male mimicry, 120
"mall invasion" actions, 186
Maltz, Robin, 119, 120, 125, 136
"mannish" women, 44, 61–62, 68–69, 123–25
Mansbridge, Jane, 121
man-woman sister acts, 47
marginalizing structures, 32
Margolin, Deb, 161
Markham, Bridge, 157
Marrero, Maria, 110n6
Martin, Karin A., 133, 170, 171, 172
"Masculine Women! Feminine Men!" (song), 74n34
masculinity: attribution of used to dehumanize women, 39n89; butch as term, 119: hegemonic, 39n90, 120, 125, 140, 164, 176; hypermasculinity, 155; inhabited by queer butchness, 120–21, 137, 141, 146; machismo, 93, 96–97, 180–82; "men's business," 63–64, 68, 152; nonman, 119–21, 136, 146; pachuco character, 93, 97, 99, 113n65, 113n73; racialized, 96–97, 186; sexless, 95–99; as something that "just is," 29; subordinated, 176–77; Westernized business attire as symbol of, 176. *See also* queer butchness

mass publics, 8–9, 28, 188; drag kinging and, 153, 160, 163; male impersonation and, 44, 57; queer butchness and, 118, 125, 139
materialist theories, 3–4, 8, 12, 18, 27–28
McKenna, Wendy, 153, 174
medical pathology, 49–50, 61
Mercer, Mickey, 130
mestiza consciousness, 35, 79, 82, 99, 101, 105–9
Meyer, Moe, 25–26
miniestrella (short luchador), 180–81
minoritarian group identity, 5, 32, 35, 117–18, 121; oppositional consciousness and, 35, 121, 143–44
Miracle Whips troupe, 167, 171–72
mitos (myths), 77, 84, 90, 93
Miz Cracker (drag performer), xi–xiv
Mo B. Dick (drag performer), 157
Mohanty, Chandra, xii
Moore, Fiona, 9
Mother Camp: Female Impersonators in America (Newton), 9, 128, 160–61
el Movimiento (Chicanx civil rights movement), 77–78, 82–83, 85, 106, 138, 147; gender conflicts within, 85–86, 106–7; labor organizing, 108

La Muerte role, 80, 99
Mundo (Reymundo Mata, character, *El fin del mundo*), 94, 97
Muñoz, José Esteban, 5, 43, 82, 156, 169; queerness as "not quite here," 32, 197
mythical sexless characters, 1, 10, 34–35, 77–114; angels, 92; as bent roles, 78, 82, 98; Chicanismo and, 102; *diablos* (devils), 35, 80, 92, 99; as gender-bending, 78–81; genderlessness, 99–102; impacts of teatrista performances, 105–9; mitos (myths), 77, 84, 90, 93; La Muerte role, 80, 99; as nonhuman, 80, 94; revisionary identification and, 25, 78–79, 81–82; Satanás role, 80, 92, 99; sexless masculinity, 95–99. *See also* calaveras (skeletons) roles; teatristas; El Teatro Campesino

National Police Gazette (newspaper), 42, 53, 58
Negra, Diane, 45
new materialist theories, 8
Newton, Esther, 4, 9, 22, 37n32, 128, 160–61; on DeLarverie, 115, 135–37
New York Clipper (newspaper), 40
New York queer community, 123
Nine AM Morning Show (television show), 102, *103*, 104, 105
nonbinary/gender-non-conforming people, 31, 146, 157
noncompliance, 121–22
nonidentity, 101
nonman masculinity, 119–21, 136, 146

"obscenity" laws, 179, 192n77
Odell, George, 66
offstage self of performer. *See* identity
"olio" acts, 46, 73n17

Olmos, Edward James, 113n73
oppositional consciousness, 35, 121, 143–44
Oswald, Vicki, 80, 92
"out and proud" rhetoric, 139
"Out of the Fringe? Out of the Closet" (Marrero), 110n6

pachuco character, 93, 97, 99, 113n65, 113n73
Papa Cherry. *See* South, Richelle (Papa Cherry)
Parkerson, Michelle, 131, 132, 138, 141
Parra, Yolanda, 80, 87, 92
Pastor, Tony, 48
penis, visible, 153, 174
Pérez, Emma, 102
performance skills: cross identification and, 40; reveals and, 25, 136, 142, 157–59
performers: distancing from role, 20–21, 24; responsibilities in gender-bending, 33. *See also* intention of performer; specific types of drag performance
Peter Pan character, 29
Piepzna-Samarasinha, Leah Lakshmi, 143
Pittsburgh Gazette Home Journal, 68
political action: counteridentification, impacts of, 137–45; drag kinging as, 5, 164–66, 182–83, 188–89; male impersonation and, 57–58, 71–72
poor, queer people of Color, 21
pop stars, ciswomen, 199–200
Portrait of a Boy in Fancy Dress (de Largillière), 14–16, *15*
Posada, José Guadalupe, 94
Powles, Matilda, 70. *See also* Tilley, Vesta
precultural self, 13

progress narrative, 118
Psychopathia Sexualis (Krafft-Ebing), 69
public gendering, 153
public gender prohibitions, 23
public outness, 139–40

Qing dynasty (ca. 1636–1912), 21
queer, as term, 6
queer butchness/queer butch acts, 1, 34, 35, 116; alignment of performer with queer communities, 128–29, 138; archive, 127–28, 131, 149–50n50, 149n44; assigned sex and, 123, 135, 145–46, 149n46; bentness of, 120, 145; butch realness, 119–20, 123–24, 128, 136, 139; drag butch, as term, 128, 160–61; formal attire and preening behavior, 120; heteronormativity, rejection of, 137, 142–43; inhabiting of masculinity, 120–21, 137, 141, 146; intention and, 118, 128–29, 135–39, 142, 146; mislabeling as male impersonation, 117–18; readable nonmale body/nonman self, 120; sexual-identity assumption, 121; similarity of butch acts and lived experience, 118, 120, 126, 149n49; as term, 119; terminology, 117, 122–23. *See also* Jewel Box Revue; masculinity
queer cultural space: ballrooms, 16, 120–21, 123, 139, 187; counteridentification and people of Color, 123–30; disidentification and drag kinging, 182–89; queer butchness and, 128–29, 138
Queer Music Heritage Archives, 131, 149–50n50, 149n44
queerness: as abjection, 32; of drag performers, 31; as "not quite here," 32, 197; radical, 32

queer theory, 31–32
queer worldmaking, 5, 11, 31, 33–35, 196; disidentification and, 187–89
quick change artists, 55–56

racial-gendered cultural power, 176–77
racial markers: bending of, 153–54; body-breaking and, 174–75; masculinity, subordinated, 176–77; passing, legal, 174; people of Color as drag performers, 176–82; police targeting and, 141, 143; racist drag under "shared queer community" umbrella, 153–54, 159–60; readability of, 141; White drag king appropriations of, 155, 169, 174–75. *See also* Black performers; body
racial solidarity, 34–35
radical queerness, 32
Rainey, Gertrude "Ma," 118–19, 123–25, 148n28
Rasquachi, Jesus Pelado (character), 100
Rasquachi, Pelada (character), 108–9
rasquachis, 113n66
readability, 139; disidentification and, 173–74; disjointedness, 33; gestus, 26, 29–30, 100; of race, 141; readable queerness, 117–20, 124
reality, 38n77; audience assumptions about, 3–4, 19–20, 22, 43; queer, 145–47; as vehicle for hegemonic consolidation, 28
realness, butch, 119–20, 123–24, 128, 136, 139
"realness," in ballroom culture, 136, 142–43
"realness with a twist," 136
Recollections of Vesta Tilley (De Frece), 63, 64, 66, 68, 72n3

Reich, June L., 175–76
repertoire, 2–3
resignification projects, 6–7
resistance: audiences, effect of drag on, 182–83; counteridentification and, 121–22, 142–43; defiance, 5, 11, 12, 121–22, 144–45; disidentification as, 167; oppositional consciousness and, 35, 121, 143–44
respectability, 53–54, 118; denied to Black women, 123–25; racial-sexual position of, 34, 41–42, 44–45, 47, 62, 64, 71, 118
reveals, 25–26; as counteridentification, 135–37, 139, 142, 144, 159; as disidentification, 159, 178–81; drag kinging and, 152–54; identification, 159; performance skills evaluated by, 25, 136, 142, 157–59
revisionary identification, 34–35, 77–79, 81–83, 138, 193–94; audience encouraged to separate lived identity from staged product, 82, 95, 97–98; growth and, 102–5; as mestiza practice, 82, 99, 101, 107; mythical sexless characters and, 25, 78–79, 81–82; personal identity as significant, 95; sexless masculinity, 95–99. *See also* mythical sexless characters; teatristas
Rivera, Sylvia, 141
Robertson, Jennifer, 23
Robertson, Pamela, 19
Rodger, Gillian, 43, 46, 52, 55–56, 62, 63, 75n58
Rodriguez, Diane, 78, 84, 87, 100, 102; as costume designer, 105; on gender-bending performances, 106; as Gila in *La pastorela*, 92; as Luzbel, 93
Rodriguez, Marco, 97

Rogers, Robin, 138
Rojas, Lillian, 104, 105
Royle, Edwin Milton, 49
RuPaul, xi–xii, 197
RuPaul's Drag Race, xi–xii, 1, 2, 2, 31, 197, 199
Rupp, Leila J., 5, 9, 31, 143, 164, 165, 167
Ryan, Annie, 58, 75n60

safer spaces created by drag, 2–3. *See also* queer cultural space; theater spaces, cordoned
Sally, Lynn, 172
saloons. *See* concert saloons
same-sex desire: discouragement of by performer, 69–70; history of, 43; masked by gender-bending performances, 56; medicalization of, 49–50
Sandoval, Chela, 143
Satanás (character), 80, 92, 99
Schacht, Steven P., 3–4, 9, 163
Schilt, Kristen, 36n8
scholarly accounts, 28; feminist scholarship, 86–89; script-analysis practices, 89–90
script analysis, 90, 91–92
scripted narrative, 23
self-determination of gender, 22–23, 120–21
self-fashioning, 12, 16
Selwyn, Blanche (male impersonator), 52, 54
Selwyn, J. H., 52
Semenya, Caster, 37n45
Senelick, Laurence, 2, 52, 154, 155, 163–64
seriocomic performers, 54
sex: binary classification, 4–5, 9, 13–17, 171–72; as biological gender,

sex: binary classification (*cont.*) 13–14; as cultural gendering, 13, 17; as form of embodied authenticity, 12; as medical classification, 5, 13, 174; as ontological, 4, 11, 17–18; as organizing factor, move away from, 32–33; visible markers of, 80, 94, 153, 157, 173–74, 179. See also assigned sex

Sex, Drag, and Male Roles (Torr and Bottoms), 9–10, 161–62

sexless, mythical characters. See mythical sexless characters

sexology, 49–50, 61, 124

sexuality: heterosexiness, 170–71, 172; penetrator sex acts, 171–72; same-sex desire, 43, 56, 69–70, 121–22, 126, 138, 160, 179

Shakespeare, William, plays of, 21, 23, 129, 198

shame, 139

Shapiro, Eve Ilana, 22–23, 164, 165, 167, 183; as Noah Boyz, 155, 189n8

Shaw, Peggy, 161, 190n21

sign-chains, 8–9

single-oppression framework, 32

Sisters of Perpetual Indulgence, 1, 189n1

situated knowledge, 8

Slide, Anthony, 56, 63

Smith, Bessie, 118, 123, 124

Smith-Rosenberg, Carroll, 49–50, 61

social existence, hailing into, 12–13, 145

South, Richelle (Papa Cherry), *166*, 168, 173, *185*, 186–88, 191n49, 192n86

Spade, Dean, 17, 21

speech acts, 28

Split Britches theater troupe, 161, 164

spreadability, queer, 5, 10, 28, 31, 34, 188, 194; end point of, 196–97

stability of cisgender identity assumed, 4, 14, 17–18, 27, 30, 41, 53, 164, 180, 196

stage practice, 194, 198

status quo: drag discourse reified by, 7, 21, 31; male impersonation's reification of, 43, 57–58, 71–72

Stonewall Inn (Greenwich Village, New York), 140–42

Stonewall Rebellion (1969), 35, 117, 122, 137–45, 147–48n7, 151n80; historical accounts, 140–41

Stonewall Veterans Association, 139

Stormé: The Lady of the Jewel Box (documentary), 123, 131, 132, 138, 141

stripteases, 152–54, 157, 171–72

Sun (newspaper), 42, 48, 53, 58, 69

survival, gender performances for, 12, 16, 21, 37n48, 139–40; as activist action, 142–43

Suydam, Levi, 16–17

tactical identification, 82

Takarazuka Revue, 23, 28

Tasker, Yvonne, 45

taxonomies, 5–7, 36n20, 39n98, 158–59, 174; bending, 17; institutionalization of, 194–95; redefinition for drag, 32–33, 194–95; resignification projects, 6–7; as spreadable, 5, 10, 28, 31. See also archive

Taylor, Diana, 2, 8, 28, 86

Taylor, Verta, 5, 9, 31, 143, 164, 165, 167, 193

teatristas, 34–35, 138, 147; Broyles-González's interviews with, 86–87; complexity of cultural and political positions, 81, 106; enjoyment of sexless character roles, 79–81; gender-bending performance process, 77–114;

gender-neutrality of term, 109n4; impacts of, 105–9; intentions of, 79, 89–95, 104–5; leadership power of, 87; misconstrued as powerless and oppressed, 89, 91, 107–8; mythical sexless roles enjoyed by, 80, 88; racial-gendered subject positions, 193–94; revisionary growth and, 102–5; roles, 79–81, 88, 91; scripts document specific performance limitations and obstacles, 90–91; technical contributions, 105. *See also* mythical sexless characters

El Teatro Campesino, 10, 34–35, 72, 77–114, 138; actor-driven model, 81, 83; archives, 83, 88–92, 95–96, 98; archives, celebration for reopening of, 105–6; archives restricted, 34–35, 78–79, 83, 88, 110n5, 112n51; Calavera (genderless character), 99–102; context and conflict, 84–89; core group, 84; early and midperiod work, 83–84, 90; gender and sexual hierarchies, 78, 106; gender-indiscriminate casting practices, 92; Huesos (Bones) character, 96–100, 101, 104; indigenismo (indigenous legacies), 77, 81; La Muerte role, 80, 99; later works, 84–85; mainstream ventures, 84–85; published works, 83; residency in San Juan Bautista, California, 84; roles, 79–81, 84, 88; Satanás role, 80, 92; scripts, 90–91; silencing of feminist cultural perspectives, 78; televised interviews, 83; tours, 84; women's view of roles, 79–80. *See also* calaveras (skeletons) roles; diablos (devils) roles; mythical sexless characters; teatristas

El Teatro Campesino: Theater in the Chicano Movement (Broyles-González), 89
Teatro de la Esparza, 87
Teatro Nacional de Aztlán (TENAZ), 86, 89–90. *See also* El Teatro Campesino
teatros, male-dominated, 87
TENAZ (Teatro Nacional de Aztlán), 86, 89–90
theater, nineteenth century, 45–46
theater history, 20–25
Theater Owner's Booking Association (TOBA), 73n6, 115–16, 123, 125, 129
theater spaces, cordoned, 19–20, 198–99; assumed to be free from punitive conventions, 22, 57–58, 199; symbolic representation and message transmission, 19, 22; willing suspension of disbelief, 19, 22–23, 199
theatrical, as term, 22
theatrical gender-bending. *See* gender-bending, theatrical
Thespis, 20
thinness, 171
Tilley, Vesta (male impersonator), 34, 40–41, 67, 71, 119; as "Algy," 65; celebrity interviews, 68; drag kinging comparison, 152–53, 161, 165; as Lady De Frece, 66, 70; on "mannish women," 68–69; memoir, 63, 64, 66, 68, 72n3; offstage identity as feminine, 63, 64, 66; reality of career, 66–68; third-person pronouns used by, 40; vaudeville process, 60–70
Titterton, W. R., 61–62, 63
Tony Pastor's theater, 40
Torr, Diane, 10, 161–63

trans people: performance of gender to access services, 17, 21; post-operative performers, 25–26
"trouser roles," 29, 47
true womanhood, 44, 48, 61, 62; denied to Black women, 123–25; marketing of, 70
Trujillo, Cecelia, 106
Twelfth Night (Shakespeare), 23
two-pillar model, 19–22, 25–26

Ubangi Club (Harlem), 124, 126
"Uncovering the Stonewall Lesbian" (Hinds), 141
Underwood, Lisa, 3–4, 9, 163
unified body-gender, 120
United Farm Workers (UFW), 85
University of California, Santa Barbara (UCSB) Library, 88–89, 110n5
Urban Dictionary, 175, 191n70
urban population increase, 45

Valdez, Luis, 78, 79, 83, 84–85, 110n5, 112n51
Valdez, Lupe, 84, 87
Valdez, Socorro, 79, 80, 87, 92; as Calavera (genderless character), 99–102, 107, 108–9; on female identity, 107–8; as Huesos (Bones) character, 96–98, 101
Valentine, David, 18
Van Ness, Joan, 158
variety shows (1860–1880s), 10, 34, 40–45; Hindle's variety process, 50–60; variety into vaudeville, 45–50. See also cross identification; male impersonation
vaudeville (1880–1920s), 10, 34, 43, 48–49; "Black vaudeville," 123, 125; butch queerness linked to, 129; drag kinging linked to, 152–53, 161, 165; family model, 49, 129; third-person songs, 60, 62; Tilley's vaudeville process, 60–70. See also identification; male impersonation
Venetian Causeway Bar (Miami), 131
Vicinus, Martha, 41–43, 44, 55–56
Victorian gender and sexual mores, 26, 41, 43; sexology and, 49–50, 61; true womanhood, 44, 48, 61, 62, 70
visibility, economies of, 174
Vivian, Charles, 48, 52, 58–59, 75n59
Volcano, Del LaGrace, 165, 190n39

Warner, Michael, 5, 34, 196
Waters, Ethel, 118, 123, 124, 148n28
Weaver, Lois, 161, 190n21
Welter, Barbara, 44, 48
Wesner, Ella (male impersonator), 47, 48, 52, 53, 60; offstage masculine appearance, 56–57; same-sex relationships, 57
West, Candace, 16, 37n43
Westbrook, Laurel, 36n8
Western theater canon, 20–21
Weston, Maggie, 60
White Horse Inn (Oakland, California), 158, 168
Wiegman, Robyn, 174
Williams, Tommy, 130
willing suspension of disbelief, 19, 22–23, 199
Wilson, James, 126–27
Windh, Indra, 165
women: bending of femininity, 100–1; not allowed to act in plays, 20–21; universalized, as White and middle class by default, 45
women performers and women's practices, 11, 28–30; Kabuki theatre

(ca. 1600–1629 CE), 21, 28; seen as more effective, 29; Takarazuka, 23, 28
women's movement, nineteenth century, 61–62
women's restroom, as example of discourse, 8–9

Yarbro-Bejarano, Yvonne, 82, 85–87
Yardley, William, 138

Zellers, Peter, 46
Zimmerman, Don H., 16, 37n43
Zoot Suit (El Teatro Campesino), 84, 85, 113n73

Meredith Heller is Lecturer of Queer Studies in Women's and Gender Studies at Northern Arizona University.

Lightning Source UK Ltd.
Milton Keynes UK
UKHW010746110921
389953UK00012B/447